The Triumph of Ethnic Progressivism

The Triumph of Ethnic Progressivism

❧ URBAN POLITICAL CULTURE IN BOSTON, 1900–1925

JAMES J. CONNOLLY

HARVARD UNIVERSITY PRESS

Cambridge, Massachusetts, and London, England   1998

Library of Congress Cataloging-in-Publication Data

Connolly, James J., 1962–
    The triumph of ethnic Progressivism: urban political culture in Boston, 1900–1925 /
James J. Connolly.
        p.   cm.
    Includes bibliographical references (p.) and index.
    ISBN 0-674-90950-X
    1. Boston (Mass.)—Politics and government.
    2. Political culture—Massachusetts—Boston—History—20th century.
    3. Boston (Mass.)—Ethnic relations.
    4. Progressivism (United States politics)—History—20th century. I. Title.
F73.5.C745   1998
974.4'61—dc21   97-38662

For Beth

Acknowledgments

No work of scholarship stands by itself. Although I take responsibility for any errors in this book, I cannot take full credit for whatever benefit the reader derives from it. Most of my intellectual debts are detailed in the notes. Those of a more personal nature follow below.

This book grew out of a dissertation completed at Brandeis University under the direction of Morton Keller. I profited immensely from his counsel. His keen judgment, insistence on clarity, and directness improved my work immeasurably. I was also fortunate to have Jim Kloppenberg serve on the committee. His careful reading improved many facets of the argument I make in the book.

Several others read some or all of the manuscript. Phil Ethington thoroughly critiqued the full manuscript, providing me with the benefit of his deep knowledge of urban political history. I am also in his debt for assistance with the quantitative analysis presented in the book. Jack Davis and Peter Hansen not only made graduate school more enjoyable, they helped me work through several intellectual puzzles as my research for this book took shape. Pete in particular read several chapters at crucial times, helping me organize my ideas and present them more effectively. The readers at Harvard University Press made a multitude of critical insights that have strengthened the book on several fronts. The editorial staff at Harvard University Press has been helpful as I prepared the book for publication.

I have also been lucky enough to receive the support and assistance of several institutions. Brandeis University made graduate study and uninterrupted research possible through the Irving and Rose Crown

Graduate Fellowship. The Massachusetts Historical Society provided an Andrew Mellon Fellowship to support research in their invaluable collections. The staff of the Boston Public Library, particularly its Microtext Department, offered friendly and efficient service in the midst of regrettable budget cutting. The staffs of the Archives of the Archdiocese of Boston, Brandeis University's Goldfarb Library, Boston College's O'Neill Library, the Harvard University Libraries, and the interlibrary loan office of Ball State University's Bracken Library helped as well. The Academic Computing Service of the University of Texas–Arlington and Brandeis University Computing Services solved numerous technical problems. The History Departments of the University of Texas–Arlington and Ball State University supplied funding for travel and research as well. Connie McComber of the Ball State Geography Department helped with the map.

Portions of Chapters 4 and 5 were originally published as "Reconstituting Ethnic Politics: Boston, 1909–1925," *Social Science History* 19 (1995): 480–509. I thank Duke University Press for permission to republish them here.

My greatest debt is to family and friends, who tolerated and even endorsed my puzzling academic pursuits. My mother, sisters, and in-laws provided unstinting support all along the way. My father died before I could finish this project. I hope it justifies his faith in me. Beth Hawke made far more sacrifices than any spouse has the right to ask for (not least of which is reading the manuscript twice). No words can express my gratitude; I will simply dedicate the book to her.

Contents

Tables

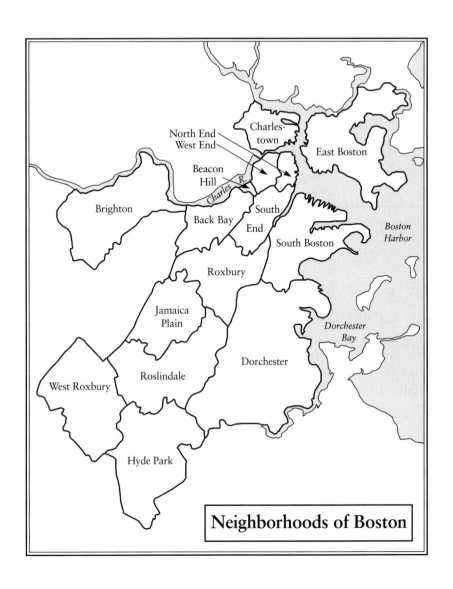

North End
West End
Charles-town
East Boston
Beacon Hill
Charles R.
Brighton
Back Bay
South End
Boston Harbor
South Boston
Roxbury
Jamaica Plain
Dorchester Bay
Dorchester
West Roxbury
Roslindale
Hyde Park

Neighborhoods of Boston

Introduction

Boston's white ethnic communities erupted when a federal judge ordered Boston to desegregate its schools in the mid-1970s. Buses carrying African-American children were attacked, fights broke out in schools, and public protests quickly evolved into riots. Many white parents placed their children in Catholic schools rather than the newly desegregated school system. Local politicians seemed intent on inciting the conflict instead of quieting it. Boston's busing crisis received national press coverage and confirmed the city's long-standing reputation for fierce racial and ethnic conflict.[1]

Scholars and commentators singled out the city's unique political culture as one cause of the tumult. They noted the extraordinary primacy of neighborhoods in local public life, the refusal of ethnic Bostonians to view the situation as anything but a political battle among social groups, and most of all, the propensity of Boston's largest ethnic group, the Irish, to see itself as an embattled minority, despite nearly a century of numerical and political dominance. Boston's Irish, as one observer commented, were "the only oppressed majority in the world."[2]

The origins of this popular mentality, all agreed, lie in the century-long cultural clash between Irish and Yankee. Begun in earnest following the mass migration of famine Irish in the 1840s, it persisted well into the twentieth century. Although immigration and a high birthrate brought political power, Boston's Irish Catholics remained excluded from the boardrooms and clubs that constituted the true centers of power. This discrimination scarred the collective psyche of Irish Boston for generations by denying it the political legitimacy and social authority that normally accompanied majority status. In response, the Irish retreated into aggressively defended ethnic enclaves, from which they viewed the rest of the world with a combination of hostility and suspicion.[3]

While such a social analysis is not without merit, it ignores the political sources of this ethnic consciousness. The origins of what it meant to be Irish in twentieth-century Boston lie neither in an anti-Catholic tradition inherited from the colonial era nor in the arrival of the famine Irish in the 1840s, but rather in the public reconception of Boston's ethnic history that occurred during the early twentieth century. Political entrepreneurs responding to the changing circumstances and structures of public life drew on the language of Progressivism to reinforce a narrative of Irish-Yankee conflict designed to mobilize voters along ethnic lines. Their predecessors, operating in a different civic environment, had created a different history, one that did not see Boston as an inherently hostile community for Irish newcomers and their descendants. That shift in rhetorical strategy played a vital role in shaping the modern identity of Boston and its Irish majority.

This book traces the political reconstruction of Boston's ethnic character. It describes changes in the city's political culture between 1900 and 1925 and examines how those changes shaped the ways Bostonians—especially Irish Bostonians—saw the city and their place within it. It rejects the traditional "machine" and "reform" categories that have informed urban political history for almost a century, choosing instead to present a ground-level analysis of the interplay between institutional change and public discourse that transformed the city's social relations.

Understanding how this process unfolded in early-twentieth-century Boston begins with an examination of the city's public life in the period that preceded it. Although scholars usually describe late-nineteenth-century politics in terms of ethnocultural conflict, Boston's party organizations actually helped keep a lid on group tensions. The city experienced ethnic and class conflict from the first influx of Irish Catholics in the 1840s, but those clashes did not define the city's public culture as the twentieth century approached. Instead, Irish politicians and elite Yankees cooperated under the auspices of the Democratic Party, an arrangement that placed party unity ahead of group interest. They created a narrative defining Boston as an increasingly harmonious community, one that had overcome the cultural conflicts of the mid–nineteenth century. Even when this alliance began to disintegrate, the entrenched place of parties in the process of distributing power ensured that most political action took place as partisan or intraparty disputes rather than as clashes among particular social groups.

A new style of public action arose to challenge partisan politics around the turn of the century. Fueled by muckraking journalism's call for a civic awakening, would-be political and social leaders in Boston began to present themselves as nonpartisan spokespersons for communal concerns doing battle against selfish interests. The definitions of community varied, ranging from the entire city to a specific neighborhood or ethnic group. Despite the differences among these efforts, their common rhetorical formula—Progressivism—created the appearance of a unified groundswell for municipal reform.

As the demand for cleaner, more efficient politics grew, the centrality of parties to public authority diminished. In Boston, this surge culminated with the revision of the city charter in 1909. Charter reform all but eliminated grassroots party organizations; in their place arose civic and business associations that relied on Progressive reform rhetoric to establish their legitimacy as representatives of communal interests. These groups assumed many of the roles once filled by parties but encompassed only a fraction of the electorate. Most voters found themselves with no institutional connections to city government. Recognizing this transformation, politicians began to pursue votes through mass publicity and broadly gauged policies designed to ignite collective action by large segments of an electorate largely cut off from the levers of power.

The most effective rhetorical tool for this new kind of politics was the increasingly popular language of Progressive reform. While Brahmin reformers used it to attack ethnic politicians, the same politicians and their supporters, led by Mayors John F. "Honey Fitz" Fitzgerald and James Michael Curley, turned it into an idiom that catered to ethnic identities and interests. The "ethnic Progressivism" they formulated cast the city's predominantly Yankee economic elite as selfish interests, greedily conspiring to deprive the city's blue-collar, immigrant majority—"the people"—of the social and political power they deserved. In a city where immigrants and their children were in the majority, this ethnic Progressivism became the framework through which many Bostonians came to understand their place in the larger community.

The intensification of group conflict after World War I takes on new significance against this backdrop. Instead of a period of reaction against reform, the 1920s can be seen as the time when the various communities mobilized by reform rhetoric began to clash. By then, the differences in their understandings of the terms of Progressivism had become evident. The battles that followed took place between versions of Progressivism rather than as a contest between its modernizing adherents and its antimodern opponents.

Two developments fueled this divergence. The first was the emergence of the cultural issues of the postwar era. As politicians grew more sophisticated in their use of the new forms of mass-mediated politics, they mixed their reform appeals with issues such as ethnic nationalism, immigration restriction, prohibition, and the rise of the Ku Klux Klan to create even more potent arguments for group mobilization. Second, middle-class migration to suburbs left urban working-class voters even more socially and politically isolated. For residents of these districts, the appeals of ethnic Progressivism proved to be especially powerful in explaining the nature of Boston's public life—a provocative story of a city torn by ethnic conflict for which Boston would become notorious.

This interpretation of Boston's Progressive Era politics inverts the usual understanding of the connections between society and politics during the early twentieth century. Scholars have typically described urban public life in this period as group conflict, with the groups shaped by immigration, urbanization, and industrialization. Analyses of Progressive Era city politics that pit some variation of the "boss-immigrant-machine" complex against native-born middle-class reformers rely on these socially driven models. This perspective assumes a unidirectional relationship between social change and political development, in which the lines of causation run primarily from society to politics but rarely the other way. A better view—one increasingly employed—insists that the political past be analyzed on its own terms, as more than a mere reflection of social developments, and recognizes that politics shaped society as much as society shaped politics. Such an argument makes sense for early-twentieth-century Boston, where the reforms of the Progressive Era altered the city's social relations by remaking its political landscape.[4]

Grasping the process through which Progressive Era political change molded ethnic identities requires an examination of the interplay between institutional structures and public discourse. The configurations and actions of the state "encourage some kinds of group formation and collective political action (but not others)," as Theda Skocpol has argued. But if institutional analysis can explain why one social group is mobilized instead of another, it cannot describe how individuals come to conceive of themselves as members of the group that is activated. Attention to the structural power of public discourse is necessary to comprehend the creation of politically active group identities. Political rhetoric gives meanings to public life, meanings that people use to orient themselves within their community. Thus a full analysis of the political sources of group identity entails both an investigation of the process by which the institutional arenas of political communication are restructured and a careful reading of the languages in which that communication takes place.[5]

A growing number of scholars have recognized the essential role publicly constructed narrative histories play in defining and politicizing collective identities. Building on the insight that ethnicity, class, and other social categories are cultural creations rather than fixed categories, these scholars argue that "identities are the names we give to the different ways we are positioned by, and position ourselves within the narrative of the past." While no two people tell precisely the same story about themselves, the narratives they create are often patterned on broader public stories drawn from fiction, history, and other public sources. When a particular collective narrative proves powerful enough to influence many life stories, it plays a central role in shaping a group identity.[6]

In many cases, more than one collective narrative may be able to explain plausibly the events and experiences of the past and present. Individual lives and the histories of social groups are, in George Steinmetz's words, "narratively promiscuous." The challenge facing the historian exploring the origins of a specific collective identity is not to determine which narrative is the most accurate but rather to explain how and why a particular one came to define the identity of that group.[7]

The process by which one collective narrative becomes more powerful than others often involves politics. Research on the emergence of nation-states in Europe has demonstrated how political leaders united populations by formulating a history that provided the citizenry of a country with a common past. These histories were created, as Werner Sollors has argued, "to substantiate politically motivated feelings of peoplehood." In the same manner, political and civic leaders in Boston crafted stories designed to mobilize ethnic groups. Successful analysis of these identities and the narratives that defined them thus requires careful consideration of the political developments that make them useful or effective.[8]

To illustrate how political change shaped group identities, I focus largely on the most famous of Boston's cultural cleavages, the clash between Irish and Yankee. Jews and Italians play lesser roles in this study, corresponding to the smaller size and limited political clout of their communities during the early twentieth century. African Americans and other groups are infrequently discussed because so few of them lived in early-twentieth-century Boston. (Blacks made up less than 2.5 percent of the city's population during the period under consideration.) The relative absence of these groups does not mean I think they are irrelevant to the city's history. Rather, I have chosen to emphasize the Irish experience because its prominence in Boston's twentieth-century public life allowed me to illustrate my argument most effectively.[9]

Any examination of urban politics in the Progressive Era must address two large and interrelated bodies of scholarly literature. The first describes the workings of city politics, which has overwhelmingly meant the activities of the urban machine. The second examines the nature of Progressivism, the complex surge of reform debate and policy initiatives during the first two decades of the twentieth century. Most urban political history imagines these two phenomena as opposing forces, each arising from specific social contexts: boss politics is inevitably linked to blue-collar immigrants, reform to the middle and upper-class native stock. Clinging to these categories, Progressive Era urban political history too often takes on a static, predetermined quality. By reconstructing Boston politics from the ground up, this study moves beyond this simplistic dualism, to present urban public life in a more nuanced, more dynamic manner.

The first step to better urban political history is to set aside ideas about big-city politics inherited from the Progressive Era itself. Jane Addams, William Riordon, Robert Woods, and Lincoln Steffens produced the dominant representations of party politics in urban neighborhoods from the Civil War to World War II. They depicted the ward boss as a one-man social service agency and argued that his persistence and power stemmed from his ability to provide for the welfare of impoverished constituents. By securing a job, a favor, or even financial assistance, the boss won the unquestioning loyalty of these voters. This caricature of ward politics survives, remarkably intact, in recent scholarly accounts of urban public life by both social and political historians.[10]

Revisionists have begun to expose the flaws in this interpretation. A growing number of studies have been devoted to dismantling the machine model of urban politics, arguing that party organizations and their leaders had far less power than is usually believed. The most forceful thrust within this writing rejects the argument that local bosses and machines persisted because they fulfilled latent social functions. Terrence McDonald and others have shown that this contention rests on an untrustworthy evidentiary base. Reformers' accounts of urban politics had a specific motivation: they sought public support for the expansion of the city government's capacity to provide social services by arguing that it would make boss politics unnecessary. If the reformers themselves, backed by the resources of the state, could provide those services, the boss would no longer be the only source of assistance. Thus weaned from dependency on corrupt politicians, voters would be free to act as independent, responsible citizens. In their effort to secure more power for themselves, reformers exaggerated both the levels of service provided by urban politicians and the control they held over their neighbors' votes.[11]

While critics of the machine model offer a convincing case that the usual picture is wrong, a great deal of work remains to be done before we have a full picture of what neighborhood politics did look like. In particular, we know little about how city dwellers were mobilized in the Progressive Era. The call for "a rejection of the assumption of the functionality of urban politics altogether" still leaves us the task of presenting a persuasive, coherent rendering of urban political mobilization from the ground up in this period. Doing so requires not only a more reliable account of the institutional aspects of ward-level public life but also a firmer grasp of the ideas and images that animated local political behavior.[12]

For the early twentieth century, a better understanding of the ideological dimensions of urban politics means tackling the issue of Progressivism. The debate over what Progressivism was and who practiced it has collapsed into confusion. Despite repeated obituaries, the concept refuses to die. Historians continue to expand its boundaries, applying the Progressive label to so many different things and so many different groups that its utility as a historical category is threatened. The challenge facing scholars of Progressive reform is to make sense of it in all its diversity, while resisting the temptation to make it either more or less than it was.[13]

If the idea of Progressivism coheres in any sense, it is as a style of political behavior, a motif of public action that took on many meanings. Attempts to demarcate it in programmatic, demographic, or ideological terms overlook this defining quality; even the most flexible threaten to rigidify an essentially malleable phenomenon. Many of the pursuits that have fallen under the heading of Progressive reform had little in common save a shared rhetorical formula. Each set of Progressives—whether settlement house feminists, elite male municipal reformers, antitrust crusaders, or ethnic politicians—presented themselves as the leaders of a communal response to the actions of illicit interests and the problems of urban-industrial life. They often drew on the language and ideas of social science to define and achieve their version of the public good, but it was the theme of united public action against corrupt forces that provided the essential common denominator.[14]

Progressivism was also defined by what it was not. Most obviously, it was not partisanship. The politicians and civic leaders who used it to depict themselves at the head of a unified communal movement explicitly contrasted themselves with the two major parties. They did not represent a "part" of the people but rather the entire public. Their primary concern was with pursuing the common good rather than with the advancement of a party, faction, or interest. In this sense, Progressivism represented a continuation of the antipartisan tradition that ran through American public life during the eighteenth and nineteenth centuries.[15]

A second foil for the Progressive style was class-based action. The wave of labor unrest that engulfed the United States from 1877 through the 1890s and the spread of Marxist-inspired ideas alarmed many observers. While generally not an explicit challenge to radical ideologies, Progressivism's emphasis on communal unity made it incompatible with efforts to mobilize people on the basis of class antagonism. By emphasizing cohesiveness, it offered Americans a way of supporting reform measures that addressed the problems of an urban-industrial society without adopting the radical posture associated with some types of working-class protest.

Progressivism's emphasis on consensus and its rejection of class appeals did not make Progressivism a fundamentally middle-class ideology. While scholars usually describe early-twentieth-century reform activism as the product of middle-class unease, it was not rooted in a specific social milieu. As a political style rather than an ideology, it was available to a wide variety of people operating in many different contexts, as long as they had access to the public sphere through the press or a civic organization. While most of those who did were members of the middle or upper classes, others with the necessary institutional resources had the opportunity to use the vehicle of Progressivism as well. The ability of Boston's James Michael Curley—hardly a tribune of the middle class—to frame the Progressive formula in ethnic terms demonstrates this point.[16]

The Progressive motif's popularity stemmed largely from its wide availability, especially in urban settings. Its origins were inextricably bound to the rise of the mass circulation press and the muckraking journalism that accompanied it. Inspired by Lincoln Steffens's series of exposés of urban corruption, big-city papers published sensational accounts of dishonest and inefficient city government as weapons in their circulation wars. These dramatic reports stoked public clamor for municipal reform in every city in the country. Boston did not escape this trend. Local papers were filled with reports of petty corruption and abusive practices by elected officials, dishonest businessmen, and political appointees. These revelations reached a large, socially diverse urban audience that interpreted them in a variety of ways to suit a variety of contexts.[17]

This popularity marks off Progressive municipal reform from earlier efforts to clean up city government and politics. Very little of the Progressive agenda was new. Calls for greater efficiency, the elimination of local representation, an end to partisan power, and the prevention of graft and other corruption echoed through urban public life over much of the nineteenth century, with limited results. The tremendous success of reformers in the early twentieth century stemmed less from innovation than from the sudden public sympathy for measures promoting a common good fueled by the spread of an independent, nonpartisan, often sensational press at the end of the nineteenth century. Party politicians had to accommodate this demand for reform or risk losing power.[18]

Progressive reform also flourished because of the blurring of traditional gender boundaries that had shaped nineteenth-century public life. Electoral politics had traditionally been a male domain, reform the supposed province of overly aggressive females and effeminate males—of "long-haired men and short-haired women," as the popular phrase went.[19] By the early twentieth century, this distinction had broken down. In *The Shame of the Cities,* his call to arms for urban reform, Lincoln Steffens celebrated the masculine qualities of his favorite reformers. His account of the origins of Chicago's Municipal Voters' League, one of the few bright spots Steffens uncovered in his investigations of big-city politics, stressed the maleness of its founders. "All they needed was a fighter," his breathless account reported, "so it was moved to find a man, one man, and let this man find eight other men." Cast in these terms, the Progressive formula became suitable for male politicians in a way that earlier reform styles had not.[20]

By the same token, urban politics was becoming increasingly "domesticated." Capitalizing on the traditional separate-spheres ideology, women activists sought to increase their political power by extending their responsibilities as wives and mothers into public life. In cities, the movement for "municipal housekeeping," with its emphasis on public health, education, and civic morality, was among the principal manifestations of this strategy. These efforts helped push new ideas onto the political agenda while giving women the opportunity to assume broader public roles. They began speaking and acting on behalf of their communities on issues considered to be within the purview of women, further expanding the possible variations on the Progressive formula in the process.[21]

Part of Progressivism's popularity also came from its connection to republicanism, one of the deepest currents in American political culture. Republicanism's celebration of civic virtue—unselfish service on behalf of a shared idea of the public good—and the vocabulary of criticism it supplied for condemnations of corruption, self-interest, and partisanship still resonated in the American public psyche long after the agrarian society that gave birth to it had disappeared. While no longer the ideological framework in which American dissenters conceived their reform efforts, if it ever was, the republican construct of a morally unified, consensual public remained a powerful rhetorical formula. This abstraction animated Progressivism and gave it cultural authority.[22]

What distinguished Progressive rhetoric from nineteenth-century reform movements that drew on republican rhetoric was the multiplicity of contexts in which it operated and thus the many meanings that it took. Popularized by a sensationalist press and muckraking journalists, the republican-style call for communal action against selfish and corrupting interests reached an increasingly fragmented audience. After a century of urbanization, industrialization, and immigration, the possible definitions of community had multiplied enormously. When mass circulation newspapers and periodicals made the notion of consensual action once again popular in the United States, enterprising political and civic leaders called numerous communities into action, using ethnicity, neighborhood, city, nation, and a host of other categories to define communal boundaries.

Herein lies Progressivism's essential irony: despite its apparent negation of class and group distinctions, it became a powerful formula for political action along many social axes. Leaders and would-be leaders of numerous and varied communities throughout Boston began using Progressivism to establish and strengthen many collective political identities. Though limited at first by the institutional structures of big-city politics, this new style would become more important as the contours of urban public life changed during the Progressive Era. Ultimately, it would emerge as the central motif of politics in twentieth-century Boston, employed by immigrant spokespersons as readily as Yankee business leaders or middle-class settlement workers. The historical significance of Progressivism rests as much in that development, in the means its many proponents used, as it does in the divergent ends they sought.

From this perspective, the frantic scramble by succeeding generations of historians to establish the Progressive credentials of different social groups has obscured rather than revealed the full dimensions of public reform in the Progressive Era. Various collections of scholars have argued that the upper class, the middle class, the working class, big business, women, ethnic politicians, native-born Protestants, and liberal Christians deserved the label "Progressive." About the only challenge remaining for this approach is to determine who was not a Progressive, and few viable candidates remain. Cumulatively, this body of work fails to persuade. It only convinces us that Progressivism was not a phenomenon that can be explained by an analysis of its social bases.[23]

Yet many scholars continue to view the demand for reform of city government and politics—a prime facet of Progressive policy innovation—as the province of some social groups but not others. Typically they have arrayed upper- and middle-class native-born reformers on one side, in favor of municipal reform, while placing urban bosses and their blue-collar, immigrant constituents on the other. Even those dedicated to rescuing the Progressivism of working-class ethnics concede that their subjects resisted most efforts to remake urban governance. Only recently has the group-based analysis of municipal reform in the Progressive Era come under systematic examination, and the results indicate that reform candidates and measures often had broad support across class and ethnic lines.[24]

If we are to move beyond the stale stereotypes that have informed urban political history, we must recognize the plasticity of Progressivism. Support for reform was not confined to particular social categories. Rather, Progressivism was a public language open to manipulation by those with access to the public sphere, including ethnic civic leaders and politicians. These men and women fashioned their own *specific* versions of Progressivism, just as their upper- and middle-class Yankee counterparts did. The several reform visions that arose in Boston included not only the Progressivisms of the city's businessmen and suburban middle class but also a series of ethnic Progressivisms, the most notable of which was an Irish Progressivism that played a central role in shaping the city's twentieth-century political culture.

This multidimensional ethnic Progressivism was not the same thing as "urban liberalism." Presenting early-twentieth-century machine politicians as precursors to the New Deal, proponents of the urban liberalism thesis note that a collection of pragmatic bosses supported many social reforms and even some political changes, so long as they benefited their constituencies and solidified their electoral base. Part humane impulse, part practical politics, urban liberalism represented the contribution of immigrant America to Progressive reform and to the expansion of the American welfare state over the course of the twentieth century. While this work properly restored immigrant communities to the annals of American reform history, its description of urban ethnic politicians in these terms also obscured an important part of their legacy. They mobilized their supporters in both ethnic and Progressive terms simultaneously. In doing so, they helped give specific meaning to the ethnic experience in Boston and throughout the United States.[25]

Recent scholarship demonstrating the specifically ethnic and racial dimensions of early-twentieth-century reform lends credence to this interpretation. African-American men and women adopted the Progressive style of political action to achieve their own particular goals. Mexican immigrants in California appropriated "new nationalism" and other elements of Progressive reform as part of the effort to create a distinctive Mexican-American identity. Even in bastions of Progressive reform such as Wisconsin, factions within the LaFollette coalition pursued specifically ethnic agendas. The significance of these efforts stems less from their immediate success or failure at the ballot box or in legislative chambers than from the role they played in defining and mobilizing groups during the early twentieth century.[26]

Approached in this fashion, Progressivism's fate in the 1920s must be recalibrated. Historians have generally imagined the twenties as a period of reaction against the apparent reform consensus of the pre–World War I era. Yet the period after the war can also be seen as a continuation of patterns set in motion before the war rather than a sharp break from them. As men and women desiring to speak for ethnic groups and neighborhoods seized on Progressivism as a tool to define and politicize collective identities, cultural clashes sharpened. For a time the coalitions that formed behind specific reform measures masked these differences, but as the differing interpretations and expectations each group attached to these proposals became evident, tensions increased.

It is important to remember that this process began during the Progressive Era itself, rather than with World War I. From this perspective the "tribal twenties" do not contrast quite so dramatically with the preceding decades. The growth of ethnic nationalism during and after World War I and the cultural and ideological controversies of the 1920s reinforced patterns established before 1917. Indeed, both the antimodern thrusts of the postwar era—prohibition, immigration restriction, even the rise of the Ku Klux Klan—and the vision of an urbanized, cosmopolitan nation that their opponents championed had distinctly Progressive roots. The cultural war of the twenties was fought within the terms of Progressivism rather than along a reform-reaction divide.

Reconceiving the reform surge of the earlier twentieth century along these lines gives us a clearer sense of the relationship between ethnic politics and Progressivism. When we relegate urban ethnics to the realm of machine politics, in which persuasion did not count and ideology did not matter, we ignore a crucial dimension of big-city public life. For it was Progressivism that supplied the political vocabulary through which ethnic and neighborhood identities came to be formulated in Boston's modern public sphere. Understanding this process necessitates more than a social analysis of politics. It also requires a political history of social relations.

Boston offers an especially fruitful place for that endeavor. The city's modern public life has been marked by powerful cultural antagonisms generally assumed to be by-products of nineteenth-century social patterns. If these supposedly deep-rooted tensions emerged from political as well as social developments, as I contend, then we must assume that politics shaped other collective identities as well. Thus a complete social history must make room for politics in its analysis of the formation of groups, whether based on ethnicity, class, race, or gender. Likewise, political history needs to move beyond a model of politics as group conflict, as its best practitioners have begun to do. The institutions, rhetoric, and activities involved in dispersing power do more than just respond to social change; they also shape it, as this study of Boston's early-twentieth-century public life will show.

CHAPTER ONE

Politics and Society at the End of the Nineteenth Century

Twentieth-century Boston's descent into a politics of ethnic antagonism was neither direct nor inevitable. Though cultural hostilities arose as European immigrants poured into the city from the 1830s onward, they did not automatically define its public life. At the end of the nineteenth century, most Bostonians—including newcomers and their heirs—described their city as an increasingly tolerant, harmonious community. The shape and character of its politics helped maintain the plausibility of that vision even amid open social conflict.

To assert that Bostonians saw their city as fundamentally peaceful does not deny the existence of group conflict. At least from the first major influx of famine Irish during the 1840s, ethnic and religious antagonism had marred the city's public life. Anti-Irish, anti-Catholic feeling periodically flared up in nineteenth-century Boston, particularly in the mid-1830s, when an angry mob attacked and burned a nearby Ursuline convent; in the 1850s, when the "Know-Nothing" Party flourished; and in the late 1880s and early 1890s, when battles over schooling, temperance, woman suffrage, and the activities of the American Protective Association (APA) heightened tensions.[1]

But what it meant to be Irish in Boston was not necessarily defined by a sense of conflict in the late nineteenth century. Instead, a narrative of diminishing antagonism and Irish progress prevailed. Despite the revival of cultural hostilities, both Irish-Catholic and elite Yankee spokesmen insisted that nativists and anti-Catholic activists did not speak for the community. Boston had moved beyond the era of "Know-Nothing" attacks, they argued; the agitation of the moment was merely an aberration. More significantly, numbers were on their side. As the Irish became a majority in the city, the threat to their interests and power would shrink even further.

This understanding persisted because parties dominated political life in Boston as they did throughout late-nineteenth-century America. A shared reliance on the Democratic Party prompted reform-minded Yankee elites and Irish politicos to cooperate and gave them reason to mute ethnic strife. They cast group conflicts in partisan terms, blaming Republicans for the anti-immigrant agitation of the late nineteenth century while depicting Boston as an essentially harmonious place as long as Democrats were in charge. And even when Yankee-Irish collaboration diminished in the late 1890s, the centrality of parties as an avenue to political power meant that Bostonians most often entered the public arena as partisans rather than as ethnic antagonists.

This is not how late-nineteenth-century party politics is typically viewed. Most scholars have followed the lead of Henry Adams, who described nineteenth-century Massachusetts politics as "the systematic organization of hatreds." While this may be a drastic oversimplification of what the progenitors of the "ethnocultural interpretation" intended, it is a perception that has dominated the historiography of nineteenth-century public life. Most scholars emphasize cultural conflicts as the essence of Gilded Age politics; even those stressing economic conflict present parties as obstacles to working-class consciousness because of their reliance on culturally divisive issues. The perception of party politics as a direct extension of social conflict governs what Richard McCormick has called "the party period in American history."[2]

A fixation with the social bases of politics has diverted attention from the creative role that parties played. The process of systematically organizing cultural hatreds into partisan loyalties did more than just reproduce preexisting social identities; it also created a new one. Party conflict was more than a surrogate for other clashes. In the late nineteenth century, partisanship was a vocabulary of public identity in and of itself. When they went to the polls, marched in torchlight parades, or attended a political rally, Americans were participating in rituals affirming their party membership. While this affiliation was inextricably bound up with other communal allegiances, it was a discrete identity as well. Few alternative forms of political identification existed in a public life dominated by parties. To act politically in this era was, for all but a few, to act as a partisan.[3]

Though a campaign of ethnic rapprochement seemed implausible for Boston as the nineteenth century neared its end, it developed nonetheless. The steady influx of immigrants, the constant remapping of the city's social geography, and the prevalence of culturally divisive issues threatened to undermine conciliatory efforts. Yet spokesmen for the city's two leading ethnoreligious groups—Irish Catholics and Anglo-Protestants—continued to emphasize comity over conflict and insisted that intergroup cooperation was now the dominant characteristic of the city's public life.

Sustaining that vision was a difficult task. Over the latter two-thirds of the nineteenth century, Boston evolved from a Yankee town to a polyglot industrial city. The migration of the famine Irish in the 1840s was but the first of several waves of newcomers who would come to Boston before 1900. Large numbers of British Americans—English-speaking Protestants who migrated by way of Canada—arrived in the city following the Civil War. Significant eastern and southern European immigration began after 1880, an influx that would peak in the early twentieth century before tapering off after World War I. Through it all, Irish immigrants flowed steadily into the city, attracted by its established Irish community. That steady flow, together with natural increase, ensured that Irish immigrants and their children would become a majority of the city's population by 1900 and its dominant ethnic group.[4]

Shifts in Boston's demographic composition took place amid a changing social geography. The growth of streetcar lines and innovations in housing construction allowed urban immigrant workers to reside in districts several miles from their workplace. Gradually, working-class Irish, who had first filled the slums of the North, South, and West Ends, moved to neighborhoods surrounding the center city. Charlestown, South Boston, north Dorchester, Roxbury, and to some extent East Boston became Irish strongholds over the last quarter of the nineteenth century. British Americans congregated in parts of East Boston, Roxbury, and Dorchester. New immigrants, particularly eastern European Jews and Italians, began to take the place of the Irish in downtown districts. A third wave of this outward migration occurred simultaneously as upper-middle-class Bostonians—including some better-off Irish and British Americans—took advantage of expanded rail transportation to move to suburban neighborhoods such as Brighton, West Roxbury, Jamaica Plain, and Dorchester, as well as nearby towns.[5]

These changes provided the backdrop for the rekindling of the anti-Catholicism that had periodically plagued the city's Irish. While Boston's tradition of Catholic-Protestant tensions stretched back to the Pope's Day rioting of the colonial era, its late-nineteenth-century manifestation had more immediate sources. The arrival of British Americans from Canada in the 1870s and 1880s on the heels of the great prewar Irish migration sparked conflict between the two groups as they wrestled for social, political, and economic advantage in Boston. It was these Canadian immigrants, rather than Boston's Yankee elite, who spearheaded the attack on Boston's Irish-Catholic community.

By the 1880s, the Irish had gained a clear advantage in this contest by virtue of their steadily growing numbers. After the Civil War, friction between Yankees and Irish began to subside, partly in response to Irish participation in the war effort. The state legislature liberalized restrictions on immigrant voting, and the fortunes of Irish office seekers began to improve. By 1870, the first Irish alderman had been elected, and in 1882 Patrick Collins became the first Irish-American congressman from Boston. Collins, a Harvard Law School graduate, and Democratic Party leader Patrick Maguire headed a small collection of Irish political leaders who carved out a solid base of political power in the city by the 1880s. Proof of their ascendance came in 1884, when businessman Hugh O'Brien became the first Irish-Catholic mayor of Boston. He went on to serve four one-year terms. These and other examples of growing Irish political power alarmed some elements of Anglo-Protestant Boston and sparked a revival of ethnoreligious tensions in the city.[6]

Conflict began in earnest in 1887 with the establishment of the British-American Society, an organization devoted to combating the rise of Irish-Catholic power in Boston. Its initial efforts were focused on school politics, a realm always fraught with cultural symbolism. With the assistance of some local Protestant clergy and sympathetic Republican legislators, the Society introduced a bill in the state legislature concerning the "employment and schooling of minors." When

Boston's Irish-Catholic community discovered that the bill allowed local school committees to inspect and even close private schools, it responded forcefully, springing to the defense of parochial schools.[7]

Though the initial inspection bill failed, another issue kept tensions alive. Later that spring Father Theodore Metcalf, a Catholic priest from South Boston, wrote to the School Committee complaining about an English teacher who was incorrectly instructing students that the Catholic doctrine of indulgences constituted permission to sin, an interpretation of Catholic canon law derived from a popular textbook. Metcalf and other Catholics demanded that the offending book be banned and the teacher punished. In June 1888 the School Committee voted to remove the text from its list and to censure the teacher. Angry Protestants reacted swiftly, forming a "Committee of One Hundred" dedicated to removing Catholics from the school board.[8]

During the summer and fall, anti-Catholic activities increased. Evangelist preacher Dr. Justin Fulton held frequent public meetings at Tremont Temple in downtown Boston to decry Irish-Catholic political power, and woman suffragist Eliza Trask Hill, daughter of a Methodist minister, led a drive to register Protestant women to vote in the fall elections. (Women had been allowed to vote in School Committee elections in Boston since 1879.) The campaign also featured English-born Margaret Shepard, a purported ex-nun and the head of the Loyal Women of American Liberty, who regaled audiences with horrifying tales of life inside a convent.[9]

Whatever its absurdities, the campaign proved effective. Despite a momentary jump in voting among Irish-Catholic women, the Republican slate of School Committee candidates endorsed by the Committee of One Hundred won, shutting out Irish candidates as well as those sympathetic to the Catholic position. The sharp rise in Protestant voting in general helped ensure the defeat of Hugh O'Brien, who was seeking a fifth term as mayor. Owen Galvin, another Irish mayoral candidate, lost by an even wider margin the following year, and Anglo-Protestant Republicans maintained their grip on the school board into the 1890s.[10]

The School Committee controversy of 1888 represented the opening salvo of a full-scale ethnocultural offensive. Like the anti-Catholic and prohibition movements that challenged the partisan system in the Midwest, nativists in Boston strove to limit Irish Democratic power. The fierce battles that resulted often translated into open religious conflict. The arrival of the virulently anti-Catholic American Protective Association in Boston in the early 1890s further fanned the flames of cultural antagonism. The School Committee campaigning of 1888 and 1889, as well as the close ties between Eliza Trask Hill (who was also a leader of the Women's Christian Temperance Union) and other leading suffragists, made woman suffrage a contentious issue. Tensions peaked in July 1895, when an APA Fourth of July parade in East Boston degenerated into rioting that caused one death and numerous injuries.[11]

Despite these battles, Boston's public life never came to be characterized primarily by group antagonism. In particular, the city's Irish Catholics, soon to be if not already a majority, did not automatically come to imagine Yankee-Protestant Boston as inherently hostile to their well-being or to the expansion of their political power. Neither Irish spokesmen nor Irish voters revolted against all things Anglo-Saxon. Instead, a description of Boston as a community that had overcome ethnic divisions remained a stock theme in the city's politics, articulated by both Brahmin and Irish leaders.

Brahmin actions bolstered this view. Their response to the School Committee controversy and its aftermath demonstrated that Protestant Boston was not fundamentally antagonistic to Irish-Catholic interests. Along with Irish leaders, several Brahmins, including the venerable abolitionist Thomas Wentworth Higginson and Harvard President Charles Eliot, testified against the school inspection measure and warned against a return to "Know-Nothing" days. Boston-born, Harvard-educated lawyer Nathan Matthews led the effort to defeat the 1888 bill and succeeded in removing clauses offensive to Catholics in a similar law that passed the following year. These and other members of Boston's Yankee elite also joined the city's Irish in denouncing the APA campaigns of the 1890s, continuing the tradition of tolerance that stretched back to the 1830s, when their ancestors had rallied behind the city's Catholic community after the burning of the Ursuline convent in Charlestown.[12]

In coming to the defense of Boston's Irish-Catholic community, these Brahmins helped articulate a public narrative of ethnic reconciliation and Irish progress. Nathan Matthews, mayor of Boston from 1891 through 1894, was among the chief optimists, confident that the newcomers would gain full acceptance. "The Puritan and the Irishman both came to this country in search of liberty denied at home," he told

Boston's Charitable Irish Society in 1891. "Both have suffered from her [England's] unjust and selfish restrictions on trade and commerce; both have struggled for the right of self government and the blessings of home rule. One has been successful; the other will be just so surely as the sun shall rise tomorrow." While such a transformation inevitably brought about conflict, he insisted that "the Puritan and the Celt as they move along the pathway of life in friendly intercourse and competition in our pleasant New England towns, will develop a race and civilization superior to all that has gone before." To another Irish-Catholic audience, he celebrated "the wholesome changes" in the character of ethnic and religious relations that had taken place in Boston in recent decades and insisted that "the darkness of those days [of conflict] . . . ha[d] disappeared and passed away forever."[13]

The rhetoric and actions of Matthews and other Brahmins allowed Irish spokesmen to maintain that anti-Catholic agitation was an aberration in Boston. The leading proponents of this point of view were John Boyle O'Reilly, editor of *The Pilot,* and Patrick Maguire, leader of the Democratic City Committee and publisher of *The Republic.* The Irish-born O'Reilly had come to Boston after a spectacular escape from British authorities, who had sentenced him to twenty years' imprisonment for his Fenian activities. Hired in 1870 as a reporter for *The Pilot,* the leading Irish newspaper in New England, he rose to editor-in-chief and co-owner with Catholic Archbishop John Williams by 1876. O'Reilly also maintained close ties to many well-known literary and political figures in Brahmin Boston. Maguire was Boston's leading Democrat. Although he held only one elective office during his political career, he was widely acknowledged as the most powerful Irish politician in the city. He used the pages of *The Republic, The Pilot*'s chief rival for local Irish readers, to present the views of Boston's Democratic leadership.[14]

Both papers sounded consistently optimistic about Irish prospects and counseled patience and restraint. During the school board disputes, *The Pilot* insisted that Boston was a tolerant place and that "an overwhelming majority of its good citizens want to see fair play all around and are tired of the bigotry of the Puritanical 17th and 18th centuries. You will see this proved if you force the issue." When supporters of anti-Catholic minister Justin Fulton evoked memories of the 1834 attack on the Ursuline convent by threatening to burn down parochial schools, O'Reilly's paper was quick to respond. "Boston is a civilized city nowadays, and thugs of your stripe, if they ventured to put their brutal sentiments into brutal deeds today, would find themselves speedily adorning the jails, if not the lamp-posts of the city," *The Pilot* somewhat paradoxically warned. Maguire's *Republic* expressed the same sentiments, even after the defeat of Irish-Catholic candidates for mayor and School Committee. The anti-Catholic movement in Boston was the work of British-American immigrants and outside agitators, the paper insisted, and did not reflect "the conservative sense of the average Boston Protestant."[15]

The stand of Irish-Catholic leaders on the question of woman suffrage, another issue of cultural contention, further underscored the confidence they had in their future. A few voices warned that the threat from "these rabid women" who led the anti-Catholic School Committee campaign was serious enough to require the votes of Catholic women to counteract them. And voting levels among Catholic women did increase in 1888 and 1889. But most Irish leaders did not shift from their opposition to woman suffrage; the surge in voting among Irish-Catholic women quickly subsided in the early 1890s and remained low thereafter.[16]

The logic of Irish-Catholic Boston's spokesmen on this issue was particularly significant. Most of them refused to abandon their position on woman suffrage because they saw no reason for alarm. Proponents of woman suffrage were anti-Catholic fanatics ("simply and solely female APAs," charged *The Republic*) who did not speak for the community as a whole. Boston's true character would soon reassert itself and the storm would pass. It was "far better for the bigots to have their own way for a year or two," declared *The Pilot,* "and the Catholics, already half the population, will be strengthened by their own reserve and the sympathy and respect of all unprejudiced people."[17]

Numerical evidence made O'Reilly and Maguire especially sanguine. In the midst of the school controversy, *The Pilot* proudly trumpeted on page one the announcement that the latest local census figures showed "children of Irish parentage now residing in Boston numerically exceed those of the children of Massachusetts by 89,763." The implications of such numbers were clear: "It is not necessary to discuss the probabilities of a growth of these ratios, nor comment upon the right of class representation." *The Republic* insisted that the city's Catholics were "perfectly capable of taking care of themselves and defending their rights." Embedded in this confident perspective was the belief that democratic institutions would ensure a smooth and legitimate transition from Yankee to Irish rule and that Boston's Anglo elite would eventually yield the mantle of leadership to the city's immigrant majority.[18]

The self-confidence of Boston's Irish leadership received its stiffest test in 1895, when a deadly ethnic riot rocked East Boston. The incident began with a Fourth of July parade staged by APA sympathizers. The marchers—most of them British-American immigrants—were members of "patriotic orders" linked to the APA. Their procession featured "a little red schoolhouse"—a well-known APA image—and a woman wearing an orange dress symbolizing Ulster Protestantism. Republican Governor Frederic Greenhalge had reluctantly granted permission for the demonstration when neighborhood organizers and city officials refused to permit the APA displays in the traditional local parade. Angry exchanges between marchers and Irish-Catholic spectators quickly erupted into fisticuffs, and gunshots followed. One man died and numerous others were injured before police restored order. The incident earned national publicity, embarrassing the city by reviving its image as a community riven by ethnic hatred.[19]

In the face of widespread claims that Boston was returning to its "Know-Nothing" past, local Irish leaders leaped to the city's defense. Patrick Maguire's *Republic* was particularly emphatic that the perpetrators did not represent local sentiment, nor were they even from Boston. In a "calm review" of the events, Maguire pointed out that most of the anti-Catholic marchers were outsiders. The riot resulted from an "un-American, un-Christian agitation . . . by a lot of anti-Catholic bigots from Ulster and Canada," his paper declared, and the man accused of killing the spectator "was an Orangeman from County Cavan, Ireland." By contrast, Bostonians of all faiths and ethnic backgrounds had attempted to prevent the parade. *The Republic* highlighted opposition to the APA parade from the East Boston organizing committee, composed mostly of Protestants, as well as the city government and the local press.[20]

For both *The Republic* and *The Pilot*, the East Boston clash did not signal the advent of full-scale cultural warfare in Boston. Once again both papers downplayed the threat and urged their readers not to respond violently or provoke further action. "The storm will soon subside," insisted Maguire's paper, and there was no need for a dramatic response. While *The Pilot* condemned the APA marchers, it also criticized Irish Catholics for not respecting the right of their opponents to parade in public and called for greater restraint in the future.[21]

This self-confident interpretation of Boston's social development did not always go unchallenged. As one commentator announced during the battle over school inspection, "I am not one of those who think that this movement is but a temporary ebullition that will run its course and finally collapse." Other Catholic voices insisted that the true meaning of the Protestant offensive was "cease to be Catholics and you will be good citizens." For some, Boston was a hostile community, and any faith in the future prospects of its Irish-Catholic community was misplaced.[22]

But the less anxious interpretation of the school crisis and the APA controversies carried more weight. As Paul Kleppner has shown, Irish voters in the city supported Yankee Democratic mayoral candidates Nathan Matthews and Josiah Quincy more strongly than they did Irish candidates. Kleppner ascribes this phenomenon to the growth of ward factionalism, which supposedly resulted in intra-Irish feuding. Regardless of its source, the willingness of Irish Boston to rally behind Brahmin candidates in nearly uniform fashion testified to their acceptance of Yankee leadership. If they viewed Boston as an ethnic battleground, it is unlikely that they would have provided this level of support to members of the opposing social group.[23]

Irish Bostonians voted with their feet as well. Part of the impetus for the 1888 school controversy was a directive by the American Catholic hierarchy insisting on the construction of enough Catholic schools to educate every Catholic child. The prospect of this parochial school offensive helped trigger demands for the 1888 school inspection bill. Yet despite the ensuing cultural controversy, and despite ecclesiastical instructions to the contrary, the vast majority of Boston Catholics continued to send their children to public schools. As late as 1908, only one of five Catholic schoolchildren in the Archdiocese of Boston attended parochial schools. While Catholic parents may have chosen public education because of its lower cost and better reputation, the willingness of so many Irish Catholics to send their children to Boston's public schools—a quintessentially Yankee institution—instead of segregating them in parish schools also suggests that they did not perceive every aspect of the city's life as hostile to their values and beliefs.[24]

No person better symbolized the idea that Boston had become a hospitable place for Irish Americans than Patrick Collins. The Irish-born Collins came to Massachusetts as a small child in the 1850s. As a young man he had firsthand exposure to the ethnic hostilities of that era, witnessing the destruction of a Catholic church in nearby Chelsea and suffering a broken arm in the ensuing riot. Even amid these tensions, Collins prospered politically and financially. After a stint in Ohio's coalfields, he returned to Boston, became an upholsterer, and began studying law. He earned a law degree from Harvard in 1871 and then began a steady rise through the ranks of the Democratic Party, propelled in part by his role in Irish nationalist politics. In 1882 Collins became the first Irish Catholic to represent Boston in Congress, where he served three consecutive terms. He withdrew from active campaigning after retiring from Congress but remained an important force in Democratic Party affairs. In 1899 he reemerged on the political scene as a candidate for mayor. Although a divided Democratic Party wrecked his hopes that year, he triumphed two years later and earned a second term by a landslide in 1903.[25]

Collins's two terms as mayor offered further proof that an Irish politician could maintain the inherited standards of Yankee Boston. His administrations were marked by fiscal and stylistic conservatism. Collins angered many Irish Democratic leaders by vetoing numerous appropriations, and he worked aggressively to cut the city's debt. He also refused most opportunities to woo political support through publicity, generally spurning the small camp of reporters assigned to city hall by the increasingly aggressive local press. Instead he preferred to govern quietly, through traditional partisan channels.[26]

With this approach Collins earned an overwhelming endorsement from Bostonians of every stripe. He swept every ward in his 1903 reelection bid, an unprecedented feat in Boston. Regression equations designed to measure the relationship between the size of a ward's Irish population and support for Collins reveal that the strength of that association dropped sharply between 1901 and 1903. (See Table 1.) Although the results suggest he maintained strong Irish support, they indicate that support had grown much stronger in non-Irish districts. His constituency had broadened well beyond the Irish core of the Democratic Party, demonstrating that even in 1903 a political coalition crossing ethnic boundaries was still achievable in Boston.[27]

Bostonians were not the only ones to see their city as well governed

Table 1. Linear Regression Analysis of Irish Vote for Patrick Collins, 1901 and 1903

Election	Regression coefficient	Standard deviation	p-value	R^2
Collins vote, 1901	.524	.171	.005	.29
Collins vote, 1903	.298	.124	.025	.20

Sources: Boston Board of Election Commissioners, *Annual Report for 1901* (Boston, 1902), p. 62; idem, *Annual Report for 1903* (Boston, 1904), p. 192. Census data for 1900 from Steven Ruggles and Matthew Sobek, *Integrated Public Use Microdata Series: Version 1.0* (Minneapolis: Social History Research Laboratory, Department of History, University of Minnesota, 1995), and from a sample of the manuscript schedule of the *Twelfth Annual Census of the United States* taken by James Connolly and Philip Ethington.

Model: percentage 1901 vote for Collins = intercept + percent Irish stock. Model statistics: intercept = .433; adjusted R^2 = .26.

Model: percentage 1903 vote for Collins = intercept + percent Irish stock. Model statistics: intercept = .536; adjusted R^2 = .17.

Note: See Statistical Appendix for a discussion of the construction of variables.

with an Irishman at the helm. During the late 1890s, when Collins's predecessor Josiah Quincy engaged in pioneering experiments in municipal welfare policy, Boston won praise as one of the nation's best-governed cities. Though most of Quincy's visionary plans failed, the victims of partisan squabbling and fiscal realities, the city nonetheless maintained its image as politically clean and well governed during the Collins administrations. Boston had avoided the major scandals that plagued other major urban centers, and Collins's popularity testified to the continuing possibility of interethnic cooperation. These circumstances elicited praise from such leading municipal reformers as Frank Parsons, Frederick Howe, and Paul Kellogg.[28]

When the National Municipal League held its annual meeting in Boston in May 1902, there was universal praise for Boston's public life. The accolades went beyond the usual polite comments about the convention's host city. Boston was repeatedly excepted from descriptions of urban corruption. "You people do not know the conditions of municipal degradation which we who come from Baltimore, Chicago, and Pittsburgh do," declared incoming League President James C. Carter. "In Boston you have a reasonably good city government. You may think this is no great thing. But in other parts of the country bribery and corruption are common." Local newspapers echoed these sentiments, as did the delegates representing Boston. When recently elected Patrick Collins greeted the convention, he proudly declared that "up in this corner of the land there is very little corruption . . . and if you should find anything wrong here in any part of it . . . come down to city hall and let me know."[29]

Collins's words represented more than just a ritual assertion of civic pride before visiting dignitaries. The context in which they were made gave them deeper meaning. Not only was the city well governed, it was governed well by an Irish mayor. And if any problems were to arise, he—an Irishman—would solve them. In making this statement to an audience of leading municipal reformers who affirmed his claims, Collins assumed the mantle of civic leadership not only for himself, but for the city's Irish population. His ability to make such declarations seriously and his extraordinary political popularity reinforced the narrative of ethnic reconciliation that now defined Boston public life.

By the time of his death in 1905, Collins's role as a symbol of Irish progress and ethnic comity had crystallized. In his lifetime "he saw New England grow hospitable, or at least less sullen, to the alien," *The Republic*'s obituary declared. "He saw the immigrant hitch up his wagon, in Emerson's phrase, to the star of American greatness. He saw opportunity 'in widest commonality spread' without lowering civic ideals of righteousness." The openness of American society, Collins's life showed, was dissolving the conflicts that plagued Boston in an earlier era. While the process was not yet complete, few doubted that the goal of ethnic harmony was in reach.[30]

Party politics played a crucial role in maintaining and promoting this vision of social progress in Boston. Parties virtually monopolized access to municipal power, an arrangement that forced Yankee and Irish leaders to cooperate and translated cultural clashes into partisan battles. Even when this coalition crumbled, ethnic conflict did not immediately become the fundamental cleavage in city politics. Political mobilization would continue to take place primarily in partisan terms until the institutional arrangements of local public life changed.

Although Boston's large Irish population assured a Democratic majority by the late nineteenth century, a defiant assertion of ethnic power never became the centerpiece of the party's appeals. Rather than rally voters by emphasizing ethnoreligious conflict, Irish Democratic leaders worked to mute cultural hostilities in the city's public life. Patrick Collins, Hugh O'Brien, party head Patrick Maguire, and others cooperated with a small group of Brahmin Democrats and mugwumps to maintain civility in Boston.

Political necessity more than mutual admiration dictated this collaboration. Irish leaders needed patronage to maintain order in Boston's vibrant local politics. Although they controlled city hall, municipal appointments alone proved insufficient for the city's burgeoning Irish political class. With the state legislature dominated by Republicans, Boston's Democratic leaders relied on nationally connected Yankee Democrats for access to federal patronage during the Cleveland administrations, a strategy that required a politics of ethnic conciliation on their part. The association with these men also conveyed a degree of legitimacy to Irish power in the city. For their part, Boston's elite Yankee Democrats, whose ranks and ambitions had been bolstered by the mugwump bolt in the 1880s, needed the Irish votes of Boston if they were to stand a chance of delivering Massachusetts to the Democratic Party in national elections.[31]

The principal architect of the Democratic alliance was Patrick Maguire. A successful real estate entrepreneur as well as a newspaper publisher, Maguire rose through the ranks of the Democratic Party, becoming the dominant political figure in the city by the 1880s. He held elective office only briefly, preferring to wield power through the Democratic City Committee, on which he served for twenty years. From that position he deftly rode herd over Boston's fractious Democratic politics, placating both the Irish leaders emerging in the city's wards and the party's small but powerful mugwump wing in his efforts to engineer Irish succession as smoothly as possible.[32]

Maintenance of this coalition required that Maguire and his fellow Irish Democrats defer to Brahmin leadership for a time. When conflicts over school issues erupted in the late 1880s, ending Hugh O'Brien's string of mayoral terms, Maguire steered the Democratic City Committee toward elite Yankee candidates who made the threat of an Irish political takeover less manifest. The initial beneficiary of this approach was Nathan Matthews, who served as mayor from 1891 through 1894. Though his fiscal conservatism and efforts to centralize power in the mayor's office placed a strain on relations between ward-level politicos and city hall, he defended Irish interests aggressively and was reelected three times with their support. The same deferential strategy persisted when Josiah Quincy, another Brahmin Democrat, succeeded Matthews as mayor in 1895, again with strong support from Irish voters.[33]

As part of this cooperative effort, both sides sought to define ethnic conflict in partisan terms. Maguire never missed a chance to blame the Republican Party for the outbreak of anti-Catholicism and the growth of the APA, a task made easier by the party's capitulation to several nativist demands, including the elimination of Catholics from the school board. While his paper praised "all things Irish," it declared "all things Republican"—not all things Yankee—"as anti-Irish." Nathan Matthews likewise blamed "the bigotry and prejudice of the Republican party" and its "ill-disguised appeal to prejudices of race and creed" for the opposition to Irish incumbent Hugh O'Brien in the 1888 mayoral election. Matthews also blamed Republicans for the movement to deny Catholics any places on the school board and to institute state inspection of private schools.[34]

By contrast, the Democratic Party represented tolerance and reconciliation. It had long "stood out against the religious prejudices of our New England ancestors," Matthews reminded Bostonians during the 1888 school conflict. Policies promoted by Democrats were largely responsible, he argued, for "the presence here of so many citizens of foreign birth and name." In effect, the Democratic Party embodied the vision of a more harmonious, inclusive Boston.[35]

Partisan boilerplate perhaps, but this rhetoric helped to develop the narrative of ethnic progress that was shaping Irish identity in Boston. By insisting that the Republican Party—in league with outside agitators—was responsible for the recent surge in anti-Catholic, anti-Irish feeling, Democratic leaders absolved the city as a whole. They could still argue that Boston was basically hospitable, that it had moved beyond the prejudices of its Puritan past. The danger of declension remained insignificant so long as the Democratic Party held the reins of power. This translation of cultural clashes into party competition did not eliminate tensions, but it prevented them from consuming city affairs.

Even when cooperation between Yankee and Irish Democrats broke down, a politics of ethnic conflict did not automatically follow. Geoffrey Blodgett and Paul Kleppner have persuasively argued that the gradual centralization of power in the executive branch of Boston's government and disputes over how the city should respond to the 1893–1894 depression lessened cooperation. But despite the fissure,

Irish leaders did not turn to a politics of ethnic animosity. Municipal affairs continued to be cast in partisan terms. Even insurgent campaigns turned into battles over control of party machinery and partisan legitimacy. The key question in city politics remained who was to represent the Democratic Party, not who was to represent the Irish or any other social group.[36]

Parties remained the intervening variable in the process of political mobilization because they controlled access to public office. Independent candidates rarely succeeded in this era of unswerving partisan loyalty and regularity; in districts where one party dominated, that party's selection was tantamount to election. And the process of claiming a party nomination was a closed one. Conventions, not popular votes, selected party nominees for state and city offices; the delegates to those conventions were chosen in ward caucuses run by the local arm of the party, the ward committee. The same local caucuses chose party nominees for the ward-based offices of state representative and common councilman.

Although caucuses were supposed to be a mechanism for polling the party faithful, those running the ward committee had considerable sway in determining winners. They appointed caucus officers, who scheduled the caucuses and counted the ballots—a practice that led to frequent charges of vote fraud by opposing factions. The ward committee also controlled access to the ward room, a meeting hall run by the party. In the weeks preceding caucuses, committee leaders often refused to allow use of the ward rooms by opposition candidates and their backers to rally popular support for their nomination bids. Control of the ward committee thus carried with it a significant competitive advantage in the battle for party nominations.

Since the support of ward delegations was usually necessary to win convention nominations, local politics revolved around battles for control of the partisan ward committee, which played so vital a role in selecting delegates. Competition was especially fierce in predominantly Irish wards, where the number of politically ambitious young men invariably exceeded the number of available offices and delegate slots. Those left out formed separate factions and wrestled for control of the ward committee and the various convention delegations. New factions formed and old ones disappeared every year, their membership changing from year to year and even election to election. This constant shifting made local political life exceedingly fluid. Only in a few central city neighborhoods where less politically active southern and eastern European immigrants made up a majority could a single organization establish itself for a significant period of time.[37]

Challenges to this ward-based system began to arise during the late nineteenth century. The principal reform effort sought to limit the patronage resources of party leaders. Mugwump reformers convinced state legislators to rewrite the city's charter, giving the executive branch more power and the City Council less, in the hopes of reducing the access of locally based party spoilsmen to municipal coffers. These reformers also placed the police department under the control of the state government instead of the city and pushed a civil service bill through the legislature. Other reforms followed at a steady clip. Beginning in 1893, elections for the Board of Aldermen were held on an at-large basis, after each party nominated seven men. And in 1895 the term of the mayor was expanded from one year to two, in the hope of further removing him from the pressures of ward-based party operatives.[38]

Though they had some impact, these changes did not fundamentally alter Boston's partisan political culture. Most of them were the work of Republican leaders in the state legislature, whose goal was to weaken the power of Boston Democrats, not to eliminate parties from public life altogether. The election of aldermen, for instance, now took place on an at-large basis, but the nominations remained in the hands of the parties. Candidates for mayor and alderman, however powerful and independent once in office, had to gain the support of delegate slates throughout the city to earn the party nomination. Though criticism of party power grew steadily by the end of the century, it remained the accepted arrangement in city politics. "The caucus is supposed to express the choice of the party," explained one defender of the status quo in 1900, "the election that of the voters."[39]

As long as parties were accepted as the primary source of a nominee's political legitimacy, even ideologically driven insurgency had to work within the system. Demands for reform inevitably became partisan squabbles in the process. Consider the local ramifications of William Jennings Bryan's 1896 presidential candidacy. Led by George Fred Williams, a mugwump from suburban Dedham who ran for governor in 1896, Massachusetts Bryanites embarked on a struggle to win control of the Democratic Party from forces resistant to Bryan's radical reforms. When his efforts met with strong opposition from Patrick

Maguire and other Democratic leaders in Boston, where Bryan's controversial and culturally alien candidacy was eyed with suspicion, Williams could not abandon organizational politics for ideological appeals to a mass public. Instead he set about recruiting disaffected factions in each ward, hoping to capture enough ward delegates to gain control of the state party organization at its fall convention. Bryan-Sewall-Williams clubs competed with regular Democratic organizations for control of the ward delegations to each convention. This process muted the ideological thrust of Bryan's campaign by making it part of the various ongoing factional battles in Boston neighborhoods rather than a reformist insurgency.[40]

Though the Bryanites lost the battle for Boston, they inflicted a wound from which the Democratic Party never fully recovered. Their efforts marked the beginning of a period of furious factional infighting in the city's Democratic wards. Among the allies Williams had cultivated was Martin Lomasney, the unchallenged political leader of ward eight in Boston's immigrant-filled West End. With Williams's support, Lomasney continued to battle against the regular Democratic Party organization and against Mayor Josiah Quincy, to whom the role of party leader had fallen after Maguire's death in late 1896. Although Lomasney's insurgency was not undertaken on behalf of the Bryanites, their maneuvering stoked the ward-level factionalism that enabled Lomasney to mount a serious challenge to Quincy and his supporters.

Quincy, who won the first of two two-year terms in 1895, quickly set about the task of restoring order within party ranks after the upheavals of the 1896 election. The scion of New England aristocrats, Quincy had come of age politically in the mugwump bolt. But he soon abandoned mugwump nonpartisanship for the give-and-take of party politics. Among his first moves as mayor was the formation of a Board of Strategy, an informal collection of ward politicians (excluding Lomasney), with whom he consulted upon various political matters. Through the deft distribution of patronage and careful politicking, Quincy won the loyalty of these leaders and maintained a semblance of the Irish-Yankee cooperation that had characterized Democratic politics in Boston for more than a decade. Capitalizing on this support, Quincy also set in motion an unprecedented experiment in municipal socialism, dedicating city government to the alleviation of numerous social difficulties in a fashion that earned Boston wide praise among social reform leaders around the nation.[41]

Forces unleashed in 1896 continued to eat away at the party, primarily through Lomasney's attempts to obtain a greater share of patronage. Although the ward eight leader refused to back Tom Riley, Quincy's Bryanite opponent for mayor in 1897, he did sponsor a separate slate of Democratic candidates for alderman, in opposition to Quincy's Board of Strategy ticket. The contest split the Democratic vote, allowing Republicans to capture six seats. Using similar tactics in 1898, Lomasney was able to negotiate enough support to elect one of his ward eight proteges president of the Common Council.

That maneuver successfully thwarted Quincy's plan for the creation of a Board of Apportionment, a formal body composed of the presidents of the Board of Aldermen and the Common Council and a third member elected by voters. The Board was a device to rationalize the city budget by removing it from the hands of locally elected City Council members. With a Lomasney man on it, its efficacy would be greatly hindered. The issue quickly became moot when Lomasney wooed Republican support in the state legislature and engineered the repeal of the law that had created the Board. The controversy and political turmoil surrounding this issue effectively crippled Quincy's mayoralty and dashed any plans he had to seek reelection in 1899.[42]

Friction came to a head in Democratic circles during the contest to succeed Quincy. Party leaders called the popular Patrick Collins out of retirement to run for mayor in the hope of unifying the party. Opposing Collins for the nomination was city Water Commissioner John R. Murphy of Charlestown, a Lomasney ally. When, after a heated battle, Collins captured the nomination at the Democratic city convention, Murphy and his supporters refused to make the nomination unanimous, claiming it had been unfairly obtained. Instead Murphy and Lomasney bolted, forming the Democratic Citizens Association of Boston, an alternative party organization that was dubbed the "Filipino Movement" in reference to recent guerrilla warfare in the Pacific. Murphy then endorsed Thomas Hart, Collins's Republican opponent. Although Lomasney did not follow Murphy's move, neither did he aggressively support Collins, and Murphy's abandonment proved enough to ensure the Democratic candidate's defeat in 1899.[43]

Perhaps the most remarkable thing about the infighting within the Boston Democracy was the absence of a serious ethnic rupture. Lomasney and his allies might have challenged Quincy's mayoralty by attempting to rally Irish support against a Yankee mayor. Instead, virtually all of Lomasney's efforts were undertaken in strictly partisan terms. In the party-centered political culture of late-nineteenth-century Boston, no other form of political action worked.

One famous episode in Lomasney's career illustrated the power of these institutional arrangements. In 1898 Lomasney and Quincy's Board of Strategy were battling over a seat in the State Senate representing Lomasney's West End as well as the North End and a portion of East Boston. Seats in the state legislature were precious for both sides, as they contested Mayor Quincy's Board of Apportionment plan. Lomasney backed Daniel Rourke, one of his ward eight lieutenants, for the spot, while Quincy and his allies promoted the candidacy of William J. Donovan of East Boston. Donovan had outpolled Rourke in the caucus voting, but Lomasney was chairman of the District Committee, the formal party organization responsible for holding the nominating convention. Since the ultimate choice of the party was made by the convention, he hoped to use the power associated with his position to capture the nomination for Rourke.[44]

While Lomasney hatched a complicated scheme designed to manipulate party rules in his favor, his opposition maneuvered to block him. With nominations due at the Massachusetts State House in downtown Boston at 5 P.M. on October 20, Lomasney scheduled the convention for 4:30 of the same afternoon and announced that it would be held across Boston Harbor, in an East Boston hotel. Since ordinary means of transportation from East Boston to downtown required forty minutes, it was widely suspected that Lomasney planned to use a ferry or another boat to deliver the nomination papers to the State House before the deadline. Donovan's supporters, fearing Lomasney would shut them out of the convention and then nominate his own man, secretly booked all the available rooms in the hotel and arranged to have men loyal to the Quincy administration manning the ferries running to downtown so they could prevent a Lomasney messenger from reaching the State House.

The result was a competition between the two factions to claim the nomination that involved parliamentary maneuvering as well as races on foot, bicycle, and boat. Rourke's delegates, led by Lomasney, arrived at the hotel late on the afternoon of October 20, where they assembled in a room Lomasney had surreptitiously booked several weeks earlier. After tricking Donovan backers into leaving the room, they quickly called the convention to order and nominated Rourke.

Not to be outdone, Donovan's delegates held a separate convention across the hall and selected their own man. A race to deliver the nominations ensued. Lomasney dispatched a decoy messenger on a city-run ferry, which was soon stranded in the middle of Boston Harbor, purportedly with engine trouble. He then sent a sprinter—a Boston College football star—to a private boat that sped across the harbor. From there, a well-known local bicycle racer pedaled the nomination to the State House, arriving at 4:49 P.M. In the meantime, Donovan's papers were rushed downtown on a second ferry and handed off to another bicyclist. But his bicycle chain broke, and he arrived three minutes after Lomasney's messenger. Insisting that the first nomination to be filed was the only legitimate one, Lomasney's forces claimed victory.

This battle over a single nomination to the State Senate is more than a colorful anecdote about machine politics. The great—and illicit—lengths to which Lomasney went to capture the official party nomination illustrate the importance placed on that credential. Rather than launch an independent candidacy for Rourke—a strategy that would soon become a preferred means of office seeking—Lomasney constructed an alternative party apparatus, which followed parliamentary procedures assiduously. Although his tactics were ruled invalid by the Ballot Law Commission, which made Donovan the official Democratic nominee, Lomasney's adherence to formal nominating procedures even while stealing the nomination reflected the degree to which the party was the principal source of legitimacy in late-nineteenth-century political culture. Without the sanction of a party endorsement, however obtained, Lomasney's candidate stood little chance of winning over an electorate dominated by unwavering Democratic regulars.

Although usually less entertaining, the rampant intraward factionalism that defined ground-level Democratic politics in Boston rarely spilled over partisan boundaries. In districts such as Charlestown's ward three, "where contests for political supremacy [were] continuous and brilliant," the losers inevitably accepted the outcome of the caucus and began preparing for the next election. Only a few candidates ran independently, and only rarely did they defeat the regular organization's candidate.[45]

Even when a disappointed caucus loser did place his name on the ballot separately, he did not ordinarily present himself as a reformer or an independent. When former State Representative Daniel Casey of

Roxbury's ward seventeen lost the Democratic nomination for alderman in 1900, he charged his opponent with winning "by unfair and dishonest methods." Instead of withdrawing, he declared himself the "Democratic Citizen's" candidate and entered the general election as a third candidate. Casey argued that he was the rightful party nominee, whose candidacy had been derailed by illicit maneuvering at the caucuses. While the use of "Citizen's" in his choice of ballot labels prefigured the reform style that was soon to become more popular, Casey's insistence that he was the true "Democratic" candidate reflected the persistent role of parties as the sole source of legitimacy for candidates for public office.[46]

Voter mobilization, too, invariably occurred within a framework of partisanship. Ward, party, and faction, not ethnicity or class, were the basic categories of political action. Democratic dominance in Boston exacerbated this situation by turning most significant political contests—especially at the grassroots level—into battles over which candidate was the legitimate party nominee. Thus most popular appeals were to party loyalty. While issues of group conflict were useful as tools to stoke party loyalty, it was ultimately as faithful partisans, not as aggrieved ethnics, that Bostonians were asked to act politically. As long as parties remained entrenched in the city's political process, social conflict was channeled into partisan competition.

The dominance of parties did not entirely preclude other kinds of mobilization. Alternatives were beginning to make their presence felt by 1900. One prominent example was the Boston Central Labor Union (BCLU), the umbrella body for many of the city's skilled craft unions. The bulk of the BCLU's membership was Irish, and many of its leaders were well connected politically. Over the course of the 1890s, the organization increased the pressure on political leaders, demanding that they support legislation beneficial to its members or risk its opposition on election day. Union leaders worked closely with the Quincy administration on numerous fronts. They even targeted individual local politicians who had aroused their ire. When Roxbury contractor and politician Harry Nawn employed men at lower wages and for longer hours than the BCLU felt was fair, the union took its case to the mayor, the Metropolitan Water Board, and the press, forcing him to adjust his employment practices or risk losing his city contract.[47]

The growing efficacy of this independent style of politics became evident in 1899, when the BCLU successfully engineered the passage of a referendum in support of an eight-hour workday for municipal workers. It lobbied the City Council, the leaders of each party, and finally candidates for office that fall, demanding that they back the referendum or forfeit the support of the BCLU's members. Its representatives also questioned each candidate for city office on the issue and then published the results of the survey in the daily press just before the municipal election. Nearly every candidate for Common Council and Board of Aldermen endorsed the idea. BCLU representatives even appeared at polling places alongside party workers, passing out cards to voters urging them to back the eight-hour measure. These tactics worked well enough to ensure the passage of the proposal by a four-to-one margin.[48]

The BCLU's success did not mark a sea change in the character of municipal politics, but it was a harbinger of the future. Union members did not seek to dismantle existing party structures; they soundly rejected proposals for an independent political committee in 1899. But the eight-hour campaign did ask Bostonians to base their political behavior on something besides partisan loyalty, a tactic that was becoming increasingly common. Educational activists formed the Public School Association in 1898 to support reform-minded school board candidates. A group of business leaders, led by lawyer-reformer Louis Brandeis, established the Public Franchise League, a body devoted to obtaining public control over the distribution of city franchises in 1900. Local woman suffragists launched the Boston Equal Suffrage Association for Good Government in 1901 to press for both suffrage and social reforms. Business leaders formed the Good Government Association in 1903. Suburban civic leaders were forming neighborhood improvement associations that lobbied elected officials and candidates on behalf of local interests. Even some of the settlement workers now dispersing through the city's urban neighborhoods tried to form independent political organizations where they lived and worked.[49]

A common thread linked these disparate endeavors: each sought to mobilize people politically on the basis of something other than partisan fealty. In some cases they involved the public interest, in others a more narrowly defined community or group goal. Each movement encouraged people to imagine themselves as members of a specific social grouping—a class, an ethnicity, a neighborhood, the whole city—and then to act politically according to that loyalty rather than as a member of a party.

As this kind of political action began to succeed, the role of partisanship as the organizing principle of municipal public life began to diminish. The structure of city politics before 1900 gave party officials almost complete control over nominations, thereby directing political insurgency into partisan competition and ensuring that the language of partisanship remained the dominant coin of city politics. But the institutional arrangements that bolstered this political culture were beginning to change, and as they did, space opened up for alternative kinds of political mobilization. This shift threatened the fragile ethnic truce that characterized fin de siècle Boston public life. Nathan Matthews, one of the city's keenest political observers, warned of this at the end of his service as mayor. He opposed the trend toward direct democracy and other political reforms that had emerged by the mid-1890s, fearing that such changes would divide voters "into classes and . . . carry the differences of social and pecuniary conditions into city politics." Parties, he argued, prevented this from occurring by organizing people along other lines.[50]

Matthews's observations would prove prescient. Party politics had helped preserve a degree of social comity in Boston, and its demise led to a redefinition of the city's social landscape. The perception of increasing ethnic harmony would fade, to be replaced in less than two decades by a new story of long-standing conflict that formed the context in which local group identities took shape. As the language of party politics gave way to the new social-political vocabulary of the Progressive Era, the city's partisan-centered public culture would begin to crumble. With it would go the fragile sense of ethnic reconciliation it had helped maintain.

CHAPTER TWO

The Dimensions of Progressivism

In the heart of the Progressive Era, Bostonians came together to define a vision for their city's future. The occasion was the creation of the "Boston—1915 Plan," a reform drive spearheaded by retail magnate Edward A. Filene and muckraker Lincoln Steffens. Launched in 1909, the 1915 Plan sought to present an image of Boston after six years of prospective reform, as a goal for all citizens of the city to pursue. Steffens argued that if people were to be lured away from allegiance to corrupt bosses, they needed another magnet for their loyalties. "If we could sketch out a picture of the city as it might be made . . .," Steffens recounted in his *Autobiography,* "the people of Boston both good and bad, both respectable and common, might become so interested that they would neither rob it nor let it be robbed." In this scenario, Bostonians would unite to combat graft not merely because it was immoral but because it blocked progress toward the ideal city they all longed for.[1]

To give this reform vision specificity, Steffens and his fellow organizers staged an exhibition. It displayed a full range of ideas for the betterment of Boston, including model tenements, parks, neighborhood centers, and schools. Various civic bodies presented demonstrations or illustrations of their current activities and their plans for the future. The fair opened with speeches from the president of the Chamber of Commerce, an organizer from the National Boot and Shoe Workers Union, social reformer Jane Addams, and Rabbi Stephen

Wise. Both the exhibition and the reform campaign it was part of won widespread praise from local and national sources. Over 200,000 people—more than a quarter of the city's population—visited the month-long display.[2]

But those who attended found many images of Boston's future instead of just one. The two hundred exhibitors included labor unions, settlement houses, neighborhood civic associations, Catholic and Protestant churches, Jewish synagogues, business and professional groups, and numerous other bodies. Within a few months, the planners had counted 1,658 different organizations prepared to reform Boston, each with its own ideas about what needed reforming and how things should look when they were finished. Few of these expectations coincided; some even contradicted each other. Not surprisingly the Boston—1915 movement faded from view within a few years, unable to unite the multiplicity of interests active within it.[3]

Though transitory, the exhibition captured the essential dynamic of Progressivism: reform entailed creating a "picture of the city as it might be made" and then joining together to make that picture a reality. But instead of forging one shared vision, Bostonians created many, each suiting particular needs, expectations, and interests. Some of these Progressivisms—particularly those formulated by business leaders, suburbanites, and middle-class reformers—are familiar to historians. Others, especially those articulated by ethnic voices, have been less fully explored. To comprehend Progressivism one must not only acknowledge its multifaceted character but embrace it as well.

The rhetorical formula that defined Progressivism made this diversity possible. Drawing from the popular journalism of Steffens and many others, self-appointed civic leaders began depicting themselves at the head of a communal response to the disorder of modern life and the greedy depredations of politicians and businessmen. But the specifics varied. They called many different communities into action against a diverse array of social problems and corrupt influences. Rarely did these responses turn into grassroots movements. More often they were the work of a few men and women claiming to speak for the city, the neighborhood, or their ethnic group, some more plausibly than others. The result was a multiplicity of distinct Progressivisms, sharing a common vocabulary but pursuing diverse ends.

This chapter surveys some of the dimensions of Boston Progressivism. It is not exhaustive, nor does it fully explore each of the Progressivisms it describes. Rather it demonstrates the extraordinary flexibility of the reform rhetoric that grew so popular in early-twentieth-century public life.

Though theirs was never the sole voice of reform sentiment in Boston, the city's business leaders often were the loudest and most prominent. Historians most commonly link the demand for the reform of urban government in the Progressive Era to organized commercial and professional groups. Samuel Hays found that members of these bodies dominated big-city reform organizations and were the strongest advocates of the centralization of city governments. James Weinstein's analysis of the commission government movement makes a similar claim. These and other studies place businessmen at the center of the crusade to redesign urban governance in the Progressive Era. In Boston, native-stock business leaders occupied a conspicuous place in that drive, though they never held exclusive rights to the meaning of urban reform.[4]

The primary instrument for businessmen's reform in Boston emerged in 1903. Representatives of seven commercial and professional associations convened after William Lincoln, the president of the Chamber of Commerce, decried the state of municipal affairs in Boston. In response to Lincoln's complaint, they formed the Good Government Association (GGA), a "disinterested organization composed of men who seek no office and have no axe to grind." The new body sought to "reform the citizens of Boston" and to help voters "secure the election of aggressively honest and capable men." They published pamphlets summarizing the records of candidates for state offices and encouraged public demand for cleaner, more efficient government.[5]

Boston did not appear to need so aggressive an approach to solving its political problems. By most accounts, Boston had entered the new century as one of the nation's best-governed cities. The reforms of the 1880s, the social welfare experimentation of Mayor Josiah Quincy in the 1890s, and the abstemious political practices of Irish Mayor Patrick Collins contributed to Boston's reputation for good government and relatively clean politics. At the National Municipal League's 1902 meeting in Boston, opinion was nearly unanimous that the host city was a model of good government. This perception so thoroughly prevailed that Boston's leading municipal reform groups of the 1890s, the

Citizens' Association of Boston and the Boston Municipal League, had withered from inactivity by 1900.[6]

With no discernible need for reform, the reasons for the GGA's creation remain unclear. Its early actions point to two possible motivations. The Association's repeated calls for a more respectable leadership may have been an effort to restore the declining civic authority of Brahmin Boston in the face of immigrant insurgency.[7] Most of the reforms advocated by the GGA were fiscal, suggesting another impetus to their reform efforts. Regulation of public franchises, social welfare, and the improvement of the urban environment—issues that concerned other urban Progressives—received scant attention in GGA literature and activities. It concentrated primarily on city finances. The drive for lower city spending and more efficient administration was designed to reduce Boston's rising property tax rate—a vital concern to the city's wealthy business leaders, who paid the largest portion of those taxes. Progressivism provided a formula for pursuing this end in the name of the public interest.

A profile of the GGA's founders is consistent with this interpretation. The twenty who came together to form the Association were Yankee business and professional men. Half did not even live in the city; those who did resided either in the aristocratic enclave of the Back Bay and Beacon Hill or in the city's most prosperous suburban districts. Six were lawyers; the remainder were officers in real estate, investment, or manufacturing firms. The original twenty included lawyers Moorfield Storey, who had cut his political teeth in the mugwump movement of the 1880s and 1890s, and A. Lawrence Lowell, future president of Harvard University. The chairman of the GGA executive committee during its first decade of existence was William Minot, the son of a prosperous Boston businessman and reformer. A real estate lawyer, he was reputed to be among Boston's largest individual taxpayers.[8]

The GGA drew a few members from beyond Brahmin business circles. Social workers Robert Woods and Edmund Billings, school reformer Samuel Capen, and crusading lawyer Louis Brandeis participated in the Association's early reform endeavors. But neither Woods, Capen, nor Brandeis became important figures in the organization, and their involvement diminished after a few years. Only Billings, the Association's first secretary, remained an influential member for most of the organization's thirty-year existence.

No man better embodied the characteristics that fueled the Association's activism than George Read Nutter. Descended from a line of Puritan preachers sharing the name Hate-Evil Nutter, he carried his ancestors' fierce morality into Boston's public life. His father was a well-to-do lawyer, and Nutter followed in his footsteps after graduating from Harvard College in 1885 and Harvard Law School four years later. The mugwump revolt against party politics during that era shaped his political ideals; decades later he would still declare "I began a mugwump and still am a mugwump." His career was marked by success in both legal and civic affairs. A successful corporation lawyer, he became a partner in the law firm Warren and Brandeis and later became president of the Boston Chamber of Commerce, the Boston Bar Association, and the Massachusetts Bar Association. He served on the executive committee of the GGA for nearly thirty years. For much of that time he was among its prime movers, both behind the scenes and publicly.[9]

Cut off from Boston's Irish-dominated partisan organizations, Nutter and other Boston business and professional men found in the reform prescriptions of muckrakers like Lincoln Steffens a way to establish an alternative source of power. Steffens, as Richard McCormick has argued, played a vital role in convincing the American public of the systematic corruption of big-city governments and of the civic inertness of most urbanites. William Lincoln's call for a municipal reform body used language popularized by Steffens and other journalists. Citing "the enormous increase of wealth, the rapid growth of our cities, [and] the vastness of corporate interests," Lincoln warned of a "decay in civic virtue." His language echoed Steffens's call for the reinvigoration of citizenship as a solution to the problem of urban life, urging that "public opinion be educated and brought up to a high standard of honour and integrity."[10]

The influence of Steffens's writings carried over into the process of organizing the GGA. It modeled itself after Chicago's Municipal Voters League, a businessmen's organization that had earned enthusiastic praise in *The Shame of the Cities*. Like the Chicago League, the GGA would take a more active role in politics, going beyond the simple compilation of information on local office-seekers—the traditional approach to municipal reform—to endorsing or opposing specific candidates. The GGA echoed Steffens's aim—"to arouse the civic pride of an apparently shameless citizenship"—when it promised to "reform the citizens of Boston" and "awaken their civic pride."[11]

At the heart of GGA reform was the claim that it operated strictly in the public interest. The Association would be strictly nonpartisan, a "disinterested organization composed of men who seek no office and have no axe to grind," in the words of its first handbill. The Association's role would be to represent the people of Boston and their undoubted desire for good government. It promised to aid voters in securing "the election of aggressively honest and capable men" and announced its intention to "open a ledger account with every man in public life."[12]

Specific assumptions undergirded the GGA's conception of its role. Its creators believed that a single set of shared civic values existed and that they were responsible for maintaining them. Through their investigations of candidates and issues and their subsequent publicity campaigns, they sought to present a clear contest between good and bad government to the public. They expected that the community would make the obvious—the only—moral choice. "The whole basis of the movement," declared the GGA's initial pamphlet, "is the belief confidently held by the promoters of it, that a majority of the citizens of Boston wish to see honest and capable men in office."[13]

That perception of unity carried with it an acceptance of hierarchy. The city's elite reformers placed themselves at the center of their solution for Boston's problems. City government needed a "more capable set of officials," declared George Nutter, but "this kind of person is never coming into office to stay until some standard is set up that demands him and some public opinion is created that will stand behind him." The GGA's directors aimed to do just that. They presented themselves as the modern version of the virtuous civic leader of republican rhetoric, responsible for articulating communal standards and then molding the public opinion necessary to maintain them.[14]

In keeping with its rhetoric, the new body at first sought to become an inclusive, grassroots alternative to the regular parties. Its original "plan of action" aimed to build up a network of strong ward committees and to expand its membership. The Association dispatched college students to every district to interview and investigate candidates for office. The results of these forays became the basis for recommending or opposing candidates.[15]

But these efforts at neighborhood activism were short-lived. The GGA quickly became a more streamlined operation, run by the lawyers and business leaders on its executive committee. Efforts to recruit new members never got off the ground; the Association relied principally on the trade and professional groups from which it was formed. Even those organizations ceded control of the day-to-day operations of the GGA to the executive committee, which formulated policy, made public pronouncements, and decided which candidates to endorse. The GGA became an operation controlled by a handful of businessmen claiming to speak in the interests of the entire community.[16]

Forsaking a grassroots approach to reform, the Association turned instead to muckraking to convince Bostonians that their city's leaders were corrupt and inefficient. In 1905 it launched its own magazine, *City Affairs,* to mold public opinion. GGA leaders filled its pages with stories of waste and dishonesty in city government. Inevitably, friendly city dailies picked up these reports, amplifying them through their headlines. It was in this fashion that the GGA helped foster popular demand for municipal reform.

After numerous minor revelations during its first two years of existence, the GGA struck gold in its investigation of the dredging of the Back Bay Fens, a swampy area adjacent to the Charles River. In 1903 the state legislature authorized $800,000 in bonds to complete the work, part of a larger project to improve drainage and sanitary conditions along the Charles River. The undertaking did not run smoothly. Two years after the initial appropriation, it was still far from completion, and city officials sought another $410,000 to finish it. Sensing an opportunity, the GGA commissioned an investigation of the project.[17]

What they found and reported to the public was an enterprise crippled by cronyism and patronage, disclosures that paralleled the depictions of urban public life by muckrakers and investigators elsewhere. *City Affairs* pointed out that the four contractors who divided up the work each had close ties to the city's Democratic leaders. One was the father-in-law of Jim Donovan, superintendent of streets and the reputed boss of the South End's ward nine; another was the former treasurer of the Democratic City Committee. Given these connections, the project inevitably turned into a patronage feeding frenzy. The engineers hired by the GGA to observe the work reported that most of the cost overruns resulted from a payroll two to three times larger than was necessary. The contractors were working on a cost-plus basis, which gave them a further incentive to pad the payroll and spend more. Surveying the situation, the GGA concluded that the result of the Fenway work was "not only disappointing, but amounted to a scandal."[18]

The Association did its best to make sure the general public came to share that sentiment. *City Affairs* maintained a running commentary on the issue through 1905, with the citywide dailies relaying every word to a wider audience. When the *Boston Post* argued that no graft had occurred, only inefficiency, George Nutter wrote a furious rebuttal for the *Boston Transcript*'s editorial page. He rejected the *Post*'s argument, claiming it "introduce[d] a distinction into graft that cannot exist." In an address to the Twentieth Century Club several weeks later, he put the issue into a broader context: "This administration of a public trust is certainly on a parallel with those administrations of a private trust which are now absorbing the attention of the entire nation." State legislators and the district attorney amplified the issue even further by commissioning inquiries of their own, which reached similar (and similarly publicized) conclusions. The result was a full-blown municipal scandal, of the kind that swept the nation's cities in the first decade of the twentieth century.[19]

Significantly, the GGA was more interested in influencing public opinion than in punishing the perpetrators. Its leaders did not pursue formal charges against the contractors and their allies. Nor did they seek to condemn particular individuals. Though Jim Donovan was at the center of the controversy, *City Affairs* insisted that he was "merely one example of a type" that had become prevalent in city government. The practices of the men running the Fenway dredging were routine rather than exceptional, the GGA argued. When another Association inquiry found misconduct in Boston's sewer department a few years later, it was deemed proof that "the Fenway graft was merely an incident in the ordinary routine of the Department." Taken collectively, the message of the GGA's revelations was that systematic corruption crippled Boston's public life and made the reform ministrations of the Association desperately necessary.[20]

The realities of Boston politics placed limits on the efficacy of the GGA reform vision. For all its success in attracting public attention, the Association realized few of its initial goals. Its endorsements had little effect on the outcomes of City Council races in 1903 and 1904, and its backing of staid Republican Louis Frothingham for mayor in 1905 not only failed to sway a majority of the city's voters but damaged the Association's credibility by linking it too closely with one party. The Association's aggressive campaign against future mayor James Michael Curley proved embarrassing as well. Curley, campaigning from a jail cell in 1904 after a conviction on charges of impersonating a civil service examinee, won a seat on the Board of Aldermen over the GGA's vociferous objections by portraying himself as the friend of the ordinary Bostonian and the foe of elites like those who launched the GGA. His win was part of a Democratic near sweep that left both the GGA and the Republican Party out in the cold. Many of the city's voters clearly did not see the GGA as a voice for their interests. Although the Association initiated the terms of Progressive debate, it clearly did not have a monopoly on popular understandings of the public good.

While Boston's businessmen fashioned one version of Progressive reform, their wives, daughters, mothers, and sisters created another. As in many cities, upper- and middle-class women established "municipal housekeeping" campaigns that translated their traditionally female household responsibilities into the public realm. While this style had roots in nineteenth-century women's voluntarism, it flourished in the proreform atmosphere of the Progressive Era. Gender served as another axis along which a distinctive variant of reform could be constructed.[21]

Building on a reform tradition stretching back to the era of abolitionism, Boston women played a central role in the development of the city's social reform movement in the late nineteenth century. The Women's Educational and Industrial Union, formed in 1877, developed into an effective force for maternalist social policies by the 1890s. Its leaders worked closely with Mayor Josiah Quincy on many social welfare fronts. Denison House, an all-female settlement established by three Wellesley professors in 1892, became a vital public presence in Boston's South End. Its residents—as well as many other women settlement workers spread throughout the city—engaged in a variety of social reform activities, ranging from child care for working women to labor organizing. These and other organizations provided public platforms for Boston's upper- and middle-class women by the early twentieth century.[22]

One of the first efforts to unite the various strands of women's activism into a municipal housekeeping movement for Boston arose among woman suffragists. A group of Boston women dissatisfied with the conservative, nativist, and increasingly ineffective bent of the Massachusetts Woman Suffrage Association established the Boston Equal

Suffrage Association for Good Government (BESAGG) in 1901. They sought to demonstrate the benefits of having women fully involved in public life. Initially they established committees for public schools, "care of the young, poor, and defective," prevention of vice, prison reform, and peace and arbitration. But BESAGG dropped most of its civic reform efforts within a few years to concentrate on direct agitation for suffrage.[23]

At about the same time as BESAGG ceased its social reform work, another group of women established the Women's Municipal League (WML). It sought to consolidate the city's women to complement the GGA. "A year ago . . . when the men of Boston, the respectable men, were all united in their effort to improve municipal conditions, it occurred, undoubtedly to a great many women, to ask themselves the question . . . whether they were doing their fair half of the work to secure better conditions in the city," declared Katharine Bowlker, the WML's first president, upon the League's founding. Noting the absence of any organization to coordinate the activities of female reformers, she proposed that the WML become an umbrella body for the many women's organizations in the city. It would serve as a clearinghouse of information, prevent duplication, and serve as the voice of the women of the city on matters of public interest.[24]

The rhetoric of Progressive reform, with its emphasis on a single, well-understood public interest, served the WML well. The League sought only those women "earnest in their wish to work for the city's good" and insisted it was a nonpartisan body. How the "city's good" was defined and by whom were never discussed. And as its name suggested, the WML claimed to speak for all of Boston's women. Like the leaders of the GGA, the founders of the League used Progressive imagery to make themselves representatives of the entire community on those issues considered part of the female domain.

The social makeup of the WML paralleled that of the GGA. Despite their claim to speak for Boston's female population, the women who founded the WML came largely from a narrow social circle. The initial executive committee roster read like a page of the *Social Register,* with such Brahmin names as Sargent, Parkman, Storrow, Higginson, Shaw, and Cabot. League President Katharine Bowlker was a member of a prestigious New England family that included GGA founder A. Lawrence Lowell. Conspicuously absent were women from the city's ethnic communities. The sole Irish-Catholic woman was the social reformer and publicist Mary Boyle O'Reilly. The daughter of John Boyle O'Reilly, revered editor of *The Pilot* and one of the few nineteenth-century Boston Irish to gain entry into Brahmin society, she hardly spoke for the mass of Boston's immigrant women.[25]

Because the vision of female solidarity embodied in the WML's rhetoric did not conform to social reality, that unity had to be created. "The great majority of women have never yet reached an adequate conception of their communal duty as corporate members of the community," admitted Bowlker, so a campaign to educate them would be necessary. The first duty of the League would be to create among Boston women "a comprehension of their civic responsibilities." Only after it accomplished this end would the League then be able to achieve its second goal, "to unite all women into an intelligent organized body of public opinion, which shall be so reasonable and so representative in its demands, that it cannot fail to compel attention and response."[26]

Despite the implicit acknowledgment that a unified female public opinion did not exist, the WML never hesitated to act on behalf of all of Boston's women. Centering its activities on the popular concept of "municipal housekeeping," the League sought to improve the conditions of urban life. Its organizational structure included committees for education, social welfare, streets and alleys, and sanitation. The sanitation committee alone devoted itself to inspecting and seeking regulations for milk, markets, ice cream and butter, infant social service, rats and flies, playgrounds, drinking fountains, and waste disposal. The women who staffed these committees and subcommittees became a regular presence at city hall and the State House, lobbying and campaigning for regulatory measures and ameliorative legislation in the name of Boston women.[27]

Their efforts proved effective. The WML helped move numerous bills through the Massachusetts legislature and the City Council, including measures to arrest litterers, make the city responsible for cleaning private ways, regulate the conditions under which food was sold, and specify how cellars were to be constructed. The League also undertook projects independently, with the hope of providing an example for local government to follow. It built playgrounds, established prenatal clinics and open-air summer schools, and inspected housing, street, and market conditions. In many cases, League inspectors were hired by the city; the WML *Bulletin* reported in 1915 that the League had become a virtual arm of the Board of Health.[28]

Women's special moral character also gave the WML a platform from which to comment on political reform. Although it avoided the suffrage issue for fear of dividing its members and never took positions on candidates or ballot measures, the League left little doubt where it stood. It offered instruction at local social centers on the evils of ward bosses and the importance of morality in politics. When the *Boston Herald* asked WML President Katharine Bowlker what she would do if she were mayor, she refused to answer. Instead, she discussed the important role women should play in municipal administration. Their inherent goodness made them ideal watchdogs against waste and dishonesty: "the business of women must be to watch lest money be wasted in matters of detail and in ways that seem trifling." As a "far reaching influence for good," women in positions of civic responsibility would help eliminate "the festering corruption of a great city."[29]

For all of its success and all of its emphasis on feminine unity, the WML never fully bridged the social gap separating its founders from the mass of Boston women. By reducing its dues payments to minimal amounts and actively recruiting women, the League increased its membership from 200 to 1,852 in just over two years. But it remained a Yankee preserve. Along with its executive committee, nearly all of its active members were upper- and middle-class native-stock women. Of the thirty-six initial members of the Committee on Public Improvements—one of the centers of League activity—twenty-two came from the Brahmin enclaves of the Back Bay and Beacon Hill, and eleven from suburban sections. The remaining three came from the polyglot South End but were settlement workers, not working-class immigrants. Numerous women signed up to keep the Back Bay and Beacon Hill safe and clean, but none could be found in the lower-middle-class Irish neighborhoods of Charlestown and South Boston. The only representatives of the poorest parts of Boston—the North, South, and West Ends—were settlement residents. Strikingly, the League's Committee on Immigration included no immigrants or children of immigrants.[30]

Though it failed to unite the city's women, the Women's Municipal League was nonetheless able to exercise substantial power. Operating outside traditional party politics, Boston's upper- and middle-class women combined the language of reform and separate-spheres ideology to win a significant public role for themselves on many social and political questions. The Progressive formula allowed them to speak for Boston's women without having to consult them.

Suburban neighborhoods provided yet another context for urban Progressivism. These expanding districts required increased levels of support from municipal governments. The desire for more and better roads, sewers, and streetcar service created new political demands in these districts. Failure to meet those expectations sparked public dissatisfaction. In this setting, the emerging national indictment of business power and city government had special resonance. The language and imagery of Progressive reform offered rhetorical tools that allowed leading suburbanites to speak for their communities in the political arena.[31]

Nonpartisan, communal action had an added appeal in these sections because it harkened back to the tradition of the New England town. The corporate political ideal had a prominent place in the political mindset of most of Boston's suburban residents. Even after 1900, a sizable number of them had lived in their neighborhoods when they were towns, before the annexation drive of the 1860s and 1870s. The members of the nonpartisan civic associations formed in the 1890s to lobby for improved municipal services consciously evoked that memory. They labeled their assemblies "town meetings" and conducted them in the open forum style of that tradition.[32]

Jamaica Plain, one of Boston's "streetcar suburbs," was fertile ground for this activity. Once a homogeneous New England village, it annexed itself to Boston in 1873. As improvements in transportation expanded Boston's urban reach, the town became a suburban neighborhood. By the early 1900s, demand for services fueled the creation of the Jamaica Plain Citizens' Association (JPCA). An outgrowth of the Jamaica Plain Businessmen's Association, the JPCA's predominantly middle-class Yankee membership included small businessmen, clergy, professionals, and politicians.[33]

The term "citizens" was misleading. The JPCA's membership hardly represented a cross section of the community. As the neighborhood had urbanized, it became more diverse. By the turn of the century, its population was almost two-thirds blue-collar and more than half its heads of household had been born outside the United States. Yet few, if any, of these Jamaica Plain residents participated in JPCA affairs. The middle-class character of the Association's activities, with its committees, motions, lectures, and formal dinners, removed it even further from working-class life.[34]

The JPCA nevertheless became the voice of the entire neighborhood. Along with social activities, it lobbied the city and state governments for improvements in street conditions and mass transportation, new playgrounds and parks, and better schools and police service, and sought legislation beneficial to the district in a variety of areas. While its efforts were not uniformly productive, the process of representing Jamaica Plain in these public forums reinforced the JPCA's self-declared role as the voice of the entire community.[35]

Mass transportation concerns energized the Association more than any other issue. As in most industrial cities, Boston's transit system underwent massive expansion in the late nineteenth century. What in 1856 had been a single horse-drawn carriage railway became by 1912 a mechanized complex that moved over 200 million passengers a year. The Boston Elevated Company presided over the final stages of this growth after it assumed full control of the city's streetcar operations in 1900. As the city's rail network expanded, conflicts between the Elevated Company and neighborhood interests grew more common.[36]

The controversy in Jamaica Plain began when the "El" sought to establish a rail link between downtown Boston and its southwestern suburbs. To do so, it proposed to run elevated tracks through the middle of Jamaica Plain. The plan prompted howls of protest from local politicians and the newly constituted JPCA, but to no avail. Matters grew worse when the railway announced in 1904 that the line would not include a station in Jamaica Plain, thus denying local residents the benefit of the new line while inflicting on them the noise, dirt, and disruption of the elevated tracks.[37]

The hated El offered an easy target for the JPCA. It had been implicated in several highly publicized bribery scandals, and its cofounder, Henry Whitney, had a notorious reputation as an inside operator at the Massachusetts State House. His ties to financier J. P. Morgan and to state and local Democratic Party officials strengthened the public image of the El as a politically powerful economic interest. Its most vociferous critic was the Public Franchise League, a reform group led by Louis Brandeis that pushed for ownership of public utilities and portrayed the Boston Elevated as a greedy monopoly, unconcerned with the common good. Whitney's bid for lieutenant governor on the Democratic ticket in 1905 ensured that old charges were dredged up just as the Elevated's plan for its new line through Jamaica Plain became public.[38]

With a villain of this sort, the issue was easily defined in Progressive terms. JPCA members described themselves as being in a battle against "the far reaching influence of the big corporations." They feared that appeals to the railroad commissioners, to city hall, or even to the legislature were unlikely to yield success. "I am willing to admit that the Elevated people have secured a pretty good grip on the streets of Boston but they don't quite own the people as yet," noted a more optimistic local politician and JPCA supporter, who nonetheless perceived the issue in the same context.[39]

Battling the corporate giant and its political servants helped the JPCA assume its role as the voice of "the people" of Jamaica Plain. When it gathered to discuss the issue, the Association's small membership suddenly became "the Citizens of Jamaica Plain in mass meeting assembled." The sympathetic *Jamaica Plain News* reinforced the impression that the JPCA spoke for the entire neighborhood. It pointed to the Association's efforts as proof that the "citizens of Jamaica Plain . . . will continue a vigorous contest for a station at Green Street." While obtaining a stop in Jamaica Plain would have undoubtedly benefited almost all of the district's residents, the campaign surrounding the question involved only a few of them.[40]

In ensuing months, leaders of the Association underscored their self-defined role as the voice of the Jamaica Plain citizenry by injecting themselves into the center of the controversy. In the campaign to win a station, its leaders testified at legislative hearings, at meetings of the Board of Aldermen, and at Railroad Commission sessions. They pressured candidates for political office to declare themselves on the issue. These activities received front-page coverage in the *Jamaica Plain News,* whose editor, L. J. Brackett, was a key member of the Association. Although they failed to prevent the construction of the elevated tracks, the JPCA and its allies finally won a station for the district in 1910. By the time they did, the Association had firmly established itself as the principal representative body of the district, even though it included just a small fraction of Jamaica Plain's citizens.[41]

Jamaica Plain's middle-class women were not among those active in the JPCA. Yet while Association membership was open only to men, some of the district's middle-class clubwomen were able to establish a degree of public authority on certain issues. The most prominent local vehicle for women's activism was the Jamaica Plain Tuesday Club, which served as a reform vehicle for some of the neighborhood's wealthier women. Originally a social and educational organization, the Tuesday Club gradually grew more involved in social reform efforts as well. Its members petitioned state legislators to limit the workweek for women and children and raised money for a new local high school. Another group of Jamaica Plain women launched the Helen Weld House (later the Jamaica Plain Neighborhood Club), a settlement devoted to assisting the local poor. And shortly after the creation of the Women's Municipal League, its Jamaica Plain members formed an affiliated branch devoted to local concerns. Reform activism by each of these organizations gave middle-class women the opportunity to speak for the neighborhood on certain issues. Yet like the JPCA, they rarely gave working-class women from immigrant families a chance to exercise political power.[42]

Patterns present in Jamaica Plain's public life were evident in other suburban neighborhoods. Most had increasingly active women's groups and virtually all had male-dominated "citizens" or "improvement" associations by the early 1900s, each presenting itself as the nonpartisan voice of the community. The Roslindale Citizens Association, for instance, was "organized solely for the purpose of protecting and advancing the interests of citizens generally, and is doing good work along that line," its president declared, summing up the attitude of every such body. The social profiles of these groups matched the makeup of the JPCA: mostly middle-class, Yankee business and professional men.[43]

Streetcar issues provided common ground for cooperation among various associations. Although civic leaders in suburban districts sometimes clashed with each other over the layout and direction of the proposed elevated line, the El's subsequent effort to extend a streetcar line to Forest Hills Square elicited a more unified response. Anxious to thwart the plan because it would disrupt local street patterns and businesses, six local civic bodies formed a "cooperative committee" that would coordinate efforts to prevent the station's construction. They succeeded in securing a hearing before the Massachusetts railroad commissioners after several months of agitation and were able to block the El's plan.[44]

The battle against the El and the public hearing on the issue provided these civic bodies with an opportunity to reinforce their self-declared roles as community representatives. The spokesman for the cooperative committee was J. J. Conway, a state representative from Jamaica Plain. In this instance, he derived his legitimacy as a witness not from his elected position, but because he was stating the views of the civic bodies. He spoke on behalf of the "citizens" of the six districts, who were presenting "a united front" on this question, the *Jamaica Plain News* reported. He cited the "authenticated records" of the various improvement groups in support of that claim, as if the sentiments of these organizations embodied the wishes of every local resident.[45]

Whether representative or not, local improvement associations gradually became more active and found more grounds for cooperation. Recognizing their common concerns and shared outlook, fourteen neighborhood civic bodies formed the United Improvement Association (UIA) in 1909. They were also responding to the encouragement of several nationally known reformers, including Lincoln Steffens, who urged the leaders of the city's neighborhood groups to combine their efforts to "express the demands of the people." The UIA quickly became a lobbying and publicity organization for the interests of suburban civic groups. As its effectiveness increased, so did the local power and prestige of the associations that belonged to it.[46]

Suburban civic leaders found the Progressive motif a useful basis for political action. As it did for the businessmen who formed the GGA, Progressivism enabled them to carve out a place for themselves in public affairs as they grew more and more isolated from traditional party politics. They became the principal articulators of local interests, not only on transportation issues but on a host of concerns, such as the establishment of playgrounds and parks, street cleaning, and telephone rates. Unlike party politicians who were increasingly crippled by the perception that they placed partisan advancement ahead of the public interest, civic association leaders could speak more credibly for their neighborhoods when they appeared before the regulatory boards and legislative committees that emerged as a central feature of urban public life during in the Progressive Era. Progressivism gave them a new route to power as old ones closed.

The language of reform had a specific resonance in Boston's immigrant communities as well. It provided an explanation for why they were excluded from public office and positions of power and influence, and why social conditions in their districts were deteriorating. Most importantly, it offered them, too, a way to construct a political identity outside of party politics. Progressivism helped leaders and would-be leaders of the city's Italians, Jews, and especially its Irish majority to establish the civic credentials of their communities. By devoting themselves to the public good, Boston's immigrants would demonstrate their willingness to transcend partisan loyalties and act as unselfish citizens. But while spokesmen for several cultural groups developed versions of reform with enough similarities to share the label "ethnic Progressivism," each was designed to suit its group's particular circumstances.

Purveyors of ethnic Progressivisms used them in a fashion similar to that of the city's business and suburban leaders and middle-class women. They legitimized their claims to be the representatives of their neighborhood or ethnic group. The Progressive fiction of a unified, morally aroused citizenry allowed small bodies of men and women to speak on behalf of particular communities. How convincingly they did so varied from case to case.

Historians have described some but not all of the dimensions of these ethnic Progressivisms. They argue that while immigrants favored social welfare reform as well as many democratizing measures, including the popular nomination of U.S. senators, direct primaries, and woman suffrage, these same immigrants opposed most attempts to remake city governments. Historians agree that the attempts of upper- and middle-class reformers to launch investigations of corruption at city hall, establish citywide elections, and remove partisanship from city politics were efforts to strip political power from working-class ethnic neighborhoods; as such, municipal reform supposedly met with strong resistance from the inhabitants of these districts. But these assumptions are based on little careful examination of ground-level, urban public life. A closer look reveals that many ethnic leaders found in Progressivism and its assault on city politics a formula with which to pursue their own ends.[47]

Though just a few miles away from Jamaica Plain, Boston's immigrant-filled North End enclosed a different social and cultural world. The home first of Irish then of Jewish immigrants, by the early twentieth century the North End had become a predominantly Italian neighborhood. Children of Italian parents constituted 60 percent of the district's population in 1905. The 1910 census classified 76 percent of the working members of that population as semi- or unskilled laborers; the remaining 24 percent had managed to climb to the higher rungs of the socioeconomic ladder. Fourteen percent were white-collar workers. Members of this better-off group spearheaded the attempt to create an Italian-American political identity in Boston.[48]

Numerical supremacy did not translate into political dominance for the North End's Italians. The principal reason for this failure was a low rate of electoral participation. "Italians without a doubt take the least interest in politics of any nationality," declared one social worker. In 1896 just 13 percent of Italian males with five years of residence in Boston registered to vote; by 1900 only 36 percent of the same group had become citizens. Nor were Italians a cohesive group. Rather, they were divided by provincial loyalties, which remained strong in the North End. Barriers of language and custom prevented them from becoming an organized political force, a difficulty many never tried to overcome because they planned to return to Italy.[49]

Nevertheless, a basic infrastructure of public leadership had developed among leading Italians by the early 1900s. Its essential building blocks were unions and cooperative societies. Forty-four mutual aid societies operated in the North End in 1908. Two years later the number had grown to one hundred. Out of this activity emerged a tier of local *prominenti*. Dominic D'Alessandro, who came from a small village near Rome to Boston in 1898, rose to prominence as an organizer of the Italian Laborers' Union. In connection with the union he established the Benevolent Aid Society, a federation of smaller mutual aid associations. He also helped found a bank and a branch of the Dante Alighieri Society, an Italian cultural organization. He was aided by George Scigliano, a second-generation lawyer with ties to the North End Democratic Party leaders and a reputation for supporting working-class causes while in the state legislature. James Donnaruma, editor and publisher of the *Gazzetta del Massachusetts*, the North End–based Italian weekly, also played a central role in neighborhood public life. Rounding out this collection of local elite were political lawyers Jerome Petitti and Frank Leveroni, and a handful of other business and professional men.[50]

By virtue of his position at the helm of the *Gazzetta*, Donnaruma became the dominant public voice in Boston's Italian community. Arriving in the United States at the age of nine, he was educated in the Boston public schools. After purchasing the Italian-language *Gazzetta* in 1897, he launched an aggressive campaign to expand his Italian audience. In 1904 he helped D'Alessandro form the Italian Laborers' Union, and relentlessly publicized its activities in exchange for the guaranteed subscriptions of its members. Aggressively marketing his paper, Donnaruma played a central role in constructing a public identity for the Italian-American community in Boston.[51]

Donnaruma and his fellow North End *prominenti* had little opportunity to translate their civic status into political power. The local Democratic organization, still in the hands of the district's Irish remnant, blocked their path to public office. John F. "Honey Fitz" Fitzgerald, who was elected mayor of Boston in 1909, was a former resident; and although its namesake had long since departed for wealthier suburbs, the Fitzgerald organization still dominated North End politics. The failure of most Italian immigrants to vote made that task much easier. The North End's Irish politicians had learned by 1900 to placate the few Italians who voted by placing one Italian candidate on the ballot each year.[52]

For the North End's emerging Italian elite, power depended on its ability to represent the community convincingly, a difficult task in a community split along provincial lines. The Fitzgerald organization's continued success made this difficult. So they turned to the Progressive formula to establish themselves as civic spokesmen. Progressivism offered a vocabulary that allowed them to speak for North End Italians and at the same time provided a rhetoric for criticizing Fitzgerald and his supporters.

The choice of Fitzgerald as villain was revealing. He had not lived in the North End for nearly a decade when he was elected mayor in 1905, but his notoriety made him an ideal scapegoat for a Progressive crusade. His political exploits first received widespread public notice in settlement worker Robert A. Woods's *Americans in Process*, a study of life in Boston's North and West Ends published in 1902. Woods depicted Fitzgerald, "the Young Napoleon of the North End," and the West End's Martin Lomasney as corrupt, all-powerful bosses preventing social progress in the city's immigrant districts. Fitzgerald and several other politicians threatened to sue Woods for libel after the book appeared. Fitzgerald's image as an unscrupulous politician grew after he was elected mayor, when a series of scandals uncovered by the

GGA and the Boston Finance Commission, a state-sponsored investigative body, rocked his administration.[53]

The attack on Fitzgerald began in earnest when several Italian leaders openly opposed his 1905 mayoral bid. Casting Fitzgerald as a political predator, a group led by Dominic D'Alessandro called on Italians to unite to help defeat him and break his organization's hold on the North End. Fitzgerald was a "dictator," they charged, whose "oppression" was responsible for the deteriorating condition of the North End. The failure of local Italians to "cooperate for the benefit of their district" in the past allowed boss rule to continue. Only when they worked together would they achieve their "political emancipation."[54]

Another prominent North End Italian, State Representative George Scigliano, joined the anti-Fitzgerald insurgency. Although he owed his seat in the state legislature to the Fitzgerald organization, Scigliano broke with it in 1905 as part of the larger factional dispute with the Democratic Party. Opposing Fitzgerald's mayoral aspirations in the name of the "Italian people," he attacked the candidate as a boss who was working "against the interests of the Italians of the North End." The momentum from Scigliano's bolt carried over into the municipal elections that followed. With Fitzgerald battling the Democratic leaders in Boston over the mayoralty, North End Italians formed a "Partito Italiano Independente" and ran two local lawyers, Jerome Petitti and Frank Leveroni, for Common Council.[55]

Although the efforts to create a distinct political identity for North End Italians originated largely from factional disputes within the Democratic Party, they received their greatest support from the *Gazzetta del Massachusetts*. The revelations of the Boston Finance Commission and the attacks of the GGA during Fitzgerald's first term received front-page coverage. The paper presented a long analysis of municipal expenditures and services under Fitzgerald taken from the Finance Commission's highly publicized findings. With the commissioners, Donnaruma concluded that "graft" was the source of the city's growing expenditures and declining local services. During Fitzgerald's term Donnaruma was quick to point out every deficiency in the North End and to blame it on the mayor. "For the people of Boston, Fitzgerald is a new Attila, a divine scourge," the *Gazzetta* concluded, though it claimed in proper reform fashion that the campaign was "not against an individual, but a system."[56]

The sound and fury generated by the anti-Fitzgerald campaign signified little in the way of votes. Fitzgerald carried the district in 1905, and his followers controlled most local offices. But he remained a useful foil for efforts to create an effective Italian-American political identity in Boston. Appeals to the "Italian independent vote" became staples of Donnaruma's editorials, with the terms "Italian" and "independent" becoming virtually interchangeable. The Partito Italiano Indipendente persisted, with opposition to boss Fitzgerald remaining the primary plank of its platform. The *Gazzetta*'s attacks on the mayor borrowed heavily from the revelations of the GGA, the Finance Commission, and the daily press. And the paper continued to present local public life as a battle between the "Italian people" and the corrupt Fitzgerald machine. When Thomas Grady, a candidate opposed to the Fitzgerald organization, won a state representative seat from the North End in 1908, the *Gazzetta* declared that he had "broken the chain" that had bound the people of the North End, and credited the upset to the ubiquitous "Italian independent vote." Grady's victory marked "the triumph of the Italians," who had represented reform in the context of the *Gazzetta*'s portrayal of North End politics.[57]

That the North End Italians' "triumph" took the form of the election of an Irishman was a good measure of their limited political clout. Despite the efforts of Donnaruma and his allies to fashion a reform-based political identity for North End Italians, the Fitzgerald forces remained in control. Grady's victory was the only defeat for the Fitzgerald organization in the North End between 1900 and 1915. The high-water mark of 1908, when Grady won and Republican (and "Italian independent") Jerome Petitti fell just ten votes short of securing the second state representative spot, soon receded. In the city elections that followed, the independent Italian candidates were defeated, and both Grady and Petitti lost in the following year. The size of the nonvoting segment of the Italian population and the willingness of the Democratic organization to nominate a few popular Italians severely restricted the ability of other immigrant leaders to develop a political base outside party politics.[58]

Nor did gender prove a useful basis for sparking political action among Italian women. Efforts to establish a public role for them were limited to a few settlement workers and had little impact. Italian-American demographics were the greatest obstacle to such efforts. The Italian migration to Boston and the rest of the United States was predominantly male. Those women who did migrate either remained at home in traditional domestic roles or performed unskilled labor. Few of them participated in the women's reform campaigns becoming so prevalent in Boston during the first years of the twentieth century.

However limited its impact in the short run, the language and imagery of Progressive reform proved flexible enough to serve the interests of North End *prominenti*. The investigations of settlement house workers, the revelations of local muckrakers, and the exposés of the daily press provided rhetorical tools for Italian spokesmen, just as they did for the businessmen of the GGA, the women of the WML, or middle-class suburbanites. Italian leaders in the North End used Progressivism to create a distinctive local Italian-American political identity and to establish themselves as the legitimate representatives of the Italian-American community in Boston. Though an ineffective fiction at first, the formula would prove more potent over the long term, when changes in the workings of politics gave nonpartisan action a more important place in urban public life.

Boston's Jewish voices crafted their own Progressivism designed to suit their particular experiences and circumstances. As in the case of Italian spokesmen, Jews' access to political power was limited. Although the roots of the Jewish community in Boston reached back further than those of Italians, they were fragile. Most of the five thousand Jews in Boston in 1880 were German immigrants who had arrived in the middle of the nineteenth century. Between 1880 and 1914, seventy thousand eastern European Jews poured into the city, carrying with them a language and customs that made assimilation into American life difficult. Their arrival also sparked tensions within the ranks of Boston Jewry, as the well-adapted Germans eyed their recently arrived coreligionists with suspicion. The effort by Jewish leaders to bridge this gap involved the creation of a clear Jewish political identity. Progressivism would be a crucial tool in the attempt to create that consciousness.[59]

Prior to the influx of new immigrants, the city's German-Jewish population experienced a fair degree of social and political success. Many prospered in local businesses and lived in Boston's growing suburban sections. They won a share of local public offices as well. Several rabbis, including reform leader Solomon Schindler, served on the School Committee, and a number of Jewish businessmen earned seats on the Common Council and in the state legislature. The most successful of them, Leopold Morse, served a term as a U.S. congressman in the 1880s.[60]

But Boston's Jews had no distinctive political identity. Jewish candidates were just as likely to appear on a Republican as a Democratic ballot. Indeed, the absence of a clear partisan loyalty or ethnic politics was perceived positively, as evidence of their successful assimilation. The city's German Jews created few specifically Jewish institutions, striving instead to blend fully into American life, in politics as well as in social activities. "We have no special Jewish interests to defend," insisted Boston's *Jewish Chronicle* in 1892, "and we would not antagonize our Christian neighbors by continually forcing our religion to the surface."[61]

The note of defensiveness in the *Chronicle*'s comment reflected the changing circumstances of Jewish Boston. The flood of new immigrants shattered any hope that Jews could slip unnoticed into the mainstream of political and social life. The distinctive customs and language of the Russian, Polish, and other Jews who flooded Boston gave Boston Judaism a markedly ethnic character. Immigration also changed the social geography of Boston Jewry, establishing ward eight in the West End as the center of Jewish life by 1900.[62] By 1910, almost 70 percent of the district's 32,430 residents were Jewish, and they represented the majority of the city's total Jewish population. Crowded into the tenements of ward eight, these immigrants became the most visible Jewish presence in Boston, particularly after Robert Woods and his South End House settlement colleagues published *Americans in Process,* their well-publicized examination of slum life in Boston's North and West Ends.[63]

With so distinctive a public image now attached to Boston's Jews, the main challenge facing Jewish leaders became the forging of a respectable public identity. On the social front they began to develop charitable institutions that cut across the boundaries between German and Russian Jews. Politically, they turned to Progressivism as a way of establishing a distinctively Jewish presence in the city's public life. While Jewish men and women worked in separate spheres, they drew on a similar reform theme—the battle against the ward boss—to claim the mantle of reform for themselves and their community.[64]

The articulators of Jewish Progressivism in Boston belonged to various reform wings. They included labor leader Henry Abrahams, Harvard professor Horace Kallen, and settlement workers Philip Davis, Eva Hoffman, Meyer Bloomfield, and Henry Levenson, all of whom concentrated on social reform. Lawyer-reformer Louis Brandeis, Zionist editor Jacob de Haas, and David Ellis, a lawyer from Brandeis's firm involved in School Committee affairs, were other key figures of Jewish Progressivism. They devoted themselves not only to social reform but also to politics and political reform, using the Progressive motif in an attempt to create a Jewish political movement.[65]

With the hope of sharpening Jewish political consciousness, political reform advocates trained their sights on Martin Lomasney of ward eight. Lomasney was not only the acknowledged political power in the West End, where the largest and most visible portion of Boston's Jews lived, but also the quintessential urban boss. Woods's *Americans in Process* had chronicled Lomasney's exploits as the "czar of ward eight" alongside its portrait of Fitzgerald's North End activities, winning Lomasney wide and unflattering public notice. His grip on the votes of West Enders became legendary. Between 1888 and 1909 Lomasney's candidates never lost a local race. He even delivered his Democratic ward to a Republican candidate in one instance. His control over a predominantly Jewish district—largely by virtue of the low voting rates of recent immigrants—made him anathema to those seeking a respectable Jewish political identity.[66]

The Jewish reform offensive began with school politics. Robert Silverman, a young Jewish lawyer and settlement worker at the West End Educational Union, accused Walter Harrington, headmaster of a nearby grammar school, of "misappropriation of funds." Harrington, who had political ties to Lomasney and whose sister Julia Duff served on the school board, escaped punishment when the Boston School Committee dismissed the charges in a narrow vote. Boston's Jewish leaders cried foul, claiming that the Committee had suppressed evidence in response to political pressure from Harrington's allies. Harrington filed suit against Silverman for libel, further fueling public interest in the controversy.[67]

Boston's Jewish Progressives mobilized in support of Silverman. David Ellis, a Democrat and member of the School Committee, deserted the party as a result of the controversy. He ran instead as an independent battling against political corruption, with the endorsement of the Public School Association (PSA), Boston's educational reform organization. Brandeis's law firm represented Silverman in hearings before the school board. Leading the way was Jacob de Haas, editor and publisher of the *Jewish Advocate,* Boston's Jewish newspaper. As the case played out over the fall of 1905, the *Advocate* repeatedly described the issue as one pitting "the people" against a political machine. Silverman's actions, it declared, constituted an "offer of assistance from the people"; the rejection of his claim, an act of "gross partisanship."[68]

De Haas and the *Advocate* used the subsequent school board election to link Jewish interests with reform. He urged Jews to vote as a bloc for Ellis and the PSA candidates. Calling the Association a defender of Jewish "flesh and blood," he told his readers that the "decent members" of the School Committee "find their efforts continuously thwarted by the evil elements placed on board by a political machine." Support for the reform candidates in opposition to those who acted as "the tools of some corporation or political machine" was "a paramount duty on the part of Jewish voters."[69]

The Silverman case blossomed into an all-out campaign by Jewish leaders against ward bosses in general, and Lomasney in particular. "These bosses are enemies of the immigrant," declared the *Advocate.* "Remember what our people suffered through the influence of ward bosses," the newspaper warned another time; "the bosses want you today but forget your interests tomorrow." When a Lomasney foe won an election, de Haas's paper welcomed the "triumph for clean politics and against the Eighth ward boss." Louis Brandeis, who was already at the forefront of political reform activities in Boston, urged opposition to machine politics in a preelection address entitled "What Loyalty Demands" before a Jewish audience in 1905. He linked Jewish ideals with principles of American citizenship and appealed to Boston's Jews to place themselves on the side of clean politics.[70]

Jewish reform activism intensified further when social worker Henry Levenson opposed Lomasney in the 1906 race for state representative from ward eight. Casting himself as the "people's independent candidate," Levenson relentlessly attacked Lomasney and attempted to mobilize Jews against him. "This is a campaign of the people against the boss," he declared, and he left no doubt who "the people" were in this instance. The campaign aimed to secure "representation for the Jews," as one backer put it. Levenson trumpeted the endorsement of prominent local Jews, including Robert Silverman, Horace Kallen, and several synagogue leaders. Lomasney was the "czar" of the West End, they declared, a term with powerful significance in a neighborhood where 60 percent of the residents were Russian Jews. Levenson's backers blamed Lomasney for the poor sanitation of the West End and the prevalence of political corruption in the district. Although Lomasney won, the campaign drew wide attention and was seen as a spur to Jewish political activism in the district.[71]

In battling bossism, the city's leading Jews also sought to create a nonpartisan, specifically Jewish political movement. They held a meeting in November 1905 to discuss plans for nominating Jewish candidates for City Council and considered the possibility of sending a delegation to the GGA to lobby for the inclusion of a Jew on its slate. Although no immediate results came of the meeting, it set a precedent for further activity. It also reflected the emerging push for political unity among Jews in Boston.[72]

As popular clamor for reform increased in Boston after 1905, the drive to define Boston's Jewish community as politically independent and reform-minded accelerated. Spearheading this effort was de Haas's *Advocate,* which claimed to speak for "the solid Jewish vote of Boston." Often citing "the natural political morality of the Jews" in its editorials and reporting, the *Advocate* insisted that its readers strongly favored clean politics. "The Jewish vote is finally on the side of morality," the paper declared in 1907. Two years later, when municipal reform fever in Boston neared its apogee, de Haas observed: "There has grown up a quiet movement which shows distinctly enough that the tendency of the Jews, now as at all times, is to combine with the forces that make for righteousness in municipal affairs."[73]

Efforts at mobilizing Jewish women also drew on Progressive themes, including opposition to ward boss Lomasney. Encouraged to organize by settlement worker Eva Hoffman and other social reformers after a series of riots over high food prices early in the twentieth century, Jewish women in Boston's West End slums finally united in 1912 to battle the "beef trust." This effort evolved into a permanent body, the West End Mothers' Club, which lobbied the state legislature for price regulation, organized boycotts, and staged protest marches. They also singled out Lomasney for sharp criticism, blaming him for the difficult living conditions in the West End. Like their Protestant and Catholic counterparts, Jewish women turned their roles as wives and mothers into a springboard to political power. But they did so separately, never joining with the WML or any of the other citywide reform bodies dominated by middle-class Protestant women.[74]

As both Jewish women and men sought distinctive political identities in Boston, Lomasney remained the biggest obstacle. He continued to dominate the political life of the West End, a symbol of the failure of efforts to wean Jewish voters away from him. While part of Lomasney's success came from his willingness to accommodate some local Jews, the primary reason for his ability to remain in power was the limited interest in voting shown by the eastern European Jews who crowded into his district. Between 1900 and 1910, voter registration in ward eight averaged just 38 percent of the district's total adult male population. A considerable number of the neighborhood's Jews either were not eligible or did not bother to register to vote. The *Advocate* estimated that only one-third of qualified Jews registered in 1905, a view echoed by other observers. With so large a portion of Jewish residents electorally inert, Lomasney faced no real threat to his preeminence.[75]

But the true significance of the Jews' use of Progressivism in Boston did not rest in election results. Rather, Boston's Jewish leaders established a model for future political activity along Jewish lines. As internal social tensions diminished, as they migrated to other parts of the city, and as new national and international issues emerged that linked them together, Boston's Jews would begin to act more cohesively in public life. The groundwork for that activity lay in the appropriation of Progressive concepts and language by the city's Jewish leaders.

For Boston's most famous immigrants, the language of Progressive reform had yet other meanings. The Irish, who made up a majority of the city's population, dominated its electoral politics. On the surface, they had little reason to embrace Progressivism. But civic authority did not automatically follow from electoral triumphs in Boston. Though the Irish governed, they struggled to win the respect of their Yankee contemporaries. It was in this context that some Irish men and women employed Progressivism as a vehicle to demonstrate their legitimacy as inheritors of the civic ideals of Brahmin Boston.

The unwillingness of the Yankee elite to accept Irish claims to social authority manifested itself outside electoral politics. Despite their numerical and political supremacy, the Boston Irish lacked entry to important corridors of social and economic power. State Street financial institutions, Back Bay clubs, and corporate law firms remained the exclusive preserves of the city's Anglo elite. Even in those areas where they gained a foothold, as in the legal profession, access to such Yankee strongholds as the Boston Bar Association was still limited.[76]

Nevertheless, they had gained considerable social and economic ground by the end of the nineteenth century. A significant number climbed to at least the middle rungs of the socioeconomic ladder. Fully a third held white-collar jobs, and more than half had graduated beyond unskilled or semiskilled labor by 1910. "Their institutions are at once the largest, strongest, and best managed that one comes upon," noted one observer of ethnic Boston. "It seems necessary to emphasize the obvious fact because so many people who should realize it have failed to do so," he added pointedly.[77]

South Boston was among the city's Irish strongholds. Located on a peninsula jutting out into Boston Harbor, it had been a prosperous Anglo-Saxon enclave in the mid–nineteenth century. Unskilled Irish laborers began arriving after the Civil War, settling primarily on the western, inland edge of the peninsula. They gradually edged the remaining native-born and a growing number of middle-class Irish toward the harbor, where the newly displaced built large houses on the wide streets of the City Point section. By 1900, South Boston was an Irish neighborhood. "The main current of South Boston life," a South End House investigator noted, "carries one into the story of the assimilation of the Irish people to the particular social, industrial and commercial conditions of Boston and New England during the past fifty years."[78]

Contrary to prevailing assumptions about Progressive Era Irish neighborhoods, the principal fact of South Boston public life was not machine politics. While the Irish influx made the district solidly Democratic, it did not yield a boss or a machine. Factionalism plagued neighborhood politics. "South Boston has not had a real leader of the 'Pat' Maguire or the Martin Lomasney or the 'Jim' Curley type," the *South Boston Gazette* noted in 1906. Each of the district's three wards had prominent party leaders, but none could unite either his own ward or the larger neighborhood into a single political machine. Factions and alliances rapidly came and went, and politicians often abruptly switched from one group to another between one election and the next. A smoothly run political organization never materialized out of South Boston's chaotic electoral life.[79]

This relentless feuding kindled dissatisfaction with local politics. Frustration over the inability of district politicians to cooperate in pursuit of common goals fed public criticism. Echoing broader calls for political reform, a local priest demanded "the sinking of all party lines and the rallying of all our citizens in support of local aims and objects for the benefit of all." Factionalism discouraged and embarrassed civic leaders. After John Fitzgerald was "hissed and disturbed" at a campaign rally in the neighborhood, the *South Boston Gazette* fretted over the damage done to the district's reputation. "It is unfortunate that such things occur to cause outsiders to talk about South Boston hoodlumism when other citizens are striving to have the district retain its good name." Ever conscious of the ongoing search for Irish legitimacy in Boston, many South Bostonians struggled to shape popular perceptions of the character of their district's public life.[80]

In their anxiety to obtain more-effective representation for their district and to refute stereotypes about Irish-American politics, some South Bostonians drew on Progressive rhetoric. The editor of a local paper and several leading legal and political figures in the district embraced reform as a way to overcome internal political feuding and to rehabilitate South Boston's political reputation. Their efforts yielded mixed results. Though reform-style candidates won a handful of elections, they did not unseat the district's dominant party politicians. Nor did they pry many local voters away from their staunch allegiance to the Democratic Party. But the activities of these candidates helped fuel an antimachine political style that would emerge more fully in later years.

A key figure in South Boston–Irish reform activism was John J. Toomey, editor and publisher of the *South Boston Gazette*. Along with his editorial duties, Toomey involved himself in local politics in the 1890s, running several times for state representative as an antiorganization candidate. He was successful in 1897 and again in 1899, when he ran as an Independent Citizens candidate after losing the Democratic nomination in a hotly contested race. While serving in the State House, he earned a reputation as a strong advocate of political reform, mainly for his outspoken backing of a measure to replace party caucuses with state-run primaries. He used the *Gazette* as a platform to rally support for political reform and clean politics in South Boston.[81]

Toomey had a number of partners among South Boston respectables in his proreform campaign, including two of the district's leading lawyers. Judge Josiah Dean of the South Boston Municipal Court led the battle against Joseph Norton, ward fourteen's most successful party politician at that time. Dean's former law partner, Charles Slattery, also joined in the fight. Slattery was a Harvard College and Law School graduate who was first elected to the Board of Aldermen in

1901, where he won widespread praise and a reputation as a clean and honest politician. His political rectitude apparently irked Norton and other South Boston Democrats, who prevented him from receiving the customary renomination for a second term in 1902. The rejection sparked a contest that thrust reform issues directly into local public debate.[82]

Declaring himself an independent candidate, Slattery ran as a reformer against the local party leadership and attacked his opponent, veteran political figure and Norton ally John E. Baldwin, as a machine politician. "I have never been a gang fellow," Slattery proudly proclaimed, as he sought to distance himself from organizational politicians. He depicted Baldwin as a greedy, self-seeking candidate, whose sole political ambition was to obtain offices for self-enrichment. For their part, Slattery's opponents appeared content to let the race develop on these terms. They attacked Slattery as an ally of the PSA and other elite reformers and as a man who was out of touch with the needs of ordinary people.[83]

Despite his break with party leaders, Slattery won by a 354-vote margin with 6,244 ballots cast. He would win a third term as well, with the backing of the Good Government Association. He also had the support of Republicans, whose leaders endorsed him when no viable alternative arose from within the party. But his triumph also illustrated the growing appeal of reform politics, even in predominantly Irish districts. Slattery's success was merely the opening salvo in a broader attempt to formulate a Boston-Irish version of Progressive reform.[84]

As in other neighborhoods, the local press played a central role in cultivating proreform sentiment. John Toomey's *Gazette* constantly decried boss rule, the convention system, and self-seeking politicians. The boss has "unhesitatingly domineered over his followers," the *Gazette* declared, "and that has always been the first indication of the unfitness of the 'boss' to rule." Toomey's paper was "pleased" at the exposures of corruption by the Boston Finance Commission and complained about the incompetence of many city employees. Toomey and his staff also regularly attacked local machine politicians, especially John Baldwin and Joseph Norton. "It's been disgusting, to say the least, the way he has run things for many years," announced the *Gazette* after a Norton defeat, "and it was just about due for the people to rise up in their might and teach him a lesson."[85]

The *Gazette* repeatedly insisted that South Bostonians were undergoing a civic awakening of the sort promoted by Lincoln Steffens. It predicted imminent defeat for "the boss" in South Boston, claiming "the people have tired of 'boss' rule where the boss thinks himself bigger than all the people." Another observer argued that "a young man has more chance to win on merit than 'boss' influence than ever before." "The Critic," the *Gazette*'s political columnist, noted defensively that "there are some . . . who think that the voters of our district can be driven into line at the word of the so-called leaders or 'bosses.' The people, however, are mindful of their own responsibilities and duties, and they think and act for themselves."[86]

The *Gazette* contributed as well to the growing clamor for efficiency and nonpartisanship in city affairs. In language that might easily have come from the GGA, it called for a "citizen's candidate" for mayor in 1907: "A non-partisan administration would indeed be a novelty for Boston. An administration where the only qualification necessary for a position at City Hall would be fitness, not whether Democrat or Republican, where the city's money would be distributed with the special desire to do the most good, and not in order to please this or that alderman, or to satisfy the most influential sections." The *Gazette*'s proreform rhetoric did not prevent it from harboring suspicions about the Brahmin-tinged Good Government Association. But the flexibility of Progressive rhetoric allowed both the GGA and the *Gazette* to give it meanings that suited their particular social and political ends.

As Progressivism's themes became more popular in South Boston, politicians began to use them more aggressively. Candidates breathlessly endorsed "ADOPTION OF THE REFERENDUM AND THE INITIATIVE" to thwart boss rule. A South Boston grocer running for reelection to the Common Council in 1903 proudly recalled his vote "in favor of investigating charges of graft in the public building department," while another office seeker frantically "pointed to the charges and evidence of graft that are rampant throughout the country" in an effort to win popular support for his reform candidacy. Others began pointing to their business acumen instead of their political experience in the hopes of convincing voters that they would be responsible and efficient leaders.[87]

This growing reform sentiment was visible in the ground-level politics of other Irish neighborhoods as well. In Charlestown, the Irish-run *Charlestown Enterprise* encouraged reform in the same way the *South*

Boston Gazette did, and politicians suddenly began to stress their independence. George Monahan, who had conducted several independent campaigns, prominently cited his fight "against machines and seasoned politicians" during his 1907 State Senate bid, while district attorney hopeful Joseph Dennison emphasized his defiance of local ward leaders in the 1902 congressional elections. Aldermanic candidate Arthur Dolan confidently declared that he would not suit "those who believe that the chief duty of an alderman is to obtain passes and patronage for their constituents." Even reputed ward boss Joseph Corbett caught reform fever, insisting that he "never cared to have anybody finance his campaigns. If he was to hold elective office he always preferred to hold it by the grace of the voters, not caring to be tied up in any way by financial assistance from friends or the public service corporations."[88]

Increased demand for good government prompted many candidates to present themselves as efficiency-minded businessmen, however convincing that claim might be. "The men who form the city government of Boston," Charlestown Alderman Edward Cauley declared, "are business directors of a stupendous corporation." During his reelection bid he naturally pronounced himself qualified for the job. "Alderman Cauley," one of his ads read, "represents that element of the community for which there is such an insistent and reasonable demand—the business man who is willing to enter public life." Another ad claimed that Cauley had succeeded in his field "by conducting his own business, by supervising every detail, and by making it a point to see that nothing is left undone which should be done for the comfort, benefit, and profit of patrons." He pledged to apply similar principles as an alderman. Of course his claims to business expertise may not have been what most people had in mind: he was a corner-store cigar dealer. Nonetheless, his aggressive presentation of himself as a business reformer reflected the growing popularity of the rhetoric of efficiency in local public life.[89]

A second Progressive theme was also present in the political culture of Boston's Irish neighborhoods. Local candidates pledged opposition to trusts and big business as often as they promised honest and efficient government. Charlestown's George Monahan warned that "corporations and trusts would find him a formidable opponent," while another candidate was outraged that "men who have spent their lives in helping great corporations defy the law have been advanced to high public places with large salaries." South Boston State Senator Frank Linehan alerted voters to their dire circumstances: "you men have no more control at the state house than a man way over in Russia," he told them; "the corporations have full control there and they completely run the state house."[90]

Perhaps the most aggressive use of antitrust rhetoric among Irish politicians was by a woman. Despite her connections to Martin Lomasney, Julia Duff found the anticorporation theme of Progressivism a useful political tool in her battles to win an at-large seat on the Boston City Council. Duff, who had long campaigned on the slogan "Boston schools for Boston girls," a not-so-subtle demand for greater employment of Catholic women as public schoolteachers, began to portray herself as a trustbuster as well. "Mrs. Duff," her supporters announced, "is backed by no machine, supported by no book trust, directed by no close corporation of politicians and financiers or educationalists. She has accomplished genuine reforms all along the line." Her campaign literature detailed her successful efforts as a member of the school board to rid the schools of out-of-date textbooks by "fearlessly" exposing the "machinations of the wealthy book trusts." Sinister forces backed Duff's opponents, her followers charged. She was "opposed solely by those influences which are everywhere shaking the foundations of our Republic—trusts and immense wealth."[91]

The decision by Duff and her Irish male counterparts to use reform rhetoric does not prove that they sincerely desired to change the city's politics and government. But it is an indication of how powerful the language of Progressivism was becoming among their supporters. Irish voters did not automatically recoil from the idea of reform, even political reform, as so many scholars have suggested. Many of Boston's Irish shared the frustration of an angry letter writer from Charlestown who insisted that machine politics made public service "subservient to petty ward factions and political revenge." Much of the political rhetoric aiming to assuage these sentiments may have been hypocritical, but the sentiments themselves were not.[92]

Another strand of Progressivism that drew Irish participation was municipal housekeeping. But like their male counterparts, Irish women in Boston created a distinct version of reform that gave them their own place in local public life. Very few joined the Women's Municipal League. Instead they participated in the activities of the League of Catholic Women (LCW), a parish-based federation of women's clubs throughout the Boston Archdiocese. The LCW provided a vehicle for Catholic women to enter the public arena based on their ethnic and religious identities as well as on their gender.

A small group of Catholic laywomen launched the League in 1910, with the support of Archbishop William O'Connell. They modeled the new organization on the recently created English Catholic Women's League in Oxford, England. But the LCW was also quite clearly the Irish-Catholic response to the growth of predominantly Yankee women's groups such as the Women's Municipal League during the Progressive Era. O'Connell repeatedly insisted that Catholic women stay out of secular women's bodies. By working to "unite Catholic women for the promotion of religious, intellectual, and charitable work," the LCW provided them with a separate public platform free of Yankee Protestant influence and of the taint of the more controversial social reform programs sometimes favored by women's groups of the era.[93]

The LCW grew quickly. In 1915 its membership had surpassed 1,700 and was climbing steadily. By 1919 the League would blossom into a federation of more than forty local societies with over four thousand members. Virtually every parish had an affiliated women's guild or club, giving the LCW a far greater presence in many ethnic neighborhoods than the WML or any other reform or charitable group. Most members were middle-class Irish Catholics. Very few Catholic women from Boston's burgeoning Italian community joined. Nevertheless, the LCW succeeded in establishing itself as the voice of Boston's Catholic women.[94]

Progressive rhetoric lent credibility to the League's claims, while allowing it to remain distinctly Catholic and Irish. Like the WML, its secular counterpart, the Catholic League saw itself as a nonpartisan organization representing communal interests. But it conceived of the community differently. When a member described the LCW as "the material expression of an ever deepening movement among our women for unity," the "our" referred to Boston Catholics, not all Bostonians. LCW leaders used the same vocabulary of solidarity as Boston's other women reformers but gave those words different meanings.[95]

The League's work also paralleled the efforts of the WML and its other Protestant counterparts. The LCW's lecture series not only helped attract new members but encouraged Catholic women to participate in public affairs and presented reports on many social reform topics, including education, prison reform, and disease control. The LCW itself created a women's employment bureau, educated immigrants, engaged in social work, and helped the juvenile courts with their probation load. It became affiliated with several nonsectarian national groups, such as the North American Civic League for Immigrants. These endeavors not only gave the League credibility as a force for reform but also reinforced its claim to be the public embodiment of the views of Catholic women.[96]

Despite shared methods and goals, the LCW and the WML rarely cooperated. Archbishop (later Cardinal) O'Connell provided much of the funding for the LCW and was thus able to keep it on a short leash. He insisted that Catholic women not join Protestant or secular groups but instead operate separately. When some members attempted to combine efforts with a Protestant charity, O'Connell was forced to remind them that the LCW was organized "to assist in carrying on the work of Catholic charities" and should not become "a sort of subsidiary to the various organizations directing these non-Catholic activities."[97]

Much of the LCW's work had a sectarian slant as well. The efforts to educate and Americanize Italian immigrants, for instance, not only served a charitable purpose but also assured that the newcomers would not be lured away from their faith by Protestant social workers. The same impulse fueled the probation work the League performed with young Catholic girls. And in addition to its standard social welfare work, the LCW also dispatched members on home visits to "backslidden" Catholics in an effort to return them to the flock.[98]

In sum, the LCW constituted a distinctive variant of municipal housekeeping. It allowed Catholic women to use the same separate-spheres strategy as their Anglo-Protestant counterparts to establish a foothold in public affairs. Yet it also represented an assertion of a specifically Catholic Irish identity.

In the voice of Boston's Irish men and women, Progressive reform thus took on special significance. For male politicians, it was a way to debunk charges that the Irish were thoughtless followers of party bosses, incapable of acting as responsible, independent-minded citizens. For Irish women, it provided an avenue for gender-based civic activism within specific ethnic and religious boundaries. The openness of the Progressive formula allowed it to fit the needs and circumstances of Irish Boston, just as it did for Brahmin Boston and for the city's other social blocs.

Social and political circumstance determined the possible variations of Progressivism. Ironically, its emphasis on a unified communal response to the corruption, self-interest, and inefficiency that seemed to plague American life in the early twentieth century was the source of its variety. In Boston, an urban setting buffeted by more than half a century of geographic expansion, spatial and social mobility, and immigration, the number of conceivable definitions of "community" was multiplying. As suburbs grew, as immigrant districts matured, as Boston's Irish became a majority, and as women became more active in public life, the openness of the political language of reform made it available to a variety of newly emerging local elites. Each set of leaders depicted themselves at the head of united political action by their own community, whether defined in neighborhood, religious, gender, or ethnic terms, or by various combinations of these elements.

None of the many versions of reform arose from a grassroots movement. Rather, each sought to create such a movement, or at least to create the impression of one. In every case, a handful of a community's most articulate leaders, usually in connection with a newspaper or publicity-minded organization, built a rhetorical facade of independent, reform-based action within their city, neighborhood, or social group. Initially, at least, none succeeded. But as the popular clamor for reform grew, and as party politicians increasingly found it useful, the new political language and the public endeavors that accompanied it became more widespread, and more powerful.

In the short run, the growing popularity of the Progressive style made possible the construction of coalitions in support of municipal reform measures. The promise of more honest and efficient government, better and broader government services, and fairer politics appealed to a wide variety of interests.

But the shared words of reform masked different and sometimes contradictory expectations. The understanding of good government espoused by a Brahmin businessman differed from that favored by an immigrant editor. Gradually, city politics came to be a competition to make these divergent visions of urban public life real in practice. During the early twentieth century, the mechanics of city politics were changing, making Progressivism a more powerful electoral tool. As it became a more central part of public discourse, the differences embedded within reform rhetoric would begin to surface. Group identities—increasingly expressed in Progressive terms—eclipsed partisan loyalty as the principal category of political mobilization in Boston. Ironically, the language of Progressivism made possible the initial expression of those disparate identities in the name of unified public action.

CHAPTER THREE

The Politics of Municipal Reform

Frank J. Linehan hardly fit the Progressive profile. A construction contractor representing ward thirteen, the most immigrant-filled and tenement-ridden of South Boston's three electoral districts, and a member of the Board of Aldermen from 1903 to 1905, Linehan had all the attributes of a machine politician. He quickly earned a reputation as one of Boston's most corrupt and demagogic public figures, particularly after a GGA investigation found that he had used his position to funnel municipal contracts to a construction company he secretly owned. These revelations prompted official charges against him, and he was ultimately convicted and sent to jail.

A proven grafter, Linehan embodied everything Progressivism opposed; yet he too found in the language of reform an effective political tool. Linehan portrayed himself as "a foe of corporations and nefarious schemes against the interests of the people." He even turned Progressive rhetoric against the GGA: "the corporations want me defeated because they cannot control me, and they use the so named Good Government Association in an effort to bring it about." He was the reformer; the GGA represented "the interests." However hollow this sounds almost a century later, it apparently made sense to many voters; Linehan was reelected to the Board of Aldermen in 1904 and won a State Senate seat the following year despite the charges pending against him.[1]

With its variable villains and vague definitions of "the people,"

Progressivism could be tapped by both Linehan and the GGA. It could take on several meanings at once, even when they explicitly opposed one another. To comprehend the politics of municipal reform, one must grasp this basic principle. The effort to remake city government during the early twentieth century was not simply the product of a single search for order by a rising middle class.[2] What from a distance appeared to be a coherent nationwide reform project was, up close, many projects, each with different understandings of what was wrong, who was responsible, and how things should look when reforms had been implemented. The success of specific measures depended on the ability of their proponents to present them in a manner broad enough to match multiple reform visions. To understand the origins and significance of the changes that took place in early-twentieth-century American public life requires an examination of the interaction among the various Progressivisms operating in particular settings.

This is not the standard view of Progressivism and the reforms it inspired. Robert Wiebe, Samuel Hays, and others have described Progressivism as a coherent ideology that arose in response to industrialization and spurred a uniform process of political modernization throughout the country, a key part of which was the centralization of city governments. These studies argue that because well-organized members of the middle and upper classes benefited most from this restructuring of early-twentieth-century public life, they must have been responsible for the changes that occurred. In this formulation the democratizing rhetoric of the Progressive Era was deceptive, obscuring their drive for power.[3]

But scholars less willing to dismiss ideological declarations as "mere rhetoric" see more complex sources of urban political reform. For one thing, in most cities, blue-collar and ethnic voters—those supposedly averse to municipal restructuring because of their allegiance to political machines—easily outnumbered upper- and middle-class native-born residents, yet reform measures and candidates repeatedly earned electoral majorities. Several studies have described broad cross-class and cross-ethnic proreform voting coalitions created in various cities during the Progressive Era, coalitions built through popular appeals rather than vote swapping among bosses. Even where municipal reform failed, as it did in Chicago, its collapse did not stem from entrenched, culturally based opposition to reform among specific social groups. Kenneth Finegold argues that it was a political failure—the inability to incorporate experts into reform coalitions—that doomed charter revision there, while Maureen Flanagan cites the inability of local political leaders to reconcile the many competing ideas of what reform meant to explain the defeat of municipal restructuring in Chicago.[4]

In Boston, too, the adoption of a new city charter reflected Progressivism's multiplicity rather than its uniformity. The city's elite business leaders pursued their own hierarchical vision in the campaign for municipal reform. But their prominence did not translate into hegemony. The language they used was so broad that they could not control the meanings other Bostonians gave to it. Members of other social groups, most notably the Irish, saw in municipal reform a vehicle for their own civic aspirations. The flexibility of the Progressive formula facilitated an alliance across class and ethnic lines by encouraging different sets of people to interpret the same proposals in different—and even contradictory—ways. The electoral coalition that resulted made charter reform possible.

If in the short run Progressivism created unity, in the long run it fueled division. The first clear hints of that conflict emerged immediately following the adoption of a new city charter, as the varying interpretations of Progressivism encouraged by the reform campaign became evident. As they did, group tensions sharpened. The reform formula provided the narrative framework in which ethnic identities and relationships began to be redefined in twentieth-century Boston.

Grasping the origins of Boston's charter reform challenges prevailing views of American political development in another fashion as well. A number of historians have regarded the Progressive Era as the time when a truly national political culture developed in urban-industrial America. Experts, communicating through such networks as the National Municipal League, began to share their ideas for reforming urban society and government. These exchanges allowed ideas pioneered in one city to be implemented in others, giving rise to a wave of municipal reform that seemingly homogenized American urban public life. But more nuanced examinations of politics in individual cities have indicated that while the same words were used to propel similar measures, municipal Progressivism was not simply a uniform national phenomenon. As Boston's experience shows, the meanings that reform supporters attached to their actions were specifically local. Several other studies have reached similar conclusions, suggesting that further investigation into the cases of individual cities and their distinctive political cultures is needed.[5]

On the face of things, the events leading up to Boston's 1909 charter reform illustrate the traditional view of Progressive municipal reform. The idea came from the Boston Finance Commission, an investigative body dominated by elite business leaders with close ties to the Good Government Association. The Commission's reports painted a picture of a thoroughly corrupt, boss-run city government desperately in need of reform. The solution they presented, a new city charter, followed the model charter of the National Municipal League. The reformers moved the fiscal portions of their proposal through a Republican state legislature anxious to restrict the resources of Democratic Boston. And when changes in the city's political structure were submitted to voters in the form of a referendum, they swayed a majority of voters to support it with promises of more-efficient municipal city government.

But closer inspection suggests the origins of charter reform were more complex. It was an Irish ward politician, not an elite reformer, who proposed the creation of the Boston Finance Commission. To fend off a hostile inquiry by the state legislature, Mayor John F. "Honey Fitz" Fitzgerald called for an investigation of city government in late 1906, which eventually yielded the Commission. He did so in part to gain some control of the process and in part to enhance his reputation as a reformer. Even when the Commission set its sights on the mayor and began painting a picture of him as a corrupt boss plundering the city treasury, Fitzgerald continued to embrace the investigation and claim credit for its findings. Two years later the by-then former mayor, along with several other Irish politicians, endorsed the Commission's political reform proposals, helping to ensure their passage in the 1909 referendum vote.

To understand the origins of charter reform in Boston, one must begin not with the rise of business reformers but with the public career of John F. Fitzgerald. The man who started Boston down the path to charter reform began his political life in the crowded tenements of the North End. Born in 1863, he was the third son of a first-generation Irish-American grocer and liquor dealer and his immigrant wife. Forced to abandon medical school after his parents died, Fitzgerald soon turned to politics, where his strong voice, quick wit, and political instincts brought him rapid success. He was elected to the

Common Council in 1891, to the State Senate the following year, and to the U.S. Congress in 1894, where he served three terms. His ultimate ambition, well known even before 1900, was to become mayor of Boston.[6]

While urban historiography automatically pigeonholes Fitzgerald as a boss, that label obscures more than it reveals. City politics was changing by the early twentieth century. A series of measures, particularly the adoption of primary elections in place of ward caucuses in 1903, weakened the institutional bulwarks that supported partisan ward organizations in Boston. Those seeking citywide office had to appeal directly to voters through advertising and publicity rather than by recruiting factional support in each ward. Fitzgerald was among the first effective practitioners of this kind of politics. His success was a harbinger of a new urban politics that relied on mass appeal as much as on organization. Ward-centered party politics still mattered but not to the degree it had a decade earlier.[7]

Fitzgerald's ascent to the mayoralty was hardly a triumph of machine politics. He won by going around Boston's Democratic organization rather than through it. In September 1905, the death of Mayor Patrick Collins presented an opportunity for Fitzgerald to fulfill his lifelong ambition. But when Fitzgerald announced his intention to run, the feuding factions within Boston's Democracy coalesced in opposition to the ambitious former North Ender. The city's leading Democrats, including Martin Lomasney, Jim Donovan, Patrick Kennedy, and Josiah Quincy, tapped Edward Donovan, a Lomasney lieutenant, for the nomination instead. Fitzgerald found himself cut off from the resources of Boston's Democratic Party.[8]

To overcome this handicap, Fitzgerald pioneered new methods of voter mobilization. He relied on disaffected ward factions where he could, promising them access to city hall should he win. But he also reached out to voters directly, through mass-media politics. Having acquired a weekly newspaper of his own in 1902, Fitzgerald had developed an appreciation of the growing importance and power of publicity. He conducted a furious campaign, traveling by automobile to as many as ten wards a night and delivering rousing speeches. This activity attracted the attention of Boston's newspapers, and thus of Boston's newspaper readers, allowing Fitzgerald to develop a public persona unlike any of his predecessors. On the eve of the primary, Fitzgerald made an unprecedented auto tour of all twenty-five wards in the city, an event that neatly symbolized the changing dynamic of city politics. Fitzgerald went directly to the voters, instead of relying on local party leaders. Structural reforms and a mass-circulation press were beginning to make ward organizations obsolete.[9]

In crafting his media campaign, Fitzgerald drew on the theme of municipal reform, which he fashioned to fit his particular situation. The opposition of the Democratic City Committee and the flexibility of Progressivism allowed Fitzgerald to fashion himself as a reform candidate. Announcing that he would eschew organizational support and conduct his campaign "single-handedly," Fitzgerald linked his efforts to other reform drives in New York, Philadelphia, and Chicago and promised "to banish graft and jail the grafters." Such promises were especially resonant in Boston at that moment, when the GGA's revelations about graft in the Fenway dredging project had reached their peak. At the opening rally of his campaign, he declared his candidacy to be "the people's cause" and his opponent to be "the people's enemy." Fitzgerald also pounced on Donovan's ties to Lomasney: "under the wool of Mr. Edward J. Donovan, look sharp and you shall find the hide and claws of Mr. Lomasney, the Boss." To be sure, Donovan responded in kind, linking Fitzgerald to corporate interests, particularly the Boston Elevated. But his ability to command public attention was no match for Fitzgerald's, and his organizational backing made such pronouncements less persuasive.[10]

Fitzgerald's use of reform rhetoric to circumvent party organization worked. He defeated Donovan by almost four thousand votes. His campaign ran well in the city's suburban districts and overcame organizational opposition in a number of inner city wards. In ward seven (the upper portion of the South End), the two dominant factions, led by John Quinn and William T. A. Fitzgerald, united behind Donovan yet failed to carry the ward for him. In Charlestown's ward five, party leader Arthur Dolan could not deliver the district for Donovan despite his firm grasp on the ward committee and the cooperation of his principal local rivals. Joseph Norton, the leading figure in South Boston's ward fourteen, failed to hold his neighborhood for the Democratic City Committee in the face of Fitzgerald's aggressive campaign. In all, Fitzgerald defeated twenty-one of Boston's twenty-five Democratic ward organizations.[11]

Fitzgerald would face an opponent in the general election who also cast himself as a Progressive. Despite his patrician background, Louis

A. Frothingham was only marginally closer to the stereotypical image of a reformer than Fitzgerald. The Harvard-educated lawyer was an inside player in state politics. He had served as Speaker of the Massachusetts House of Representatives and was a political protégé of Massachusetts Republican leader Henry Cabot Lodge. Nevertheless, Frothingham found Progressivism's antiboss motif congenial to his battle with Fitzgerald. Bolstered by a GGA endorsement, he used charges of corruption and dishonesty to undercut Fitzgerald's Progressivism. Citing "fraud in payrolls" and "lavish expenditures to favored contractors," Frothingham announced that "the sole supreme issue of the campaign will be clean government and honest municipal reform."[12]

Even amid such attacks, Fitzgerald refused to abandon his own reform themes. His supporters formed a "Citizens Committee" of their own, calling it a "new reform movement," and he continued to distance himself from the Democratic City Committee. He repeated his promise to "put an end to machine and graft rule and to prevent our city from falling prey to political bosses and grafting experts." The endorsements of Yankee reform Democrats, including Josiah Quincy and Nathan Matthews, gave credibility to Fitzgerald's position. Fitzgerald was helped, too, by the fact that Republican mayoral aspirant Judge Henry Dewey refused to accept his narrow primary defeat and ran as an independent candidate. Dewey spent most of his time on the stump accusing Frothingham of vote fraud, a charge that weakened the Republican nominee's claim to political purity.[13]

This contest between two reformers better represents the typical municipal election of the period than the customary image of a boss-reformer battle. As a style of public action rather than a coherent program, Progressivism was available to politicians of all stripes, even those in opposition to each other. By 1905 even New York's Tammany Hall, the quintessential political machine, was couching its appeals in the language of reform. This does not make such rhetoric meaningless. Rather, comprehending the significance of municipal reform requires an exploration of the various specific meanings invested in particular versions of urban Progressivism.[14]

The results of the 1905 election offer the first hints of the different Progressivisms at work in Boston. Fitzgerald carried the city's immigrant neighborhoods, including Charlestown, South Boston, the North and South Ends, and Roxbury. His success in these sections—

without the full support of the Democratic organization—suggests that his Progressive appeals were effective, especially among the Irish Democratic voters who constituted the backbone of his support. As an Irishman and a reformer, Fitzgerald embodied the drive for civic respectability that appealed to so many Irish. Frothingham ran strongest in suburban and upper-class neighborhoods, where his version of Progressivism, critical of the city's Irish Democratic leadership, undoubtedly attracted many Yankee voters. Competition between these two conceptions of reform would dominate Boston's public life after 1905.[15]

The Irish—or more accurately, the specifically Boston-Irish—character of Fitzgerald's Progressivism came sharply into focus in his inaugural address. Pointing to the city's history of "liberty, commercial enterprise, [and] intellectual distinction," Fitzgerald declared that Boston's "abiding spirit" remained despite changes in its physical condition and "racial complexion." He called for a new generation, his own, to live up to the city's "splendid past." Although Fitzgerald nominally spoke for all of the immigrant groups that had altered Boston's "racial complexion," his remarks were aimed most obviously at the city's Irish majority. His rhetoric offered a way for them to establish themselves as the legitimate inheritors of the mantle of civic leadership.[16]

In celebrating this generational shift, Fitzgerald included a subtle dig at Boston's Brahmin elite that foreshadowed changes in the city's ethnic relations. Citing Boston's recent economic stagnation, he promised a "bigger, better, busier Boston" under his leadership. By implication, Boston's Yankee elite were to blame for past difficulties. Now that more aggressive Irish leaders had taken charge, the problem would be solved. These comments marked a departure from the conciliatory rhetoric of Patrick Collins and his generation of Boston-Irish politicians.[17]

Fitzgerald's articulation of a Boston-Irish version of reform was not compatible with the Progressivism of the Good Government Association. Indeed, in the new mayor's hands, it often became a weapon used against Brahmin reformers and their brand of Progressivism. When the GGA attacked Fitzgerald as a corrupt patronage boss, he used Progressivism's anti–big business theme to counterattack, pointing to GGA leader William Minot's connections with the New York, New Haven, and Hartford Railroad, which was negotiating a development contract with the city. Fitzgerald drew attention to Minot's role in the transaction to discredit the GGA, painting a picture of a collection of manipulative insiders fronting for powerful corporations and opposing Fitzgerald's initiatives on behalf of the ordinary citizens of Boston.[18]

Competing efforts to manipulate public opinion in this fashion became an increasingly central element of city politics. One episode illustrates how these contests worked. The GGA maneuvered Fitzgerald into a corner by asking permission to investigate the graft and inefficiency in the sewer department. If the mayor refused, he would look like he had something to hide; if he agreed, the GGA might be expected to find evidence of corruption that would embarrass his administration. Fitzgerald agreed to the investigation but soon found a way to defuse its impact. Two weeks later he asked the reform group to examine the workings of the city's tax assessors office as well.

In part, this ploy diverted attention from the sewer investigation, but the maneuver had a subtler impact as well. In calling for a probe into the tax department, Fitzgerald implied that it had allowed landowners in the city to avoid paying their property taxes. He also wanted the GGA to address the question of "betterment assessments" on Back Bay property that had increased in value after the construction of the Charles River Basin. When the GGA's leaders refused the mayor's request, as Fitzgerald undoubtedly knew they would, their credibility, particularly among ethnic working-class Bostonians, was damaged. The GGA appeared willing to investigate a city department that employed a large number of blue-collar workers but unwilling to examine another branch that appeared to favor the comfortable Brahmins of the Back Bay.[19]

The Boston Finance Commission (BFC) is better understood as a product of this contest to shape public opinion rather than simply as a tool of organized economic interests trying to remake municipal government to their benefit. The BFC was contested terrain from the start, as both Fitzgerald and elite reform leaders, particularly the GGA, tried to influence its findings and, more importantly, the public perceptions that followed therefrom. From this perspective, Boston's inquiry has implications for urban reform in other cities, where similar bodies were established for the same purposes.[20]

John Fitzgerald officially proposed an investigation of Boston's municipal finances in late 1906, in the hope that he would benefit from it. The desire to head off a more hostile inquiry by the Republican-dominated state legislature undoubtedly prompted his announcement. But dismissing his proposal solely as an act of political self-preservation ignores the fact that it took the form of a reform measure. By putting the inquiry under city auspices, he hoped to be able to control it and thus to receive credit for whatever results it yielded. Fitzgerald's alienation from Democratic Party leaders, which made his reputation as a reformer crucial to his political fortunes, eased his decision. Conducted as he wished, the investigation could be used to punish Fitzgerald's political enemies and enhance his Progressive image.[21]

The Boston City Council granted Fitzgerald's request, ordering the creation of the Finance Commission on March 7, 1907. Its charge was to "examine into all matters pertaining to the finances of the City." In particular it was to examine the question of what government expenditures should be financed by taxation and what should be paid for by borrowing. State legislation followed that June, giving the new body the authority to summon witnesses, enforce their attendance, and administer oaths. The Commission was to complete its investigation by the end of 1908.[22]

Although initially wary of a Fitzgerald-controlled inquiry, the Good Government Association warmed to the idea when it had the chance to influence the Commission's membership. The GGA's Republican allies in the State House blocked the appointment of Fitzgerald supporters by threatening to deny the BFC subpoena power. Only when the mayor capitulated, appointing men acceptable to the GGA, did the legislature provide the necessary authority.[23]

The final result was a body allied with the GGA instead of the mayor's office. By the summer of 1907, George Nutter of the GGA was privately pronouncing the Commission members "altogether a good lot—better than we had reason to expect when we started." He declared that three of the seven members were "distinctly with us," and a fourth was generally sympathetic. Two others, Democrats John A. Sullivan and Nathan Matthews, were known to favor reforms, but their partisan ties left Nutter and the GGA unclear of their intentions. Only John F. Kennedy, the representative of the Boston Central Labor Union, remained "an unknown quantity altogether" to the GGA leader.[24]

Though it was not the pliable body he hoped for, Fitzgerald still tried to use the BFC to enhance his reputation as a reformer. Apparently confident of his ability to benefit from the inquiry, Fitzgerald refrained from criticizing the Commission even after its initial reports reflected badly on his administration. When a dispute with the Board of Aldermen arose over his $300,000 loan order for water main construction, Fitzgerald turned to the BFC. The Commission agreed to the loan but limited it to the far smaller sum of $75,000—a decision that Fitzgerald earnestly claimed vindicated his position but that his critics used as evidence of his profligate spending habits. The mayor even hoped to put the BFC to partisan uses: when state Republican leader Henry Cabot Lodge made accusations of fraud and corruption in Boston's government, Fitzgerald urged the investigative board to repudiate the charges.[25]

The Commission ignored Fitzgerald's overtures and instead focused on his administration. It portrayed a city government riven by corruption and inefficiency. The commissioners called for a hiring freeze and the withdrawal of all pending appointments, implying that the city payroll had reached excessive levels. The BFC then unleashed a series of headline-grabbing reports describing the corrupt behavior of a variety of administration officials.

Anxious to sell newspapers, the press seized on these revelations, often inflating them beyond their original meaning. After the BFC called for public scrutiny of municipal real estate transactions, the *Boston Herald* announced that the Commission had asked the mayor "to put a stop to land graft in private deals," as if illegal exchanges were the norm for city business under Fitzgerald. Even more sensational were the September 1907 "coal graft" hearings, which featured dramatic testimony from Michael J. Mitchell, head of the city supply department and a close friend of the mayor, who described the regular distribution of city coal contracts to political allies without the required public bidding process. The local dailies closely followed the hearings, with several weeks of breathless headlines describing the "Latest Developments in the City Coal Inquiry" and front-page sketches of nervous witnesses testifying before the Commission. Although the actual discoveries were relatively minor and Fitzgerald was never implicated, they undermined his image as a reformer.[26]

Others hopped on the anti-Fitzgerald bandwagon launched by the BFC. John B. Moran, Boston's version of the crusading district attorney, announced his intention of summoning the witnesses who appeared before the Finance Commission to testify to a grand jury. Within a week of the coal hearings, the GGA released the report of efficiency expert Richard T. Fox, imported from Chicago to examine Boston's street department. Fox's report further embarrassed Fitzgerald by describing the department's "inefficiency due to bad methods and lax discipline." The *Boston Herald* published two full pages of photographs and detailed analysis of the reports, laboriously depicting the proper and improper methods of street cleaning. Mitchell resigned his supply department post the same day, fueling speculation about wrongdoing at city hall.[27]

In part the Finance Commission's anti-Fitzgerald publicity campaign grew from election-year exigencies. As the December 1907 municipal election approached, the BFC continued to expose instances of petty graft and low-level corruption in city government. One report decried the "swollen" municipal budget and blamed it on the "reckless use of the City's debt," a direct thrust at the Fitzgerald administration. Though the mayor was never conclusively linked to any illegal actions, the cumulative weight of these reports severely hurt his chances in the coming election. The BFC's findings prompted the GGA to release a statement on the city's financial condition in late November that singled out Fitzgerald for condemnation. Just four days before the election, the Finance Commission struck its final blow against the incumbent mayor. In a suspiciously timed set of public hearings, the BFC accepted testimony that described the granting of city contracts by members of Fitzgerald's administration in exchange for bribes. This last-minute move erased any doubt that the Commission's investigation was aimed directly at the incumbent mayor.[28]

The finance commissioners and their allies thus successfully crafted an image of Fitzgerald as a corrupt political boss. "For the first time a man was elected to the office of Mayor whose aim was not merely to use or perfect the political machine then in existence, but to become the machine itself," the commissioners announced. "Under this administration, the spoils system was developed, concentrated in the hands of the Mayor, and pushed to its logical end—waste, inefficiency, corruption, and fraud."[29]

Hyperbolic though it was, this rhetoric helped Boston's business reformers undercut Fitzgerald's Progressivism, even in ethnic quarters. It merely confirmed the suspicions of the middle-class Yankee residents of Jamaica Plain and other suburbs. North End editor James

Donnaruma found in the Commission's report new ammunition in his battle against Fitzgerald, and he featured the reports of the finance commissioners prominently in his *Gazzetta del Massachusetts.* Most significantly, the mayor's role as a symbol of Irish Boston's civic aspirations was damaged. The political commentator of the proreform *South Boston Gazette,* who strongly backed Fitzgerald in 1905, declared himself pleased at the revelations of coal fraud and incompetency at city hall, and the paper sharply criticized Fitzgerald's conduct as mayor.[30]

The *Gazette*'s defection was part of the larger abandonment of Fitzgerald by the city's middle-class Irish during his 1907 reelection bid. The regression model reported in Table 2, designed to measure the relative strength of Irish and working-class support for Fitzgerald, points to a strong relationship between the size of his 1905 vote and the proportion of Irish in a given ward. But in 1907 the strength of that relationship diminished, while the association between Fitzgerald's vote and the size of the working-class population in a ward was now significant. These results suggest that the municipal reform issue peeled away middle-class Irish voters from Fitzgerald while their working-class counterparts remained faithful to him. The better-off Irish in Boston were especially sensitive to anything that threatened the civic legitimacy they sought, and they quickly abandoned Fitzgerald when he ran into trouble.

Table 2. Multiple Linear Regression Analysis of Vote for John F. Fitzgerald, 1905 and 1907 Mayoral Elections

Election	Percent Irish	Percent working class	R^2
1905	.56 (.15)[a]	.39 (.25)	.48
1907	.37 (.14)[a]	.52 (.23)[a]	.42

Standard error in parentheses.
a. Significant at $P < .05$ or better.

Sources: Samuel H. Preston, "United States Census Data, 1910: Public Use Sample" (Ann Arbor: Inter-University Consortium for Political and Social Research, 1989; ICPSR 9166); Boston Board of Election Commissioners, *Annual Report for 1905* (Boston, 1906), p. 171; idem, *Annual Report for 1907* (Boston, 1908), p. 210.

Model: Percent vote for Fitzgerald = intercept + percent irish + percent working class. Model statistics: N = 25; adjusted R^2 (1905) = .43; adjusted R^2 (1907) = .37; intercept (1905) = .14; intercept (1907) = .07.

Note: See Statistical Appendix for a discussion of the construction of variables.

As this analysis suggests, Irish Progressivism could become two Progressivisms divided along the fault line of social class. Fitzgerald used the antibusiness, prolabor theme—he labeled his 1907 Republican opponent "antagonistic to labor and against progressive legislation"—and his reputation as a generous dispenser of patronage to maintain the support of blue-collar Irish. But their middle-class counterparts, longing for respectability in public affairs, could not stomach Fitzgerald's blackened reputation. They deserted him in favor of Republican George Hibbard or John Coulthurst, a third-party candidate running with the backing of William Randolph Hearst's Independence League. Coulthurst's presence on the ballot in particular allowed Irish voters to back a reform candidate without completely betraying their party loyalty.

The formation of the Finance Commission and the results of its initial investigation represented a triumph for the city's elite reformers. Through a well-crafted publicity campaign they succeeded in projecting an image of Fitzgerald as a machine politician. That representation crippled Fitzgerald's efforts to construct himself as an Irish reformer, at least in the short run.

Having shaped public opinion well enough to defeat Fitzgerald in 1907, Boston's business reformers set about the task of institutionalizing their reform vision along the lines followed in many other cities. Through the BFC they proposed an overhaul of the structure and mechanics of Boston's municipal government based on the National Municipal League's model charter. Their recommendations included an increase in the state legislature's power over the city's finances, civil service controls over city employment, a simplified ballot, the abolition of party names in city politics, a small unicameral City Council, the concentration of executive power in the mayor's office, the expert administration of departments, and a permanent Finance Commission. The BFC's final report promised that "these measures will enable a good mayor and city council to give the citizens a really good administration."[31]

Though these plans fit neatly into the common pattern for Progressive Era municipal reform, their triumph cannot be explained without reference to the local context. Proponents used the broad language of Progressive reform to explain the need for charter reform. In doing so, they allowed other social groups to develop their own understandings of why charter reform was necessary and what it would accomplish. If upper- and middle-class Yankee civic leaders saw the restructuring of city government as a way to end Irish machine rule, Irish voters saw it as the means by which they could legitimately govern the city. Still others could imagine the proposed charter as the solution to the particular problems their communities faced. It was this multiplicity of specific, often locally defined interpretations that made the construction of a pro–charter reform voting coalition possible. Comprehending this process begins with a close analysis of the arguments used to enlist popular support for charter reform.

At their core was the reconceptualization of corruption and its causes that had developed during the Progressive Era. Borrowing from the language of social science, muckrakers and reformers described corruption as a systemic problem, whereas previous generations had defined it as an individual moral failing. The BFC's report followed this new reasoning, insisting that the sources of Boston's problems were primarily structural rather than the product of individual misbehavior, and that reforming the city's governmental system would automatically restore its civic morality. The final report of the commissioners argued that the city's "electoral machinery" had proven "unsuited to the requirements of successful municipal government through popular suffrage." Current methods of electing city officials prevented "the best and most representative citizens" from serving, "increased the power of money in elections," and "practically handed the city over to ward politicians." It was a system that tended "to create bad government no matter how badly the people may desire good government."[32]

Implicit in the BFC's diagnosis of Boston's problems was the belief in a shared understanding of the common good. The corrupt politicians who had so damaged the city would never have been elected "if their constituents knew the facts and could vote for anyone else," their report declared. Voters would make the proper choice if an election were presented as "a contest between candidates known to represent clearly and unequivocally the opposite sides of the issue of honest government." Believing "the questions affecting the proper administration of the government" to be "far removed from political questions," the finance commissioners defined the problem to be simply a case of efficiently delivering services. Thus they saw a need for "more effective supervision by the central government, the importance of trusting the administration to experts, and . . . eliminating the spoils system from democratic institutions." The guiding assumption in these pronouncements was that almost every Bostonian had the same ideas about which policies should be pursued and in what manner. Seen in this light, the new city charter was an attempt not simply to remake government but also to restore its proper relationship to a virtuous people.[33]

The issue of leadership was at the center of this formulation of Boston's problems. Boston's current system "debarred the best and most representative citizens from participating in the government." Party primaries "operate[d] to make the nomination and election of representative citizens to the elective offices of the city government more difficult." Since national parties offered "no municipal policies capable of formulation," men who owed their allegiance to the party rather than the public were ill suited to govern the city. In the place of "competent and representative citizens" seeking to perform their "civic duty," Boston was getting venal party politicians, "men who had brought such discredit on themselves and the city of Boston."[34]

This call for a government run by "representative citizens" had strongly hierarchical connotations. It did not refer to a broad cross section of the city's social life but to an elite who would "represent" the city most respectably. They were to be "busy men"—in short, businessmen—a group dominated by Boston's Yankee upper and middle classes.[35]

The Commission's model was adopted, but through a process that cost them control over its meaning. Six of the seven finance commissioners and most of the GGA's executive committee wanted the state legislature to rewrite the city's charter without in any way consulting the people of Boston. But charter revision faced stiff opposition from leaders of both parties, who were hostile to the plan to do away with partisan control of the nomination process. After several months of legislative wrangling, Boston reformers and the Republican leadership struck a compromise: the leadership would push through the legislature those portions of the BFC's recommendations that gave the state government greater authority over the city budget and hiring in exchange for submitting the proposed political reforms to the voters of Boston for approval.[36]

The citizens of Boston were to be offered a choice between two plans through a binding referendum. Plan One was an alternative to the Finance Commission's offering. It included a weaker mayor; a thirty-six-member City Council, with some members elected by ward; and the retention of party labels. Plan Two—the reform plan—featured a stronger executive department and a nine-member City Council elected on an at-large basis. Most importantly, it would replace partisan nominations with a petition process. Candidates for mayor could receive a place on the ballot by collecting five thousand signatures from registered voters; those seeking a City Council nomination needed two thousand names.[37]

Although most of Boston's elite reformers opposed a popular vote on any aspect of the new charter, some of them recognized that the referendum was an opportunity to mold public opinion. By engaging in a public campaign, they could reinforce their message that the problems Boston faced lay in its politics, not in its people. "We believe the fact can be driven home that in civic affairs the interests of all good citizens from the humblest to the most exalted are identical," declared civic reformer James J. Storrow. Storrow proposed to send a copy of the final report of the Finance Commission to every citizen of Boston. GGA leader George Nutter privately agreed, favoring a citywide vote for its "educational value." The GGA began orchestrating a publicity campaign in March 1909, including the mailing of an abstract of the Finance Commission's report to every voter. The political compromise that yielded the referendum thus intensified the effort to popularize reform.[38]

To attract widespread support, Plan Two's promoters presented the referendum in the broadest terms possible, as a choice between clean government and corrupt bossism. "When Fitzgerald, Lomasney, Curley, Timilty, 'Jim' Donovan, 'Charlie' Innes, and 'Harry' Atwood are lined up together where do you, Mr. Citizen, wish to stand? Where do you think your interests lie?" asked a pro–Plan Two advertisement (ignoring Fitzgerald's endorsement of the reform measure). The supporters of the reform charter claimed that it would eliminate a litany of evils, including "the Municipal Boss, the Auction Sale of Delegates, . . . the Money Bought Nomination, the Party Serving Officials . . . [and] the Wasteful Division of Funds." The new charter would "Place Power in the People . . . Make Way for Honest Candidates . . . Fix Official Responsibility . . . [and] Make for a United Boston."[39]

Plan Two proponents also attempted to dispel any claims that charter revision was the work of any one social group or political party. Although upper- and middle-class Yankees made up a majority of the handpicked "Committee of 100," its membership also included several prominent Irish Catholics and Jews. Representatives of both major parties belonged as well.[40]

This aggressive campaign convinced a slim majority of Bostonians to support Plan Two, which captured 39,170 votes to Plan One's 35,276. A surprisingly strong showing by the reform proposal in several blue-collar ethnic districts made its success possible. It ran strongly in the city's two largest Irish neighborhoods, garnering a majority in Charlestown and falling just short in South Boston. Plan Two edged Plan One (880 votes to 803) in the North End. These totals enabled it to overcome staunch opposition in Martin Lomasney's ward eight and a few other sections. Though Plan Two did not get a majority of the votes of blue-collar and immigrant Boston, it won enough to ensure its passage. Charter reform in Boston was not simply the triumph of upper- and middle-class Anglo-Protestants.

More systematic analysis underscores the inadequacy of a group-based explanation of Plan Two's success. Support from Yankee professionals, businessmen, and property owners was not the foundation of charter reform's electoral triumph. The regression model summarized in Table 3 indicates no significant relationship between the size of a ward's vote for Plan Two and the percentage of native-stock or white-collar residents in it. Nor were suburban voters seeking to improve city services and reduce property taxes principally responsible for the reshaping of Boston's municipal structure. The variable for the degree of suburbanization included in the regression equation does not predict how a ward voted on the charter question.

Plan Two's triumph did not necessarily mean that a majority of Bostonians shared the Finance Commission's reform vision. It won because it was framed in broad terms, allowing alternative interpretations of reform to develop simultaneously. The commissioners' promise of more efficient, democratic, and responsive municipal government resonated among constituencies with various grievances already conditioned by the language of reform. Ambitious politicians such as John F. Fitzgerald and Charlestown's John R. Murphy, both of whom hoped to run for mayor in 1910, recognized this appeal and stumped the city endorsing the reform proposal. Even ward leaders Martin Lomasney, James Michael Curley, and James Timilty flirted with Plan Two before endorsing Plan One at the last minute.[41]

The efforts of the two mayoral aspirants proved crucial to Plan

Table 3. Multiple Linear Regression Analysis of Plan Two Vote,
November 1909

Predictor variable	Regression coefficient	Standard error	p-value
Percent U.S. stock	.32	.22	.16
Percent white-collar	−.16	.04	.55
Suburban variable	.04	.07	.63

Sources: Samuel H. Preston, "United States Census Data, 1910: Public Use Sample" (Ann Arbor: Inter-University Consortium for Political and Social Research, 1989; ICPSR 9166); Boston Board of Election Commissioners, *Annual Report for 1909–1910* (Boston, 1910), p. 129.
Model: percent vote for Plan Two = intercept + percent U.S. stock + percent white-collar + suburban variable. Model statistics: $N = 25$; $R^2 = .13$; adjusted $R^2 = .01$; intercept = .46.
Note: See Statistical Appendix for a discussion of the construction of variables.

Two's success. Murphy campaigned aggressively for the reform charter, especially in his home district of Charlestown, where he had been a prominent political figure for two decades. His efforts helped swing the neighborhood's three wards into the Plan Two column. And Fitzgerald repeatedly argued that charter reform would "place all citizens upon an equality at city hall." His calls clearly swayed voters as well, particularly in his old home, the North End, where Plan Two won despite the opposition of the *Gazzetta del Massachusetts* and Italian leaders who feared an at-large system would prevent the election of Italians to the City Council. Without the votes provided by Fitzgerald's and Murphy's campaigning, Plan Two would have failed.[42]

Bossism does not explain the ability of these politicians to persuade voters. While Fitzgerald's connections to ward six through the agency of his brothers' political organization helped deliver a majority of the votes cast in the North End, other party leaders were less effective. John R. Murphy was a well-respected figure in Charlestown circles, but by no means did he dominate its highly factionalized politics. Charles Innes, the reputed Republican boss of ward twelve, could not carry his district for Plan One. Nor can Plan Two's strong showing in South Boston's ward fourteen, where it ran almost evenly with its alternative, be explained by neighborhood political alignments.

Plan Two attracted enough ethnic and working-class support to win because its sweeping promise of a more honest and effective government was open to a variety of interpretations. The lone dissenting member of the Finance Commission had already demonstrated how the language of charter reform could have multiple meanings. John F. Kennedy served on the BFC as the representative of the Boston Central Labor Union. He refused to go along with the Commission's final report because he considered it too critical of the Fitzgerald administration. But for all his disagreements, he concurred with his fellow commissioners on one issue: charter reform.

Kennedy believed that a more open and democratic political process and a more responsive government would benefit Boston's working class. Under the reform charter "the various interests of the city will have a better chance of obtaining proper representation in the city government. And labor," he added, "the greatest of these interests and possessing by far the largest voting power, can well take care of itself under the new system proposal." Kennedy confidently predicted that "the economic and social issues which will come to the front will certainly be of more vital importance to our citizens than the party issues which tend to obscure them under present conditions." Like his fellow finance commissioners and Plan Two proponents, Kennedy expected the public to express its desires more effectively under a new system. But his understanding of what those desires were clearly differed from that of his Commission colleagues and the GGA.[43]

Though Kennedy referred specifically to Boston's workers, his argument had wider implications. The promise of democracy and efficiency made the adoption of Plan Two attractive to a variety of interests, each of which could conclude that a new charter would serve its particular agenda. Suburban improvement associations found the promise of lower property taxes and the efficient delivery of government services appealing. The *Jewish Advocate*, which had long identified municipal reform with Jewish interests, strongly endorsed Plan Two in large part because it would make possible the election of a Jew to the City Council. Robert Woods, Meyer Bloomfield, and other settlement workers believed that a reformed charter would eliminate ward bosses and create a government that more effectively delivered social services to the urban poor.[44]

Women reformers were conspicuously absent from the Plan Two campaign. Unlike cities such as Chicago, Boston's leading women's groups did not assume a significant role in the debate. Although a number of women's reform organizations had expressed sympathy for political reform in general terms, they maintained their policy of avoiding all electoral contests. The one group that might have jumped into the fray, the Boston Equal Suffrage Association for Good Government, had by 1909 shifted its emphasis almost entirely to suffrage work.[45]

The most important interpretation of Plan Two's promise occurred among its Irish supporters. If, as Plan Two proponents argued, the fault lay not in the people but in a system that perpetuated boss rule, then Boston's Irish, who constituted the majority of the city's electorate, were its primary victims. Manipulative bosses "frequently acted directly contrary to the known wishes of the people they were supposed to represent," observed John Toomey's *South Boston Gazette*. They denied Irish voters the chance to elect respectable and public-spirited leaders from their communities. The restoration of democratic municipal government would confer legitimacy upon Irish leaders. Instead of being stereotyped as corrupt bosses, Irish-Catholic politicians elected under the new system would govern with the same communal authority their Yankee predecessors had wielded in the past. "We have men here in South Boston who are able, aggressive when need be, honest and willing to serve the public, yet who would not venture, under the present mode of electing, to go before the people." Revising the political process would allow this set of "respectable men" to assume power in the city.[46]

The major attraction of Plan Two in Irish quarters was its shift to direct nominations by the people. If popular nominations were the sole feature of the new charter, it would win by a ten-to-one margin, declared the *South Boston Gazette*. "The first and most important question to be considered is as to whether the people are to control or self-appointed bosses are to continue to manipulate." John R. Murphy cited the elimination of boss-run nominating conventions as a primary reason for his support of the reform charter. "Under Plan Two," he explained, "the citizens nominate directly by petition who shall run for mayor, who shall run for council, a step in the direction for which democracy has fought so long." For Boston's Irish majority, charter reform promised a restoration of democracy, and the chance to govern effectively and legitimately.[47]

That Irish and GGA enthusiasm for charter reform stemmed from different reasoning became clear in the ensuing municipal election. Only nine weeks after a cross section of the city's voters endorsed political reform, they split sharply along ethnic lines in a battle between a party politician and an elite nonpartisan reformer. Boston's Irish did not back Plan One, the antireform plan, but they did unite in support of John F. Fitzgerald's mayoral candidacy two months later. As Table 4 shows, a regression model measuring Irish and working-class support for Plan One found no significant relationship between the size of either group in a ward and the vote in that district for the antireform plan in November 1909. But the same model indicates strong Irish backing for Fitzgerald in January 1910. After watching his ethnic political base crack in 1907 and remain divided on the question of charter reform, Fitzgerald now patched it back together.

Although it is tempting to assume Fitzgerald restored Irish political cohesion by reviving the Democratic machine, that was not the case. While most of the city's Irish ward leaders (with the notable exception of Jim Donovan of ward nine) backed him, their influence is easily exaggerated. In 1907 the same ward leaders rallied behind his incumbent candidacy but failed to deliver a majority. There is no reason to think that their power had increased over the intervening two years. The voters whom Fitzgerald had brought back into the fold—the middle-class Irish—were least likely to have been swayed by a boss.

Fitzgerald rebuilt his voting base by reestablishing himself as a symbol of Irish political aspirations in Boston and by reframing those

Table 4. Multiple Linear Regression Analysis of Vote for Plan One (1909) and Vote for Fitzgerald in 1910 Mayoral Election

Election	Percent Irish	Percent working class	R^2
Plan One vote (November 1909)	−.07 (.16)	.07 (.26)	.01
Fitzgerald vote (January 1910)	.53 (.16)[a]	.34 (.26)	.43

Standard error in parentheses.

a. Significant at $P < .05$ level or better.

Sources: Samuel H. Preston, "United States Census Data, 1910: Public Use Sample" (Ann Arbor: Inter-University Consortium for Political and Social Research, 1989; ICPSR 9166); Boston Board of Election Commissioners, *Annual Report for 1909–1910* (Boston, 1910), pp. 129, 142.

Model: Plan One/Fitzgerald vote percent = intercept + percent Irish + percent working class. Model statistics: N = 25; adjusted R^2 (1909) = .08; adjusted R^2 (1910) = .37; intercept (1909) = .47; intercept (1910) = .20.

Note: See Statistical Appendix for a discussion of the construction of variables.

aspirations in the language of reform. Boston's immigrants, and especially its Irish, were the majority—"the people," in Fitzgerald's Progressive formulation—while his opponent James J. Storrow and his Brahmin allies represented private, selfish interests plotting to deny the majority their right to rule themselves. Faced with such a threat, the Irish coalesced. But their support for Fitzgerald did not constitute a rejection of reform. In the same election, they also helped elect seven of the nine City Council candidates endorsed by the Citizens' Municipal League, the GGA-backed municipal reform body.[48]

It appeared at first that Storrow would be able to restore the sense of ethnic cooperation that had characterized Boston public life a few years earlier. The wealthy Brahmin-born banker had a record as a conciliatory force in Boston's public life. Along with numerous philanthropic endeavors, Storrow had helped to form the City Club in 1906, one of the few civic organizations that truly sought a socially diverse membership. He also reconstituted Boston's Chamber of Commerce, turning the moribund Yankee enclave into a more open and active organization. Most importantly, as chairman of the Boston School Committee, he demonstrated a capacity to forge agreements on the delicate cultural issues arising in school politics. His performance as Committee chairman even earned him effusive praise from *The Pilot,* still the leading Irish-Catholic newspaper in the city.[49]

The essential strategy of Storrow and his GGA backers was simple: to portray Fitzgerald as a corrupt boss and Storrow as an honest reformer. They used the reports of the Finance Commission as ammunition to attack the former mayor as a municipal plunderer. In numerous ads headlined "FITZGERALDISM," the Storrow forces revived testimony from the coal graft hearings and other BFC investigations. In contrast, they portrayed Storrow as the upright steward of the municipal interests, who had managed "$10,500,000 of the people's money" as School Committee chairman without any hint that even "a single postage stamp or a single cent was used except for the benefit of your children."[50]

The emphasis on fiscal responsibility was only part of Storrow's larger emphasis on the unity of interest among Bostonians. As in the charter campaign, Storrow and his supporters argued that an honest, efficient government promised benefits to every citizen. Storrow underlined this theme by campaigning actively not only in the boardrooms of State Street and the clubs of the Back Bay, but also on the sidewalks of the North End and in the meeting halls of South Boston. Speaking in frigid temperatures to factory workers, Storrow insisted that his conservative fiscal policies would attract a "higher class of industry" that would pay better wages, allowing working-class women and children to stay home. It was the "dishonest contractor, not the honest laborer," who would be the real beneficiary of a second Fitzgerald administration. "There is an attempt being made by my opponent and his backers to split us up into a lot of discordant factions," the candidate told a group of freight yard workers, "and by us I mean the people of Boston."[51]

Storrow's charge was accurate, but he never recognized that his own rhetoric helped make Fitzgerald's divide-and-rule strategy possible. As in 1905, when he had also faced an opponent presenting himself as a reformer, Fitzgerald refused to concede the reform issue to his opponent. Instead he restated it on his own terms: Storrow became the tool of monied interests, Fitzgerald the voice of the people. "I have had to fight more money in this campaign than has been expended in city campaigns in Boston for the past five campaigns put together," Fitzgerald declared. Storrow's ties to big business meant that he could not have the interests of ordinary people at heart. "If not for the complete indifference on the part of James J. Storrow and his banker friends," the former mayor told an audience of longshoremen as he pointed toward the harbor, "there would be 50 ships there instead of just one." Under a Fitzgerald administration a "large representation of the real population will have the say in the investment of the moneys" of the city.[52]

Fitzgerald summed up this appeal with the phrase "Manhood against Money," a slogan that sharpened his reform appeal. It not only underscored his charge that Storrow represented the interests of wealthy Brahmins, it also cast the contest in gendered terms. One source of the persuasiveness of Progressivism was its masculinization of the idea of reform. Nineteenth-century portrayals of reform as the effeminate, overly moralistic antithesis of the pragmatic, male-dominated realm of electoral politics gave way in the early twentieth century to Progressivism's self-image of masculine practicality. Fitzgerald took advantage of this change by splashing the "Manhood against Money" assertion across his campaign advertising and repeating it in his stump speeches, a sensible strategy given the all-male municipal electorate. The implication of this gendered appeal gave it added punch: Fitzgerald the reformer represented the masculine side of the contest, while Storrow and his supporters were cast as effeminate and ineffective.[53]

Progressive reform in Fitzgerald's hands also took on an ethnic dimension. Although much of his public rhetoric centered on Storrow's wealth and his connections to trusts, Fitzgerald was able to translate these issues into ethnic terms by carefully targeting his audience. Fitzgerald's biographer claims that he perfected the technique "of submitting one speech to newspapers and delivering another behind closed doors in friendly territory." Storrow accused Fitzgerald of doing just that in an underground campaign that included appeals to racial and religious bigotry. While Storrow's allegations—which in themselves raised the ethnic issue—remained unproven, another Fitzgerald tactic suggests that they had some merit. In public speeches and comments to be carried by the largely hostile daily press, Fitzgerald stuck mostly to standard reform rhetoric, focusing on Storrow's wealth and influence. But in *The Republic,* a weekly paper he purchased in 1902 and that catered to the city's Irish population, he gave the same attacks a much sharper ethnic tone.[54]

In his own paper Fitzgerald ridiculed Storrow's efforts to encourage ethnic harmony. One report mocked the Yankee's awkward attempts to connect with a South Boston audience by introducing them to his dog—an "Irish Bull," the paper joked. "His hearers saw through Mr. Storrow, and also through his mascot," *The Republic* account declared. For Roxbury, Dorchester, Brighton, and other WASP-tinged suburbs, Storrow had another mascot, a "golden calf." The banker-candidate came in for further lampooning when he reminded a North End gathering that he too had been born there and could lay claim to being a "Dearo," Fitzgerald's affectionate name for his fellow North Enders. "James J. Storrow is 'a Dearo.' Who would have thought it?" asked *The Republic* derisively, noting that he had "been rather slow in pressing these claims of kindred." All the while, the paper denied that Fitzgerald was using ethnic appeals, asserting that it was Storrow himself who had injected the issue into the contest.[55]

Fitzgerald's newspaper also attacked Storrow's record as head of the School Committee, despite his efforts toward ethnic accommodation while in that position. Citing the complaints of Catholic priests, *The Republic* deplored the condition of many schools in Charlestown, Dorchester, the South End, and other ethnic districts. The source of this neglect was Storrow, the "dominant, economical, multi-million-aire, who never having known the hardships of the struggle for life, believes that almost anything in the shape of the schools is good enough for the children of the people." By injecting this class rhetoric into the culturally charged issue of school politics, Fitzgerald was providing an ethnic as well as an economic dimension to the identity of "the people."[56]

On the eve of the election, *The Republic* stressed ethnicity (over class) even more explicitly in its attack on the city's Brahmin elite. Unlike their predecessors, who founded the nation on egalitarian principles, Boston's twentieth-century Yankees wanted to "make a little House of Lords here, and hold class dominance by money power," a reference to aristocratic English government sure to resonate among its Irish readers. This new generation of Brahmins sought "to keep the self-respecting wage-earner, and by this word we mean not only the laborer and the mechanic, but the teacher, and the struggling man of all other professions out of the public service." It was these old-stock "multi-millionaires," led by Storrow, who were trying "to hold Boston at any cost for the rich." The stewards of Boston's immense fortunes were using their inherited power to block the ascendance of the city's new ethnic (and predominantly Irish) majority. They were "the interests" in Boston.[57]

It is important to emphasize that Fitzgerald did not reject the traditions of the founding generations of Bostonians; it was only Yankees of a more recent vintage he decried. "This little group," his newspaper insisted, "is in no wise representative of the hardy old-Yankee stock which laid 'the ribs and keel' of the ship of state in Massachusetts." They were "never ashamed of humble birth and honest labor." In differentiating between original Yankees and their descendants, Fitzgerald refused to reject the communal ideals that had long been celebrated in New England, ideals closely linked with the nation's founding. Instead, in a new twist on the ethnic Progressive narrative, he claimed that the present group of Brahmin reformers had abandoned that heritage by seeking to prevent the representatives of the new majority from taking their rightful place in the city government. The current Yankee elite were the betrayers of the public interest in Boston, which in *The Republic*'s formulation became the interest of the city's ethnic majority.[58]

Fitzgerald also sought to discredit the Finance Commission, whose reports were Storrow's chief weapon. He made "Vindication!" another slogan of his campaign, vindication from the biases of the BFC investigators, who *The Republic* claimed were led by "members of the old time school of New England anti-Catholic bigots." The newspaper also pointed to the lack of convictions in the antitrust cases stemming from the Finance Commission's exposure of the "Boston Agreement," a price-setting deal among large manufacturers doing business with the city. If the evidence compiled by the BFC in that case was insufficient, then its investigation of Fitzgerald's administration must also be inadequate, *The Republic* reasoned. On the stump, Fitzgerald trotted out John F. Kennedy, his lone ally from the Commission, who accused his fellow commissioners of treating the ex-mayor unfairly. These charges were effective; three days before the election, the GGA's George Nutter reported in his diary that the Storrow campaign was "deathly afraid of talking too much of the Fin. Com."[59]

With this offensive, Fitzgerald fully broke with the conciliatory tactics of his Irish predecessors. He abandoned the social narrative of ethnic cooperation emphasized by Democratic leaders a decade earlier, replacing it with an account emphasizing the declining moral character of Brahmin Boston and increasing discrimination against the Irish. This reformulation of the city's past and present proved temporary, a way station en route to an even harsher version of Boston's ethnic history that would follow in a few years. Fitzgerald's efforts to mobilize Irish support in 1910 set the stage for the further redefinition of Irish identity in Boston in coming years. Ironically, it was Progressivism's emphasis on communal action, and the structural reforms it encouraged, that fueled this transformation.

Boston's 1910 election thus saw the sharpest divergence of the city's principal Progressivisms to that date. Fitzgerald's restoration of Irish political unity followed from his reassertion of the central element of Irish Progressivism: that the Boston Irish could legitimately inherit the reins of municipal government. He reclaimed his role as the embodiment of those ambitions in 1910. But he did so in a more aggressive manner, sharpening ethnic battle lines by now portraying the city's Brahmin elite as uniformly hostile to Irish aspirations. By the same token, the Storrow campaign's attacks on Fitzgeraldism and Fitzgerald's subsequent triumph confirmed middle-class Yankee suspicions that the city's ethnics, and especially its Irish, were implacably hostile to honest and economical government. While these twin perceptions were not unprecedented, their emergence as the defining feature of Boston's politics contrasts starkly with the conciliatory character of local public life a decade earlier.

Charter reform in Boston was simultaneously unifying and divisive. The drive to establish a new municipal structure knitted together a contingent coalition based on the language of Progressivism. But embedded within this language were multiple visions of the city's past and future, visions informed by social experience and quickened by the campaign for municipal reform. Progressivism's open-ended rhetoric made possible the development and momentary unification of those differing representations. But the Plan Two voting coalition was a volatile mix. Its divergent expectations grew clearer, and the conflicts between them emerged more fully after 1909. The possibility of temporary alignments among varying Progressivisms remained. But the likelihood of angry splits increased as the pursuit of specific municipal policies made these alternative visions more explicit.

CHAPTER FOUR

The New Urban Political Terrain

Boston's 1909 charter reform sharply divided the city's political history. Parties, the central institution of nineteenth-century American politics, dominated public life before Plan Two's passage. Afterward, the nonpartisan, communal style of politics that emerged with the rise of Progressivism became the dominant mode of local public action. From then on, the city's political culture more closely resembled the late-twentieth-century pattern than it did the highly structured world of nineteenth-century parties and elections. To be sure, the change was not quite so abrupt. The trend toward a public life dominated by interest groups and mass appeals was under way before 1909, and the legacies of partisan power persisted well beyond that date. But the institutional arrangements and political styles that mark modern urban politics became firmly rooted in Boston's public soil at that moment.

Changes in Boston reflected a nationwide pattern. Though parties remained the central institution of American politics, they began to grow weaker in the early twentieth century. Levels of voter participation declined, the beginning of a century-long trend only temporarily reversed during the 1930s. When people did vote, they were more likely to split their tickets, as partisan loyalty began to wane. It was around this time that new modes of mass politics began to flourish as well, as advertising and mass appeals based on personality superseded caucus battles and calls to partisan arms. Finally, interest groups multiplied and began to occupy an even more conspicuous place in American public life than before.[1]

City neighborhoods were the crucibles for many of these developments, yet they are often ignored in urban political history. Scholars have focused on the consequences of political changes at the social and political center, while devoting less attention to what occurred on the periphery. The neighborhood, Samuel Hays has concluded, was no longer a "creative urban force" but now "an object of action generated elsewhere."[2] Historians of urban politics turned their attention to the large social and economic interests deemed to be the mainsprings of urban public life—railroads, utilities, chambers of commerce, women's groups—and the issues that arose around them. They have ignored ward politics, assuming that stereotypes about bosses and immigrant voters applied equally before, during, and after the institutional upheaval of the Progressive Era. A closer look suggests that a significant alteration in ground-level urban public culture occurred, one that sharply and permanently reconfigured neighborhood political life.

Had they examined grassroots politics in Boston, historians would have discovered that the structural reforms of the Progressive Era created a distinctly modern political pattern at the local level. The shift to nonpartisan, at-large City Council elections eliminated the monopoly the major parties held on municipal offices. The power and significance of ward-level partisan machinery withered, and nonpartisan civic organizations became the most effective intermediaries between the government and the neighborhood, not only in middle-class suburbs but in ethnic districts as well. Even in the wards where bosses were supposedly entrenched, charter reform created space for these alternative forms of political action. Like the contemporary interest groups that litter the urban political landscape today, these neighborhood and ethnic associations involved a relatively small number of people who proposed to speak for the "community" as they defined it.

If institutional change made the new form of politics effective, the malleable and increasingly popular Progressive style made it possible. By 1910, the new political environment created by charter reform made the image of cohesive communal action more attractive and more persuasive than ever. As parties faded, it became the dominant form of political action, with distinctive consequences for the social dimensions of local public life.

To some extent the changes sparked by charter reform in Boston are consistent with the prevailing social history of Progressive Era political development. Numerous scholars have argued that the decline of ward-based party politics and the growth of organized interest groups and centralized bureaucracies cut off the working class and immigrants from power.[3] Boston's structural revamping clearly gave an advantage to middle-class associational politics at the expense of more-inclusive party bodies. But as subsequent chapters will show, new institutional arrangements created new opportunities for political entrepreneurs as well. Employing carefully crafted public appeals, James Michael Curley and others were able to mobilize many of those left out of the new politics as well as some of those operating within Boston's new regime, with distinctive consequences for the city's social character.

This chapter traces the transformation of Boston's ground-level political terrain following charter reform. It examines three distinctive neighborhoods: Brighton, Charlestown, and the West End. Brighton, jutting out to the west from central Boston along the Charles River, was part of the outermost suburban portion of Boston, where middle-class Yankees still dominated. But Anglo-Saxon hegemony had begun to fade, giving way to a steady influx of middle- and working-class ethnics, especially Irish Americans. Brighton was one of the few parts of town where local politics still featured serious two-party competition in 1910. Charlestown, a crowded neighborhood across the Charles River from downtown Boston, was largely Irish and primarily blue-collar, though a remnant of middle-class Yankees remained from its days as a separate town. Its three wards were overwhelmingly Democratic, although the intraparty feuding was rampant. The West End was one of the three crowded neighborhoods immediately adjacent to Boston's central business district. Like the South and North Ends, it was filled with new immigrants, in this case mostly Jewish. It was also the home of Martin Lomasney, bane of political reformers. If any party politician was equipped to weather the storm of charter reform, it was Lomasney.

Before delving into Boston's grassroots political culture, a brief examination of the impact of charter reform on the citywide political scene is in order. Efforts to limit party power did not begin with the passage of Plan Two. An 1885 revision of the city charter set in motion the process of centralizing municipal power in the mayor's office. Measures establishing the Australian ballot, replacing caucuses with primaries, lengthening mayoral terms, and altering the means of electing aldermen followed. All of these reforms weakened political parties and encouraged alternative forms of political organization. The approval of Plan Two was the final, most powerful thrust in this direction. By removing party designations in city elections, replacing district-based elections with at-large contests, and cutting the City Council to just nine members, charter reform severely curtailed the significance of parties in municipal politics.

A different kind of organization arose to fill the void created by the demise of traditional parties. The Citizens' Municipal League (CML), a nonpartisan nominating body created by the GGA, became the most significant force in local electoral politics. Although its choice for mayor, James J. Storrow, lost in 1910, the League controlled access to the new nine-member City Council. A CML endorsement became a virtual guarantee of a seat, and the Council became the center of reform activism in the city. Meanwhile, the Democratic Party, long the majority party in Boston, lost its fundamental role in city politics, opening up room for the local and group-based political action already encouraged by the spread of Progressivism.

The CML fashioned itself within this framework. "Our appeal," declared Richard Olney, former U.S. attorney general and chairman of the League's original Committee of 25, "is to that overwhelming majority of Boston's citizens who know they are misgoverned; who have no interest except to be well governed." Olney explained the theory of this new municipal movement: "Some man would be deemed so desirable for mayor or for the Council by 5,000 of his fellow citizens that they would spontaneously put him in nomination by signing the requisite papers." It was this image of a morally aroused, united citizenry that lay at the heart of Progressivism and animated the CML. To preserve it, the League crafted a platform that promised "a constructive and progressive city government," a proposal so broad and vague that nearly anyone could interpret it to his or her own satisfaction.[4]

Whatever its rhetoric implied, in practical terms the League was a child of the city's economic elite and their particular Progressivism. The GGA's officers, seeking to avoid an open convention that they could not control, chose a Committee of 25, which in turn selected 180 "representative men" to be members of the League. Of these, 106 came from either the Back Bay or one of the city's wealthier suburban districts. Their ranks included seventy-two lawyers, thirteen physicians, and twelve real estate agents. Though membership remained open to the public, successful applicants required the endorsement of a current member and the approval of a majority of those present at a League meeting. While the League sought out people from all parts of the city and from various ethnic groups, its control remained largely in the hands of a few men. The nomination of James Jackson Storrow, the GGA's handpicked choice, in a meeting that lasted just fifteen minutes and considered but one name, revealed the fundamentally closed character of the new organization.[5]

Despite Storrow's defeat, the League became the dominant force in city politics over the next five years. CML-backed candidates won seven of nine Council seats in the 1910 election and sixteen of twenty-one available spots in the first five years under the new city charter. The reform organization's hold on the Council was so strong that few regular party politicians even bothered to seek a seat. Nineteen men competed for the nine openings in 1910, and ten pursued the three Council spots available in 1911; seven candidates ran for three seats in 1912, and in 1913 only one candidate not endorsed by the CML entered the race. In 1914 six candidates ran—three League endorsees and three party politicians.[6]

The League's appeal was strongest in the suburban neighborhoods within the city. In the five City Council races from 1910 to 1914, CML-endorsed candidates carried these districts in nearly every case. Non-CML candidates finished among the top three vote getters in any of these wards four out of a possible thirty-eight times. Even Irish Democrats from other parts of the city ran well in these predominantly Yankee Republican districts if they carried the League's seal of approval.[7]

Superseded by the Citizens' Municipal League, the parties no longer controlled access to city hall and quickly became irrelevant to municipal affairs. With far fewer nominations to distribute after charter reform, the role of neighborhood party organizations was limited, and competition for their control quickly diminished. Battles for the ward committee occurred in only three of Boston's sixteen Democratic wards in 1911, a far cry from a few years before, when the annual fight for control of the ward committee was a conspicuous feature of political life. "There isn't much demand for places on the ward committee as there formerly was," one observer noted; "the ward committee, as an instrument for political power, is becoming a vain and empty thing."[8]

Charter reform eroded another municipal institution that fueled political activity on the neighborhood level. The dismantling of the Common Council meant the elimination of seventy-five entry-level political offices, three from each ward. Competition for these seats had been fierce. In 1908, 183 men sought Democratic nominations for the Common Council. They formed clubs, held rallies, and knocked on doors; one 1908 aspirant shook hands with more than five thousand voters. A year later all this activity had ceased, abruptly severing the intimate connection between politicians and voters fostered by this annual flurry of electioneering.[9]

Not surprisingly, the eclipse of grassroots political contests reduced voter participation. Both turnout and registration of adult males were dipping in municipal elections even before the new city charter. A variety of factors, including an influx of eastern European immigrants and the growing number of one-party wards, contributed to the decrease. But as Table 5 indicates, the structural changes brought about by charter revision had the clearest impact. Between 1908, the last City Council election before the implementation of the new charter, and 1911, the first nonmayoral election under the reformed system, the turnout level of registered voters plunged 12 percent, by far the largest drop after 1900. In following years the steep decline persisted, a result of the waning influence of local party machinery.

The fall in turnout and the rise of the CML were part of the larger decline in voter participation and partisanship occurring throughout the nation from the 1890s on. Scholars have attributed diminishing voting rates in the early twentieth century to the absence of significant competition between parties in local settings after the realignment of 1896, to the decline in "spectacular politics," or to changes in election rules that restricted the number of people eligible to vote. The Boston case suggests another cause as well: Progressive structural reforms and the new political techniques they engendered. The changes that charter reform brought about in the city's grassroots public life badly damaged local party organizations, the principal mechanism of voter mobilization at that time.[10]

Charter reform did more than undercut the significance of parties and elections. It also favored political action framed in Progressive

Table 5. Voter Turnout in Nonmayoral Municipal Elections, 1900–1914

Year	Percent registered[a]	Percent voting[b]
1900	62	70
1902	64	59
1904	59	63
1906	57	68
1908	55	64
1911	54	52
1912	53	45
1913	52	42
1914	50	45

a. Percentage of adult males registered to vote.
b. Percentage of registered voters casting ballots in municipal election.
Sources: Boston Board of Election Commissioners, *Annual Reports for 1900, 1902, 1904, 1906, 1908, 1911–12, 1912–13, 1913–14, 1914* (Boston: 1901, 1903, 1905, 1907, 1909, 1912, 1913, 1914, 1915).

terms. This development was evident not only in the sudden emergence of the Citizens' Municipal League but also in local settings. The political style that characterized the Jamaica Plain Citizens' Association began to flourish throughout the city. These groups assumed many of the roles once assigned to partisan ward organizations. As the number of boards, commissions, and legislative committees regulating various aspects of urban life multiplied—a phenomenon reinforced by charter reform's expansion of the municipal executive branch and transfer of power to the state government—middle-class leaders of local civic bodies became the most effective representatives of community interests. Unlike party politicians, these men and (in some cases) women were not handicapped by the perception that they sought partisan advantage, a quality that made them more plausible than party officials as neighborhood spokespersons. They also assumed a key role in the electoral process, using their nonpartisan credentials and the social connections of their officers to secure CML endorsements for local politicians.

Neighborhood civic groups had a vehicle for cooperative citywide action as well, the United Improvement Association. Inspired by Lincoln Steffens and other social reformers, the UIA became a powerful lobbying force after 1910. Its representatives became regulars at State House and City Council hearings, and Mayor Fitzgerald consulted the Association on numerous occasions during his second term. In many areas the UIA proved effective. During the five years following charter reform, it helped shape the City Planning Board's program for street construction, accelerated the process of burying electrical wires in suburban districts, won legislation requiring the attorney general to investigate high consumer prices, helped block a property tax hike in Boston, and persuaded the state to shift responsibility for telephone rates from the Highway Commission to the (hopefully more responsive) Public Service Commission.[11]

Most of the UIA's agenda reflected the concerns of the members of its constituent bodies. Property tax rates, telephone rates, and the removal of electrical wires from residential streets were issues that most directly concerned middle-class homeowners. In only a few instances did the UIA push social reform measures likely to appeal to working- as well as middle-class Bostonians, such as its endorsement in 1910 of sealed milk bottles to ensure clean milk for babies.[12]

The rise of the UIA and local civic associations had sharp consequences for the social character of Boston public life. Parties were, by definition, coalitions, incorporating both working class and middle class, immigrant and native. Though neither an egalitarian force nor the social welfare agency described by some historians, parties did provide relatively open access to political power. With their demise, and with the growing power of more exclusively middle-class civic associations, the corridors of municipal power narrowed.

On the surface, the adjustment to the new political order proceeded more smoothly in Boston's predominantly middle-class suburban neighborhoods than in other parts of the city. In suburban districts the new forms of political action encouraged by Progressive rhetoric had increased in importance even before 1909. Like most big cities, Boston had annexed nearby towns during the late nineteenth century. The legacy of New England town meeting politics endured in these districts, a tradition that encouraged a corporate rather than a partisan political style. The predominantly Yankee Republican character of these neighborhoods, which isolated them from Boston's Irish Democratic political mainstream, also made alternatives to party organizations attractive. Thus a group like the Jamaica Plain Citizens' Association was a significant public presence in its neighborhood before the passage of Plan Two. After charter reform, these civic bodies assumed an even greater role in local public affairs. But their claim of representative status was increasingly at odds with the rapidly changing social environment in which they operated.[13]

Brighton was one of the outlying districts in which charter reform bolstered local civic group activism. A suburban town annexed to Boston in 1873, Brighton and adjacent Allston by 1909 formed a rapidly growing residential area that constituted ward twenty-five, the western wing of Boston. Although the neighborhood still had a reputation as a Yankee preserve, as early as 1905 60 percent of its 21,806 residents had foreign-born parents, the largest portion of whom were Irish. As respectable Yankees edged westward beyond the city limits, they were gradually replaced by working- and middle-class Irish, and by smaller numbers of Jews and Italians as well.[14]

Brighton was one of the few parts of Boston where politics remained competitive after 1900. The Board of Election commissioners reported 1,909 registered Democrats and 1,684 Republicans in 1908. Despite these numbers, Republicans appeared to have a slight advantage in actual votes. Theodore Roosevelt led Alton B. Parker by 2,113 votes to 1,761 in 1904, and William Howard Taft defeated William Jennings Bryan by 2,303 to 1,441 in 1908. But Democrats succeeded in Brighton as well: in 1905 the party's gubernatorial candidate and two nominees for state representative swept the district. This roughly equal mix of Democrats and Republicans made electoral politics an active and important part of Brighton's public life.[15]

Despite this vibrancy, alternative forms of political action arose in the district. The most prominent of these was the Faneuil Improvement Association (FIA). Launched in 1895, the Association was a nonpartisan organization formed to "promote the welfare of the western section of Allston-Brighton." During its first dozen years, the group helped secure repairs for local streets, blocked the erection of a streetcar station at an undesirable site, prevented the construction of a soap factory, and obtained improved postal and newspaper service. By 1906 it had committees devoted to streets, parks, and public buildings; rapid transit; police and fire service; schools; local improvements; and water, sewers, and lights. The FIA established its importance in Brighton's public life well before charter reform.[16]

The Association derived its sense of itself as the most legitimate representative of local interests from the growing clamor for reform in the city and the nation. Guest speaker Lincoln Steffens told its members in 1908 that improvement associations "bring a consciousness of the ward as a whole" to their endeavors and therefore had a duty "to express the demands of the people" to elected officials. The formation of the UIA as a coordinating body for local groups spurred the ambitions and activism of the Faneuil Improvement Association. Even before the passage of charter reform, the FIA declared itself the representative body for all of ward twenty-five and stepped up its activities on a number of fronts. In late 1909, with the new city charter about to take effect, the Association held its largest meeting ever, a reflection of its expanding role in neighborhood affairs.[17]

What Progressivism enlivened, charter reform institutionalized. After the passage of Plan Two, the FIA became Brighton's primary representative body. As one city councilman told the Brighton group, there was "no better way to present the needs of a district to the City Council than through improvement associations." With no Brighton man on the new nine-member Council, the Faneuil Improvement Association declared itself responsible for presenting "the needs and requirements of our district to the government at City Hall." At the suggestion of the UIA, it created a "budget committee" that would present the desires of the district to municipal authorities, a tactic local groups throughout the city adopted. Recognizing the effectiveness of this form of political action, civic leaders in Allston, the eastern end of ward twenty-five, formed their own organization, the Allston Improvement Association, in early 1910 to represent their neighborhood at city hall.[18]

The ascendancy of the FIA in neighborhood affairs quickly became evident. When Mayor Fitzgerald held a series of "town meetings" in early 1910 designed to solicit requests for municipally sponsored improvements from each district, Association officials spoke first and dominated the proceedings. While they were not the only group to speak for the neighborhood, clearly theirs was the loudest voice. Their emphasis on street repairs, school construction, and improved city services was consistently echoed by other speakers. But what was said was less important than who was saying it. The prominent role assumed by the Association in this public forum signaled a shift in the distribution of local power. From now on, the FIA would act as the primary voice of neighborhood interests.[19]

The frequent appearances of FIA officers at city hall and the State House during the years after charter reform underscored the Association's growing influence. Its representatives testified to the Board of Aldermen as to the need for street repairs and public bath improvements in Brighton; conferred with the mayor on the necessity of widening Faneuil Street, one of the district's principal arteries; and lobbied school commissioners to investigate conditions at local schools. The Association also took on the Boston Elevated Railroad Company and the Massachusetts Public Service Commission, expressing dissatisfaction with subway service to the district. Although its efforts met with uneven success, the Association's constant presence in these public settings and on the front page of the neighborhood newspaper left little doubt about where local political power now resided.[20]

Meanwhile, partisan politics nearly faded from view in Brighton public life. Republican and Democratic organizations remained in existence but devoted themselves primarily to state and national politics. Local Democrats made an appearance at the mayor's "town meeting" in the form of the Fitzgerald Club of North Brighton, but the FIA's rapidly rising star eclipsed all partisan bodies; which had become less effective as local representatives in the harshly antiparty climate of the Progressive Era. With electoral politics increasingly irrelevant to the distribution of local power, voting rates dropped in Brighton as they did all over the city, and the array of activity that had formerly accompanied city elections abruptly stopped.[21]

The decline of party-centered politics dramatically reduced the number of participants in local public affairs. Whereas the pursuit of votes necessarily involved large numbers of people, Brighton's nonpartisan groups succeeded in part by restricting membership. The Faneuil Improvement Association accepted only those who were willing to pay dues and who received the approval of a majority of the existing membership. More than four years after charter reform, the Association still had only two hundred members, a tiny fraction of the 6,597 registered voters in Brighton. Yet it was this small group of people, without any wider consultation, who now spoke for the district in most matters.[22]

The people doing Brighton's talking were overwhelmingly Yankee, despite the growing numbers of Irish in the neighborhood. As late as 1919, when the Irish had become a clear majority in the district, the Association's membership remained 85 percent Yankee, and only one non-Yankee served on the executive committee. Nearly all of Brighton's growing ethnic population found itself cut off from this increasingly powerful form of politics.[23]

The social exclusivity of the FIA manifested itself in class as well as ethnic terms. The formation of the Brighton Workingmen's Association in 1912 was a response to the absence of workers and working-class concerns from the membership and agendas of neighborhood improvement bodies. Created "to better the condition of the working-man," the Workingmen's Association raised issues that differed significantly from the concerns of the Faneuil Improvement Association. It pressed political candidates to state their positions on wage increases and pensions for city laborers, the advisability of using day rather than contract labor on city projects, and the construction of a municipal building for ward twenty-five. Aside from the municipal building, none of these questions was likely to be raised at an improvement association meeting dominated by middle-class property owners and businessmen. Although the Workingmen's Association appeared on Brighton's public stage only briefly, its presence (and its rapid demise) highlighted the absence of a working-class voice in neighborhood activism after charter reform.[24]

This was part of a larger pattern in post–charter reform Boston. The city's biggest and most powerful labor organization, the Boston Central Labor Union, had grown steadily in the early twentieth century; by 1913 its 350 locals had over 96,000 members. But the BCLU, like its parent organization, the American Federation of Labor (AFL), had allied itself to the Democratic Party, and the decline of parties in Boston meant a diminution of the union's power as well. Its Irish leadership had purged the organization of its more radical elements between 1900 and 1910, part of the process of establishing closer ties to the Democratic organization. Ironically, by excluding socialists such as Henry Abrahams and Jack O'Sullivan, the BCLU had eliminated links to settlement workers and reformers such as Louis Brandeis who might have been helpful in Boston's changing political environment. The AFL's craft-based approach also excluded most unskilled workers, including women, eastern European immigrants, and African Americans, leaving those groups with few organizational resources. Most workers, both in and outside the BCLU, found themselves cut off from many of the new forms of municipal politics that emerged after 1909.[25]

The character of Progressive-style politics handicapped working-class activism as well. Speaking on behalf of a class of people, unions and workers' associations could not easily act as the voice of a unified community. A group such as the Brighton Workingmen's Association could lobby, but as the arm of only one segment of the community, it could never develop the clout wielded by neighborhood citizens' associations at "town meetings" and official hearings. This is not to say that the Progressive formula was never available to workers or that working-class groups could not support reforms seen as beneficial to their interests, but only that Progressivism could not serve as a means of political action based explicitly on class interest.

The Faneuil Improvement Association, like most local civic bodies, also excluded women. But the mothers, wives, sisters, and daughters of Association members had an alternative source of power, the Brightelmstone Club. Formed in 1896, the Club served as a female alternative to the FIA. While the men of that group pursued purportedly masculine issues such as street repairs and subway service, the women of the Brightelmstone Club took the lead in public activities that extended their traditional domestic roles: public health, education, and sanitary conditions. They called for reforms such as cleaner public schools, pure food and milk, the regulation of child labor, and the creation of a district nursing station. Charter reform, which put a premium on extraelectoral lobbying tactics, spurred an increase in the Club's activities and a corresponding expansion of the group's local clout.[26]

Ethnicity and class circumscribed women's activism in Brighton, much as it did men's. The Brightelmstone Club, like the FIA, allowed only a limited number of members and drew them from a restricted social circle. In the words of the neighborhood's historian, "the Brightelmstone Club was as thoroughly Yankee in 1923 as it had been in 1896," despite the growing number of Irish in the district. Middle-class Irish-Catholic women did have their own organization, the Brighton Women's Catholic Club, an affiliate of the League of Catholic Women. They eventually launched a second, secular body in 1924, the Brighton Women's Club. Even these groups were predominantly middle class, leaving poorer immigrant women without a voice in local public life in the years after charter reform.[27]

Most women's activism in Boston after 1909 mirrored the Brighton pattern. Groups such as the Women's Municipal League increased in power, but ethnic and class boundaries sharpened as well. Although the WML continued to act as the voice of all Boston women, it remained almost entirely Yankee throughout the 1910s. When it opened a branch in Irish South Boston, for instance, it found only five women willing to join, just one from an Irish-Catholic family.[28]

The "class-bridging" efforts of other women's organizations also declined in the new political environment, as Sarah Deutsch has noted. The Women's Educational and Industrial Union professionalized its staff and increased its ties to leading businessmen and reform leaders, particularly in the years following charter reform. It became less an institution designed to draw together women from different backgrounds than a platform from which a handful of experts and well-connected activists claimed to speak for all women. In similar fashion, the female-run Denison House settlement in downtown Boston established a men's auxiliary in 1910 that included members of the GGA, the president of the Chamber of Commerce, and several prominent lawyers and doctors. While these links increased the settlement's political pull, they undercut some of its more aggressive efforts on behalf of working women.[29]

Charter reform clearly benefited middle-class men and women in Brighton. By placing the Faneuil Improvement Association and the Brightelmstone Club in positions of power, it allowed the district's middle-class Yankee residents to reaffirm their dominance of local affairs just as they faced a challenge from incoming Irish Democrats and working-class groups. In other neighborhoods, where Yankee power had already faded, the impact of the new forms of city politics would be even sharper.

Boston's transition to a new municipal system had its most obvious impact in predominantly Irish neighborhoods. A lively, competitive Democratic Party had thrived in these sections during the late nineteenth century and into the first decade of the twentieth. But charter reform eliminated much of the public activity associated with parties, while allowing Progressive-style political action to flourish. The result was a sudden alteration in the distribution of power, as exclusive civic associations replaced relatively inclusive party organizations at the center of local public life.

One neighborhood where this process occurred was Charlestown, an Irish district lying just north of central Boston. Settled before Boston, its neighbor across the Charles River, Charlestown remained for much of the nineteenth century an independent town. But by the time of its annexation to Boston in 1874, its character had begun to change. The first Irish began to cross the river in the 1860s, mostly to escape Boston's North End slums. As the Yankees fled Charlestown, the Irish gradually came to dominate the district. By 1905, 48 percent of the population was either born in Ireland or had parents who were. Even the middle-class Yankee enclaves atop Bunker and Breed's Hills had been invaded by some of the more successful Irish.[30]

The rise of the Irish in Charlestown placed the district's three wards firmly in the Democratic column but did not bring political unity. Factional disputes constantly plagued the party in all three Charlestown wards (three, four, and five), often preventing the unified backing of local candidates and the coordinated pursuit of municipal policies to benefit the neighborhood. At the turn of the century, Joseph Corbett and Peter Tague, both of ward three, led the two dominant factions. Corbett—a lawyer, a member of the Democratic City Committee, and later a municipal court judge—was Charlestown's most prominent politician. But neither he nor anyone else was able to unify Charlestown's Democrats.[31]

Constant factional competition, whatever its inefficiencies, gave Charlestown a vibrant political life. In the 1908 city primary, the last before charter reform, twenty-seven candidates sought the nine available Common Council seats, and four men pursued Charlestown's single aldermanic nomination. Most of these were well-educated young men seeking public office for both political and financial advancement. Each formed clubs, held rallies, dispatched people door to door, and scoured his ward for votes. Charlestown's political life also featured fierce competition for control of the three ward committees, the official party body in each district, and thus the access point to the resources of the local and state Democratic organizations.[32]

Charter reform wiped out all of this activity. With the elimination of partisanship from city elections and the rise of the Citizens' Municipal League, the control of ward committees became irrelevant to city elections. The dissolution of the Common Council and the institution of at-large voting for the new City Council ended much of the district's grassroots electioneering. Young office seekers combing the district abruptly faded from view, much of the neighborhood's vibrant political scene disappearing with them. "There is not the backbone for a good old fashioned contest in an off year under the new charter," the *Charlestown Enterprise* observed in 1912, nicely summarizing the impact of structural reform on local political life.[33]

As in Brighton, a small body stood poised to fill the void left by the decline of partisan activity: the Charlestown Improvement Association. Though in existence since 1892, the Association's "WASP-tinged" character prevented it from credibly representing its Irish-Democratic district. Even as the organization gradually came to include successful Irish, it maintained a Yankee flavor in conflict with the district's ethnic character. But charter reform allowed the Association to become the dominant power in local affairs. Its size, activities, and importance rapidly increased after 1909. Membership rose from 134 in late 1909 to 258 by 1914, a 93 percent increase. By 1914 the Association proudly and justifiably declared that "its powerful influence has been amazingly felt in every important movement to improve local conditions."[34]

Association leaders drew on Progressivism's antiparty theme to enhance their organization's status, contrasting its apparent unanimity with the district's faction-ridden politics. "Here in Charlestown," an Association member complained, "there is already enough of politics and too little neighborhood spirit—a working together for public improvements by men of all parties and all factions, regardless of the petty political strifes which look so small after they are all over." Evoking the image of corporate unity embedded in its legacy as a New England town, the Charlestown Improvement Association called its monthly gatherings "town meetings." The organizers of the Charlestown Business and Professional Men's Association, launched in 1910 as an adjunct to the Improvement Association, insisted that their group was "not formed for political purposes," nor was it created "for the purpose of advancing the interests of one, two, or half a dozen."[35]

As did its Brighton counterpart, the Charlestown Improvement Association was able to maintain this unified front by limiting its membership. The Association described its participants as "representative men," the same phrase used by the Finance Commission to describe those who governed after charter reform. Like the charter architects, Improvement Association leaders were not describing a cross section of Charlestown's population when they used the word "representative," but rather the men who would present the best possible image of the district to the public. To preserve this image, the Association selected its members carefully. Only those "whose nomination shall have been approved by the Executive Committee, and who shall receive a majority vote of the members present and voting at any regular meeting" could join. In practice, this meant the neighborhood's civic and economic elite, who conveyed the most respectable picture of the district to the wider public.[36]

The result was a roster top-heavy with civic, political, and business leaders, including many Yankees who had not yet fled the neighborhood. The Association's roster included "over 250 citizens prominent in the various walks of life: leaders in professional, financial, commercial, social, and public affairs." A number were important politicians—including Judge Corbett, City Councilman Daniel McDonald, and former State Senators Richard Teeling and David B. Shaw—who recognized the Association's growing authority. Social and business leaders such as John F. Flanagan, editor of the neighborhood weekly, the *Charlestown Enterprise;* George T. Horan, owner of the local department store; Reverend James Phelan, pastor of one of the district's Catholic churches; and Dr. Joseph Duff were active in the organization. Reverend Philo Sprague, a Protestant minister; Augustus A. Fales, a local banker; and General William Oakes led the Association's disproportionately large Yankee contingent. Fales served several terms as president after 1909.[37]

Under the auspices of the Improvement Association, these men led the public effort to ameliorate the problems of urban life in Charlestown. The agenda of just one Association meeting included discussions of streetcar service, utility rates, street repairs and improvements, school issues, and the dredging of the adjacent Mystic River. To every public hearing, legislative session, or commission meeting dealing with these and other issues of local significance, the Charlestown Improvement Association dispatched one or more officials to speak for the district. Its presence in these settings as the voice of Charlestown interests secured the Association's standing as the neighborhood's principal representative organization. At public hearings and private consultations, dutifully reported by the sympathetic *Charlestown Enterprise,* its leaders spoke and acted on behalf of the district.[38]

Much as the Jamaica Plain Citizens' Association had done a few years earlier, the Charlestown Improvement Association used transportation issues to establish itself as the neighborhood's mouthpiece.

As part of the Boston Elevated Company's continued expansion of rail service in the city, it completed an elevated line to the city's northern suburbs that cut directly through Charlestown. The mammoth elevated structure towered over homes and businesses, including part of the local business district. Its presence reduced property values, forced some retailers to close down altogether, and fueled a powerful feeling of neglect in the district.

Local leaders directed this anger at the Boston Elevated, still a classic Progressive Era corporate villain and the perfect foil for the construction of a nonpartisan political movement. "Railroad corporations have either encroached upon or disregarded Charlestown interests ever since the first rack was laid on the outskirts of the community," wrote John Flanagan, the editor of the *Charlestown Enterprise* and an Improvement Association leader. The paper insisted that the drive to eliminate the overhead railway was "genuine and not political," because, it explained, "the removal of the Elevated structure from Main Street and the construction of a subway is a platform upon which every Charlestown citizen stands firmly and unflinchingly." The presentation of the issue in these terms created a context of political unity that allowed the Improvement Association to act on behalf of the entire neighborhood.[39]

The Association did just that, taking up the battle against the El in a fashion that firmly established its role as the voice of Charlestown interests. Association leaders testified at numerous hearings, met repeatedly with Elevated Company officials, and instructed elected representatives to vote for or against particular measures. At one point the *Enterprise* even urged Charlestown's citizens *not* to attend a public hearing, fearing that an angry, oversized crowd would represent Charlestown less effectively than an orderly delegation of civic leaders. The Association also pushed for a referendum calling for the removal of the elevated line. When they failed to secure this, local retailer George Horan, an officer of the Association, filed a lawsuit seeking its dismantling. The organization's leaders did win a small increase in local service in the form of a belt line around the neighborhood, but it came at the expense of a reduction in service to and from downtown Boston. Despite such frustrations, the Association profited from the publicity it received in this highly visible battle.[40]

One occurrence neatly captured the ascent of the Charlestown Improvement Association and the corresponding decline of party politicians. In late 1910 Mayor Fitzgerald proposed to combine funds ear-marked for a bathhouse and a branch library into an appropriation for a long-desired playground. Always eager to distance himself from party politicians, Fitzgerald ostentatiously contacted the Association, stating his desire "to test the public sentiment of the people of Char-lestown through your association, which is composed of the most representative business and professional men of the district." Had the Democratic mayor sought such advice a few years earlier, he would have worked through Joe Corbett or other local party leaders. Asso-ciation leaders replied by sending a delegation to the mayor's office made up of a doctor, a Protestant minister, a Catholic priest, the local newspaper editor, and a Yankee businessman. None of these men would ever hold or even seek elective office, but in Boston's revamped public life they had become Charlestown's most powerful public voices.[41]

Charter reform also gave local civic leaders a central role in selecting the recipients of Citizens' Municipal League support. With the rise of the CML and the decline of party organizations, a district's ability to secure a place for one of its own on the City Council depended on the links forged by local leaders with the citywide reform body. Only four of the original 180 CML members came from Charlestown. All of them were members of the Improvement Association; two were Prot-estant Republicans. None were significant players in local electoral politics. Since neighborhood civic organizations like the Charlestown Improvement Association had closer connections to the CML, they— rather than party officials—became the natural conduit for local poli-ticians seeking the League's support.[42]

In Charlestown, these circumstances led to the rapid ascension of an unlikely political wire puller. Augustus A. Fales, a well-connected Yan-kee Protestant Republican businessman and the president of the Char-lestown Improvement Association, had no influence whatsoever in the Irish-dominated circles of the local Democratic Party. But when the CML named him to its City Council nominating committee in late 1909, he suddenly became the key broker between Charlestown and the new center of electoral power in Boston city politics. From that position Fales was able to secure a League endorsement for a Char-lestown man, a task that proved difficult when the CML insisted that all nominees should be opposed to the election of John F. Fitzgerald. Anti-Fitzgerald men were hard to find in Charlestown, but after several weeks of infighting Fales placed Daniel J. McDonald, an organized labor official and politician with a clean reputation, on the slate. With the backing of the citywide reform forces, McDonald was assured a seat on the new City Council. Fales's backing earned McDonald CML endorsements in two subsequent reelection bids as well.[43]

The relationship between civic groups and elected representatives did not fade away after election day. The doctrine that the local improvement association acted "as a natural advisory body of the city council" gained wide currency in this suddenly nonpartisan political atmosphere. With no real party organization to rely on, McDonald and Timothy Buckley, another city councilman from the district, cultivated a close relationship with the Charlestown Improvement Association. McDonald worked to secure city money for playgrounds, a library, and numerous other items on the Association's wish list. His efforts earned the group's endorsement in each of his reelection campaigns. McDonald declared himself "at the command of the association at any time I am called upon," a statement that underscored his dependence on the Association's support.[44]

Charlestown voters hinted at the ballot box that they were not satisfied with this arrangement. If it had been left to them alone, McDonald would not have been elected. In 1910 and 1911, Charlestown had a pair of local residents serving on the City Council, Daniel McDonald and Timothy Buckley. But the two men traveled distinctly different routes to city hall. The Citizens' Municipal League included McDonald on its reform slate at the behest of Fales and the Charlestown Improvement Association. Buckley's candidacy carried the endorsement of the Lomasney-Curley ticket, widely perceived to be the Democratic, anti-CML slate. Though both men won the at-large election, Buckley received nearly two thousand more votes than did McDonald in their home district. Without the votes from other parts of the city won by virtue of his presence on the reform ticket, McDonald's bid would have failed.[45]

As these results suggest, the Improvement Association did not always speak for a unanimous Charlestown public. But the institutional environment created by charter reform and the wider public atmosphere conditioned by the language of Progressivism enabled the Association to become Charlestown's most effective representative. Party politics, which had incorporated large numbers of participants in the process of distributing power, had lost much of its local significance.

The new style of political action that replaced it left most of Boston's lower- and middle-class ethnic population without any direct institutional connections to the centers of public power.

At first glance, charter reform seemed to have little effect on the political life of the neighborhoods that formed central Boston. Martin Lomasney's ward eight, roughly comprising the West End, seemed especially resistant to the structural changes brought about by the passage of Plan Two. Lomasney, the prototypical ward boss, remained the dominant political figure in the neighborhood long after 1909, his grip on the votes of the district unshaken.

Nevertheless, Lomasney's power and significance in municipal affairs diminished markedly after 1909. When he cosponsored a City Council slate for the first election under the new charter, it won only two of nine seats. John Fitzgerald and James Michael Curley, the first two mayors after charter reform, viewed Lomasney as a potential rival and supplied him with little, if any, of the patronage under their control. This hostility, and his inability to secure a Council spot for any of his ward eight entourage, left Lomasney largely cut off from city hall and its political resources.

The ward eight leader remained a political force only by shifting his base of power from city hall to the State House. After several years out of political office, Lomasney returned to the State Senate in 1909 and remained there for close to a decade. With municipal elections out of the hands of party leaders after charter reform, the legislature was a more effective venue. It was there that Lomasney achieved the legislation that would earn him a reputation among historians as an urban liberal. He quickly secured a seat on the Senate's Committee on Metropolitan Affairs, where he led an aggressive campaign to repeal charter reform and weaken civil service restrictions that cramped patronage politics. The state legislature remained accessible—even when city hall was not—because ward eight elected a state senator and two state representatives on its own. Lomasney and his lieutenants were guaranteed election within ward eight, something denied them in the at-large elections for City Council.[46]

Charter reform also increased the power of his local opponents. The four ward eight men included among the CML's charter members were all lawyers active in local reform circles. Three of the four lived in a sliver of wealthy Beacon Hill that lay within ward boundaries.

The only West Ender to serve on the City Council between 1910 and 1915 was a settlement worker famous for opposing Lomasney. Ernest Smith, a founding member of the West End Improvement Society and the West End Voters Club, won a three-year City Council term in 1911 with the backing of the Citizens' Municipal League. He had first come to the public's attention when he was assaulted by one of Lomasney's henchmen while endeavoring to ferret out illegal voters on election day in ward eight (a popular sport in elite reform circles). With his Harvard pedigree and settlement house credentials, Smith was hardly a typical West End resident. Indeed, in the 1911 ward eight returns he finished a distant fourth in a three-seat race, his 447 votes more than a thousand less than the top vote getter. But it was his social and political connections outside the West End, not his local popularity, that assured him a place on the CML ticket and thus a seat on the City Council.[47]

The new city charter opened the way for the West End Improvement Society—the ward eight parallel to the Charlestown and Faneuil Improvement Associations—to expand its public role. At a "town meeting" staged by Mayor Fitzgerald for the North, South, and West Ends in February 1910, the Improvement Society spoke first on behalf of its district. Two of Lomasney's allies followed, but they merely echoed the proposals already made by the Society. It quarreled with the Boston Elevated, seeking better service and a new station in the West End. As always, the El was a perfect foil for action on behalf of the entire community, allowing the Improvement Society to define itself in Progressive terms, as the representative of "the tens of thousands of people" of the West End doing battle with Boston's leading corporate behemoth. On such issues as street cleaning and repairs, the need for a new school and a new bathhouse, unhealthy tenements, and the inadequacy of police protection in the district, the Improvement Society took the lead, establishing itself as the West End's public voice in the process.[48]

While the West End Improvement Society's activism mirrored the work of other neighborhood civic associations, the gap between its leaders and local residents was even wider. The Society was primarily a tool of local settlement house workers. They created it, following the lead of Robert Woods of the South End House, and they ran it. The Society's leadership and most of its public spokesmen were social reformers, including longtime Lomasney opponent Robert Silverman,

City Councilman Ernest Smith, Reverend Christopher Eliot, and several Jewish social workers. Many of the group's meetings were held at the Frances E. Willard settlement, a house staffed and run by women. (The West End Improvement Society had female members, unlike most of its counterparts, though none became especially prominent in its activities.) Very few of the people responsible for running the Improvement Society were drawn from the immigrant ranks that made up the bulk of the West End's population.[49]

Charter reform encouraged another form of political action that affected the public life of the West End. The passage of Plan Two intensified efforts by Jacob de Haas and others to mobilize Boston's Jews. The development of Roxbury and Dorchester as the center of Jewish life in Boston had begun, but ward eight still had the largest number of Jews and was the city's most obviously Jewish district. It thus remained the base for efforts to establish a distinctive public identity for Jews in Boston.

The attempt to organize Boston's Jewry into an electoral force did not succeed. In the wake of charter reform, de Haas and the Hebrew Independent Club created a citywide Jewish political organization. The group remained active for several years but achieved little. Jewish leaders also attempted to create a "Jewish Alliance of Massachusetts" in 1910, which the *Advocate* insisted would work for "specific communal, nonpolitical purposes." It too foundered when its leaders endorsed the Republican ticket that fall, forfeiting the support of those who advocated nonpartisanship.[50]

Jewish leaders did persuade the Citizens' Municipal League to endorse Mark Stone, a Prussian-born lawyer from Roxbury. But the GGA refused to back Stone despite the CML endorsement, a snub that undercut Stone's credibility as a reform candidate and hurt him with many voters. And he failed to win enough Jewish support to overcome the GGA's rejection, finishing a lackluster tenth in ward eight and eleventh in ward six, the two most Jewish sections of the city. The voters in these districts remained loyal to the Democratic candidates backed by the Lomasney and Fitzgerald organizations.[51]

On a few issues, would-be Jewish spokespersons were able to make their presence felt. They formed a *kehilla,* a united organization of Jews, in response to a proposed measure regulating the slaughter of animals that threatened Jewish kosher practices. The group persuaded state legislators to revise the law so as to avoid outlawing Jewish food preparation traditions. Jacob de Haas led a delegation of prominent Jews that pressured Boston Elevated to dismiss two anti-Semitic employees and improve the treatment of Jewish passengers. Several rabbis formed a Jewish Central Committee in late 1912 to deal with questions of education and juvenile delinquency among Jewish children. Boston Jews also pulled together to assist newly arrived immigrants and to establish Beth Israel Hospital, which opened in 1917.[52]

Those Jewish endeavors that worked did so because they included only a few people and limited their focus to specifically Jewish concerns. Dispatching a delegation to city hall, the State House, or corporate offices required only a handful of participants. Charitable committees drew more people together but hardly reached out across Boston's entire Jewish population. Most of the people involved in these activities were middle-class German Jews. They found it easier to speak and act for an imagined Jewish Boston than to undertake the formidable project of uniting a Jewish community still divided by class and ethnic background. On relatively uncontroversial questions, such as assisting Jewish immigrants or securing fair treatment on streetcars, this kind of public action was both possible and profitable. Translating it to a broader political unity proved more difficult, as Martin Lomasney's persistence in predominantly Jewish ward eight demonstrated.

The continued power of the West End boss did not mean that most of the immigrants in his district were well integrated into the political system, despite the prevailing assumptions of urban political history. A central tenet of the machine model is that the ward boss actively mobilized newly arrived immigrants as quickly as possible through the distribution of the jobs and services they needed to survive. In exchange for such patronage, they provided the votes necessary to keep him in power. But Lomasney—whose conversations with Lincoln Steffens formed the basis upon which Robert Merton and others have hypothesized the latent functions of the urban political machine—survived charter reform not because he integrated so many of his immigrant neighbors into the American political system, but because electoral politics involved so few of them.[53]

Lomasney's district had large numbers of immigrants, but few voters. Between 1900 and 1908, turnout in city elections averaged 75 percent of those registered, and 75 percent of those eligible to vote had actually registered; but the level of participation among West End residents was low. Most of them were immigrants who either were not able or did not bother to vote, and their numbers grew as immigration increased. An average of just 28 percent of ward eight's adult men actually voted in the nine city elections held during this period. Lomasney needed only a majority of these voters to maintain control of his ward. Without any serious political competition in the neighborhood, he had no need to mobilize the remainder.[54]

The extent of Lomasney's political control becomes less impressive in this context. He delivered his ward to Republican mayoral candidate Louis Frothingham in 1905: a feat often cited as proof of the iron grip he held over the votes of his ward. But Frothingham won only 2,101 votes, or 18 percent of ward eight's adult males. Several hundred of those votes would have gone to the Republican candidate regardless of Lomasney's position—the 1907 Republican mayoral candidate received 841 votes from ward eight without Lomasney's help—further reducing the number of votes actually delivered by the West End boss. Most of the municipal candidates that he backed had similar levels of support. Lomasney's political power was not an illusion, but the argument that he maintained it by integrating immigrants into the American political system is false.[55]

Charter reform actually reinforced this arrangement. Lomasney was able to remain in power locally because even fewer West Enders voted after 1909. Between 1910 and 1914, ward eight turnout in city elections fell to 63 percent of those registered to vote, and just 22 percent of all adult males. Voting in state elections fell at a similar rate. A smaller electorate made the ward easier to control, as did the alterations in city politics that channeled his opposition toward nonelectoral political action. The redesign of ward boundaries in 1916 further entrenched the West End boss by stretching his district to include a large portion of Boston's nonvoting new immigrant population. As a result, his string of triumphs in local elections remained intact into the 1920s.[56]

Contrary to the prevailing view of boss politics, Lomasney did not provide an effective link between the poor urbanites of his neighborhood and city hall or the State House. Nor did the new forms of political action in Boston's restructured political environment successfully integrate large portions of the local populace into the political system. Even more than their counterparts in other parts of the city, the poorer residents of the West End found themselves increasingly isolated from the newly defined corridors of municipal power.

Yet the triumph of Boston's new political order was upheld in 1914, when voters rejected an attempt to change the charter reform of 1909. Lomasney and his allies succeeded in placing on the ballot a referendum offering Bostonians a chance to restore district-based municipal representation. Boston's elite reformers and local improvement associations fended off the challenge through an aggressive campaign. They convinced a majority of voters that charter reform had yielded a political system in which every part of the city received fair consideration.

The defenders of the city charter turned the election into a referendum on how fairly each neighborhood had been treated. The Charter Association, created by GGA leaders and other elite reformers to block attempts to dismantle the Plan Two system, distributed fliers describing the municipal benefits received by each district. The United Improvement Association issued a detailed report making the same claim. Both groups insisted that city money had been equitably distributed to the various parts of the city.[57]

Most local improvement groups endorsed this argument because it implied that their efforts had borne fruit. Leading members of the Charlestown Improvement Association used these arguments to justify Boston's new political order and their privileged place within it. Former Association President Augustus Fales and City Councilman Daniel McDonald, who owed his election to Fales and the Association, campaigned against changing the 1909 charter, insisting that the neighborhood had received "fair treatment" under the new system. The *Charlestown Enterprise,* whose editor was a prominent member of the Improvement Association, agreed and republished the UIA's list of city expenditures for Charlestown, which totaled over $400,000. "Political orators" had produced the scheme for a new City Council, the paper concluded, and it should be rejected because Boston had been "well governed during the past half dozen years" and Charlestown had "received excellent service." The narrow 2,319 to 2,102 rejection of the Lomasney proposal in Charlestown, despite support from numerous party politicians in the district, was in this context a victory for the Improvement Association.[58]

The attempt to change the 1909 charter lost by more than twenty thousand votes. Statistical analysis of voting for the Lomasney plan backs the argument that Charter reform had benefited Boston's Anglo middle class. Table 6 presents the results of a regression equation designed to measure native-stock and white-collar voting on Lomasney's proposal. It indicates a strong connection between the percentage of people voting against his charter changes and the proportion of people with native parentage in that district. No clear relationship is evident between opposition to Lomasney's system and the size of the white-collar population in a ward. Nevertheless, it seems likely that most of those who wanted to keep the 1909 arrangements in place were middle and upper class.[59]

In approving the reformed city charter, voters endorsed the nonpartisan mode of political action that had prospered under it. More importantly, they rejected the party-centered politics that preceded it. The new form of representation, rooted in the Progressive image of consensual politics, made neighborhoods and ethnic groups—not partisanship—the principal building blocks of voter mobilization in city elections. The organization of city politics into a clash of parties—a process that had once helped preserve ethnic comity in the city—had been substantially weakened.

Despite its rhetoric of unity, this new politics did not represent all segments of the community equally. The demise of party politics and the rise of local interest groups relegated all but a few to the sidelines. Most isolated were working-class ethnics; neighborhood associations

Table 6. Multiple Linear Regression Analysis of "No" Vote on 1914 Charter Referendum

Predictor variable	Regression coefficient	Standard error	p-value
Percent U.S. stock	.737	.16	.0001
Percent white-collar	.125	.19	.53

Sources: Samuel H. Preston, "United States Census Data, 1910: Public Use Sample" (Ann Arbor: Inter-University Consortium for Political and Social Research, 1989; ICPSR, 9166); Boston Board of Election Commissioners, *Annual Report for 1914* (Boston, 1915), p. 162.

Model: percent voting "no" on 1914 charter referendum = intercept + percent U.S. stock + percent white-collar. Model statistics: N = 25; R^2 = .13; adjusted R^2 = .01; intercept = .46.

Note: See Statistical Appendix for a discussion of the construction of variables.

neither included them in their deliberations nor addressed their concerns. Local civic bodies often had a distinctly Yankee flavor, even when the Irish or other ethnic groups made up a majority of the district's population. In cases when Irish civic leaders did play a significant role in an organization, as in the Charlestown Improvement Association, a disproportionate number of native-stock residents still occupied positions of power. Nor did women's organizations successfully integrate poorer immigrant women into public life after charter reform.

The exclusion of so large a portion of the population made Boston's new political order a fragile one. Although many working-class Bostonians evidently supported reform ideas and candidates, they did not gain direct access to power from them. Political leaders able to mobilize those cut off from the reconstituted corridors of power had an opportunity to create a broad electoral coalition. John F. Fitzgerald began to do so in his 1910 mayoral campaign. His successor, James Michael Curley, mastered the reformed political environment even more fully. He constructed a widely appealing ethnic Progressivism that would decisively shape the city's public culture for much of the twentieth century.

CHAPTER FIVE

James Michael Curley and the Politics of Ethnic Progressivism

Lincoln Steffens's attempt to muckrake Boston neatly summed up the city's politics of Progressivism. Steffens arrived in Boston in the autumn of 1908 at the behest of several wealthy GGA leaders, who had offered him $10,000 to spend a year studying local political conditions and then to publish his findings. They hoped that the nation's leading investigative journalist would do for Boston what he had done for urban politics generally in *The Shame of the Cities:* spark a popular groundswell in support of reform and reformers. To maximize its impact, the GGA planned to distribute an initial five-cent edition of Steffens's book at newsstands around the city on the eve of the 1910 mayoral election. Its effect would be "psychological," the GGA hoped, shaping both public opinion and the ensuing election results.[1]

In summoning Steffens, the GGA recognized that mass persuasion was now the primary tool of politics. As one of its leaders observed, the secret of the new politics was to "get current with the rest and advertise. That is, to study the people psychologically and move them as our opponents move them by feelings, even by their prejudices." While late-nineteenth-century party politics certainly relied on group appeals, it did so largely through decentralized party organizations. The reforms of the Progressive Era eliminated the partisan middleman, at least in Boston, making collective mobilization through publicity the fundamental means of urban political action.[2]

Steffens's dalliance with Boston's reformers ended up foreshadowing more than changes in the mechanics of city politics. What he wrote reflected the ongoing redefinition of the city's social character and history precipitated by the rise of Progressivism. After repeated delays, Steffens finally submitted a manuscript to the GGA in 1913. It was not the book his employers expected. Instead of condemning Boston's party politicians and their ethnic constituents, Steffens blamed the city's problems on "the ideals of the reformers," which he linked to flaws in the city's Puritan heritage. The conception of "good government" that drove elite reform, Steffens argued, "helps businessmen and represents the financial, commercial and employer classes," while ignoring "any legislation for labor or for humanity." He even called the Puritan ministers who founded Boston "bosses." Needless to say, the wealthy businessmen who ran the GGA did not find this analysis congenial, and they refused to publish Steffens's book. But the linkage of the city's economic elite with a hypocritical Anglo-Protestant tradition would become the central theme of Boston's increasingly belligerent public life.[3]

The principal proponent of that perspective was James Michael Curley. Few individuals have defined the public life of a big city more than the legendary Curley, whose half-century-long political career included four terms as mayor, two terms in Congress, one term as governor, and two terms in prison. Like John F. Fitzgerald, Curley created a social narrative designed to define his constituency and mobilize it. But Curley's story was harsher, echoing Steffens's indictment of Boston's Puritan past as well as its Brahmin present and making cultural antagonism the defining feature of the city's public sphere. His depiction of a Boston long riven by ethnic hatred provided the framework within which Bostonians came to understand themselves and their city, fully eclipsing the more conciliatory vision promoted by late-nineteenth-century Irish spokesmen. Even at the end of the twentieth century, journalists, analysts, and most Bostonians imagine ethnic conflict as the essential fabric of Boston's social and political history, testimony to Curley's extraordinary ability to define the context in which he acted.

Curley could reinvent the city's public culture because he had mastered its new political environment. The institutional terrain created by charter reform opened up a space in which he could fashion himself as the voice of ethnic Boston. With party organizations all but gone, and with the local civic groups that now dominated neighbor-

hood public life aggressively seeking a greater share of municipal resources, Curley used the expanded fiscal power of the mayor's office
and his unequaled rhetorical skills to mobilize electoral support. Targeting those left out, he cast himself as the advocate of blue-collar,
ethnic Bostonians who had been deprived of power by a pervasive,
enduring Brahmin conspiracy. From his first election to office in 1899
to the publication of his memoirs in 1957, Curley constantly strove
to shape popular perceptions of himself, his city, and its history in
these terms. Though later described as one of the "last of the big city
bosses," Curley is better understood as one of the first of a new breed
of urban leaders.[4] He was among the earliest masters of the new mass-
mediated, candidate-centered politics ushered in by Progressive reform. His principal method was not patronage but publicity. From the
earliest stages of his public career, he demonstrated a talent for shaping public opinion. While Curley did many of the things that made
political bosses famous—from distributing patronage and social services to bribery and graft—his successes rested largely on his manipulation of public discourse rather than on the strength of a well-honed
political organization.

The core elements of Curley's rhetoric came from Progressivism. He
consistently cast himself as the voice of "the people," whom he defined
as Boston's ethnic, mostly working-class population. His opponents
were "special interests," particularly Boston's Brahmin elites and their
representatives in the GGA. Curley offered an angrier ethnic Progressivism than Fitzgerald, one that placed greater emphasis on class inequities. This portrait of Boston's social and political life became the
accepted one by the end of the Progressive Era, blocking any hope of
ethnic reconciliation.

Curley's career illustrated a broader shift toward personality-cen-
tered, publicity-oriented politics that drew on Progressive rhetoric and
tactics to shape the terms of public life. This change was evident on
the national scene, where the "rhetorical presidencies" of Theodore
Roosevelt and Woodrow Wilson pioneered the process by which presidents went "over the heads" of Congress and party leaders to appeal
directly to the people. State Progressives such as Hiram Johnson of
California and Wisconsin's Robert LaFollette prospered through similar approaches. Mayors, too, adroitly crafted public images as reformers. Detroit's Hazen Pingree, Toledo's Samuel "Golden Rule Jones,"
and Cleveland's Tom Johnson pioneered an urban reform style that

even organizational politicians borrowed. Edward Crump of Memphis, William Hale Thompson of Chicago, and John Hylan and Jimmy Walker of New York's Tammany Hall thrived in part by presenting themselves as social reformers working on behalf of the poor.[5]

Curley's origins were those of the stereotypical ward boss, but his political talents carried him far beyond his district. His grasp of the techniques of politics in the first age of mass publicity distinguished him from his rivals. He used those skills to craft an image of himself as the champion of Boston's downtrodden, a reputation that ultimately propelled him to the mayor's office and helped him redefine the city's social character.

Curley himself was one of Boston's dispossessed. Born in 1874 to poor Irish immigrant parents in Roxbury, "the corned-beef and cabbage riviera" as he later called it, his early life was a struggle. His father, a laborer, died when Curley was ten; his mother scrubbed floors to keep the family afloat. From his father's death until his early twenties, Curley took a succession of jobs as a newsboy, a delivery boy, a drugstore clerk, a machine operator in a piano factory, and a traveling salesman.[6]

Politics offered Curley a way up. He ran for Common Council in 1897 and 1898 without the backing of either of the district's feuding Democratic factions and lost. Learning from the experience, he secured the endorsement of a local party leader, captured the nomination, and easily defeated his Republican opponent in 1899. His election to the Council began a stretch of eighteen straight years in elective office.[7]

No organization could hold the ambitious Curley except his own. He deserted first one faction and then another before finally launching his own, the Tammany Club, which he operated from a rented hall over a bakery. The Club defeated its main rivals in ward seventeen by 1903, and Curley established himself as the leading political figure in Roxbury. From this base he would go on to win at-large seats on the Board of Aldermen and reformed City Council, a seat in Congress, and election to the mayor's office in 1914. He would remain dominant in his home district until ward lines were redrawn in 1916.[8]

Curley's political ascent was a raucous one. He participated in more than his share of riots and brawls, usually as an instigator. A squad of policemen once had to forcibly remove him and a Tammany Club confederate when they charged the stage at an opposition rally during a Roxbury campaign. In another instance he sparked a near riot in Democratic City Committee headquarters by attacking onetime ally, by then rival, Thomas Curley (no relation) when the two men crossed paths in the hallway. And when the three-hundred-pound brother of Boston Congressman Joe Keliher decked Curley in the bar of the Parker House Hotel in downtown Boston, apparently in revenge for a political slight, the Roxbury politician responded in kind. Most reports had Curley getting the better of the ensuing fistfight.[9]

What marked Curley's political character most, however, was his reputation for generosity. At Christmas he distributed baskets of food to the needy and served holiday meals to poor children. While serving in the Common Council and the state legislature, he achieved a strong record as an advocate of measures to aid workers and poor people. Curley also made great efforts on behalf of the unemployed in his neighborhood, a district that suffered a sharp economic decline after several local factories closed. He bragged to the *Boston Post* in 1903 that he had found work for more than seven hundred men. When a representative of the GGA visited the Tammany Club to interview him that year, Curley told him the GGA did not understand the situation in his ward. "There are six hundred men . . . wholly out of employment," Curley told the reformer, "and the greater part of the work of the Ward 17 Tammany Club is in seeing them, looking out for them, and trying to get them places." The GGA, he observed in a criticism that he would voice more sharply in future years, "might spend its money and energy more to advantage in looking after these men."[10]

Neither fists nor favors were Curley's most effective weapon. The ability to manipulate rhetoric and images was the essence of his political method. During the years of Curley's ascent in Roxbury, a few observers began rehabilitating the reputation of ward bosses. More-sympathetic renderings replaced the scathing portraits of urban politicians created by Thomas Nast, Josiah Strong, and James Bryce. Jane Addams's explanation of why Johnny Powers ruled ward nineteen in Chicago, Robert Woods's report on the effectiveness of Smilin' Jim Donovan in Boston's South End, and William Riordon's portrait of George Washington Plunkitt of Tammany Hall held that the ward boss persisted because he provided social services. Clearly conscious of this emerging popular image, Curley took the notion of the ward boss as a benevolent figure and used it to craft a popular persona.[11]

Curley's manipulation of one incident early in his career undoubtedly won him more votes over the years than a thousand favors ever
did. In 1904 Curley and a political ally were convicted and sentenced
to two months in jail for impersonating two applicants in a civil service exam. He won reelection to the Board of Aldermen while campaigning from a jail cell in 1904, finishing fifth in a citywide race for
thirteen spots. The political capital that Curley extracted from this
event served him throughout his public life. Rather than sweep his
criminal record under the rug, he celebrated it as proof of his devotion
to the poor. "He did it for a friend" became his rallying cry, and he
regularly alluded to the incident on the campaign trail. In one instance
when a member of a South Boston audience (probably planted by
Curley) brought up the subject, candidate Curley explained that he
took the exam "for a man who had a wife and five children starving
for want of food and who had not earned a dollar in many months."
The *South Boston Gazette* reported that "he then forgave his dis-
turber amidst great enthusiasm," a scene often repeated during Curley's career.[12]

Curley of course actually did do many of the favors and provide
many of the services for which urban politicians of that era were
famous. At the same time, he exhibited an increasingly sophisticated
understanding of the need to enhance his reputation through the press.
While running for mayor in late 1913, Curley heard of a Roxbury
woman, Mrs. William Doane, whose husband had died just before
Christmas, leaving her penniless. He gave her the money to pay for the
funeral and to buy the clothes she needed, the kind of gesture that
earned ward bosses their reputation for generosity. But he did not
present the money directly to Mrs. Doane. Instead he handed it to
a newspaper reporter, who in turn delivered it to her and reported
the favor in his newspaper. Curley became famous for his generosity
through such publicity. Developing the image of a benefactor mattered
more than actually delivering services, especially as Curley began competing for citywide offices. His skillful use of mass media in this fashion paved the way for his subsequent political triumphs.[13]

Curley's publicity skills carried that reputation beyond local con-
fines. When the *South Boston Gazette* conducted a series of man-in-
the-street interviews during Curley's 1910 congressional campaign,
his supporters almost unanimously cited his aggressive efforts on be-

half of the downtrodden as their reason for backing him. "Because he's always been a friend of the poor in Ward 17," one South Boston man responded when asked why he was voting for Curley. "He has a heart and mind willing to suffer for the oppressed," declared another. These respondents were not from Curley's home district and were not likely to have received any favor or service from him directly. It was his reputation, not his actions, to which they responded.[14]

The ability to project a benevolent persona throughout the city earned Curley the mayor's office, where he gained even more power to shape popular perceptions. Seizing on the rhetoric of Progressivism, he made himself the representative of Boston's ordinary citizens as they battled corrupt, hostile Brahmin interests. This image became reality for most Bostonians, a convincing explanation of the city's social order and their place within it.

His first run for mayor in 1914 demonstrated his persuasiveness. Not only did he win, he even carried South Boston, his opponent Thomas Kenny's home district, by more than 1,000 of the 8,400 votes cast. In doing so, he overcame the opposition of local newspapers and the leaders of the South Boston Trade Association and the South Boston Citizens Association. He accomplished this feat without significant organizational support. In other districts, a similar story could be told. Curley triumphed with the support of few, if any, of the civic leaders who had risen to prominence after charter reform. Although many of them would support Curley and his policies in coming years, his initial mayoral victory came through direct appeals to voters rather than through the influence of prominent local figures.[15]

Nor were ward-based party organizations of any material assistance to him. Stripped of power by charter reform and the other antiparty measures, local party officials had little influence on the voters in their districts. The *Boston Globe* reported that many reputed party leaders backed their neighbor Kenny to no avail. In Charlestown, despite the opposition of "almost all the leaders," Curley carried the district by more than two thousand votes out of five thousand cast. Nor could Patrick J. Kennedy, the supposed boss of East Boston, hold off the Curley onslaught. In the black precincts of Roxbury's ward eighteen, voters defied the wishes of local leader Joseph Timilty by supporting Curley. He carried Jewish districts by solid margins with little formal support. The avenue of political mobilization now ran directly from candidate to voter, without the old detour through a party organization.[16]

A politician of Curley's talents naturally recognized the efficacy of Progressive rhetoric in this era. He used it during his mayoral campaign to cast himself as a reformer working in the interests of ethnic Boston. The city's working-class ethnic majority were "the people" and Curley was their champion. Perhaps more significantly, Curley drew a verbal picture of his opponents as a handful of wealthy Brahmin businessmen conspiring to control the political, social, and economic life of Boston at the expense of its ordinary citizens. This characterization proved persuasive enough to earn Curley an electoral majority in 1914 and a loyal following for three decades.

Presenting himself as a reform candidate for mayor became easier when his opponent found himself entangled in a brewing controversy. The state legislature was at that time conducting hearings that publicized the illegal practices of the New Haven Railroad. William Minot, a leading figure of the GGA, was connected to the railroad, as was Richard Olney, head of the Citizens' Municipal League. To make matters worse, Olney was famous for breaking the 1894 Pullman strike as attorney general under Grover Cleveland, an accomplishment that hardly added to his popularity in working-class Boston. Since both the GGA and the CML had endorsed Kenny, Curley could now link him to illicit corporate interests.[17]

It was an inopportune moment to be seen in such company. Big business and its political allies were among the main villains of the Progressive Era, and Curley wasted no time in exploiting the connections between Kenny's backers and powerful financial interests. "I ask every God-fearing citizen to save Boston from the banks and railroads," he proclaimed during the campaign. "I want to know," he asked, "why the banking interests, the railroads, and the corporations are so anxious for Mr. Kenny's success?" Kenny could only muster up ineffectual, defensive replies: "In my entire career in public office, I have never had any relations with the New Haven Railroad of any kind whatsoever." The issue served Curley well, allowing him to present himself as the true reformer, the representative of the people. "I want the opposition of the corrupt bosses and leaders," he declared proudly, "and I want the saleable and purchasable element to be opposed to me."[18]

Curley's past record on reform issues lent credibility to his assertions. He had supported numerous Progressive measures in Congress, including child labor restrictions, judicial recall, and labor arbitration. His platform, promising economical and honest administration of city business and emphasizing measures to improve the city's economic condition, differed little on the surface from Kenny's. But unlike Kenny, Curley could talk about reform without offending working-class and ethnic voters suspicious of the GGA. Curley's reputation as a champion of the underdog put his promises in a different context, making them reforms that would benefit the average citizen instead of businessmen and other powerful interests.[19]

Curley also strengthened the ethnic dimension of his Progressivism by touting his record of opposition to immigration restriction. As a congressman, he had played a highly visible role in the battle against the establishment of a literacy test for prospective immigrants. He gave ringing speeches on the floor of the House, claiming among other things that eight of the signers of the Declaration of Independence were Irish. For his efforts, he received a pen when President Taft vetoed the bill. Always conscious of the importance of publicity, he worked closely with the ethnic press, particularly the *Jewish Advocate* and the *Gazzetta del Massachusetts,* in rallying public opposition to the bill in Boston. They reciprocated by praising Curley as a staunch friend of the immigrant. Curley revived this issue during his mayoral run by circulating his congressional speeches on the topic. He also organized a "Citizens' Immigration League," a group whose name reflected his marriage of ethnic and reform themes. Though Kenny was himself the son of immigrants and noted so in his campaign literature, he could not match Curley's barrage, and observers credited Curley's use of this issue as a decisive factor in his victory.[20]

An analysis of election results confirms this assessment. The presence of another Irish candidate, especially one with legitimate reform credentials of his own, prevented Curley from monopolizing the Irish vote. Table 7 shows results of a regression equation indicating that Curley's support came from a broad cross section of Boston's immigrant population. The higher the percentage of immigrants and their children in a ward, the more likely it was to give Curley a majority. Social class, by contrast, had little effect, suggesting that his broadly worded appeals to immigrants and their descendants had, at least for the moment, more effectively politicized ethnic than class identities. In

Table 7. Multiple Linear Regression Analysis of Curley Mayoral Vote, 1914

Predictor variable	Regression coefficient	Standard error	p-value
Percent foreign stock	.66	.20	.004
Percent working class	−.13	.27	.6

Sources: Samuel H. Preston, "United States Census Data, 1910: Public Use Sample" (Ann Arbor: Inter-University Consortium for Political and Social Research, 1989; ICPSR 9166); Boston Board of Election Commissioners, Annual Report for 1913–1914 (Boston, 1914), p. 129.

Model: percent vote for Curley, 1914 = intercept + percent foreign stock + percent working class. Model statistics: N = 25; R^2 = .35; adjusted R^2 = .29; intercept = .16.

Note: See Statistical Appendix for a discussion of the construction of variables.

a race between two Irish Americans, Curley managed to make himself the ethnic candidate.[21]

As mayor, Curley faced the same political challenge he had overcome in getting elected: how to reach the voters without benefit of a grassroots organization. He did not object to machine-style politics; he simply found it inadequate in a changing urban political sphere. He bullied city workers, manipulated civil service rolls, and cut deals with corrupt contractors. But even with the expanded fiscal powers of his office, he could hardly employ a majority of the city's voters, a fact he openly acknowledged. "Here's the way I figure it," he explained during his first term; "the population of Boston is about 740,000 and there are 14,700 people on the payrolls." Those 14,700, he calculated, had an average of five family members and friends dependent on them. Another 6,000 or so lawyers, contractors, and vendors had business with the city, making a total of 103,500 Bostonians with "a personal interest in the payroll or expenditure of the city." The remaining 636,500 "were only interested in the honest and efficient conduct of the city." With the support of that number, Curley declared, "no man need fear for his political future."[22]

These figures can in fact be read in two ways. One hundred thousand people was hardly an insignificant number in electoral terms; Curley won the 1914 mayoral race with 43,262 votes.[23] Patronage undoubtedly remained an important political tool. Yet Curley had a point. The vast majority of Bostonians were not directly linked to city hall in this fashion. They backed (or opposed) Curley because of his policies, his image, or his reputation, not because of any favor or service he provided directly. The localized structure of nineteenth-century politics required only that a politician's reputation be spread through the neighborhood. The broader arena of twentieth-century urban public life made it necessary for politicians to project their personas far more widely. Mastering the art of publicity became an essential skill for political survival.

Curley grew even more proficient in the art of mass urban politics as mayor. During his first term he used tactics that foreshadowed the news-cycle management of the television age. Boston in Curley's day had a half dozen or more daily papers, some delivered in the morning, others in the evening. Many people read one of each. The leading members of the GGA and other reform groups were generally businessmen whose work schedule forced them to pursue politics at night. These "evening politicians" prepared their public statements late in the day for consumption in the next morning's papers. Curley was a full-time politician and acutely aware of the need to mold public opinion. He made sure to respond to morning-edition attacks in time for the afternoon paper. Boston's newspaper readers often had his counterattack in hand even before they had encountered his opponents' charges. Meanwhile Curley's salvos went unanswered until the next day, giving them time to settle in the public mind. With this kind of sophistication, he adroitly shaped popular perceptions on the key questions of municipal affairs.[24]

From the start, reform was a central tenet of Curley's public pronouncements. In his inaugural address he bitterly attacked his predecessor Fitzgerald as a corrupt boss, whose pursuit of a "policy of discharging political debts through the mediumship of the city treasury" had bankrupted Boston. He promised clean and efficient government that would make "the city's business the property of all, rather than office holders alone." His first message to the City Council called for a series of changes designed to promote "the highest efficiency" in city government, including the creation of a central purchasing office that used a "modern system of auditing," a monthly planning conference for the city, new methods of street construction, and professional approaches to juvenile delinquency and alcoholism. Above all, he promised to end the "cancer" of "special privilege," because "the welfare of the entire community is paramount to the wishes or welfare of a particular element of the community," a Progressive theme to which he would return constantly throughout his career.[25]

Curley followed up these assertions with well-publicized actions. He immediately fired Fitzgerald's building commissioner, promised to remove one department head a day, eliminated pay hikes made by Fitzgerald just before leaving office, vetoed a $500,000 loan order, chopped $2 million from the municipal budget, and promised to reduce the number of city workers by five hundred. A month later he fired a slew of Park Department employees who had been hired by the Fitzgerald administration, the first in a series of dismissals.[26]

These tactics achieved several political ends, only some of which were advertised. Of most immediate importance to Curley, they damaged Fitzgerald, his principal political rival in the city and likely opponent for reelection in four years. The cuts and firings also removed the former mayor's loyalists from city hall, freeing up municipal positions for Curley's allies and helping him establish a personal patronage network. Within a year Curley had restored all of the pay cuts he had made, expanded the city payroll, and outspent his predecessor's outlay of the previous year by $540,000. But in the short run at least, these cutbacks validated Curley's claim to the mantle of reform.[27]

Bashing Fitzgerald was not the only way Curley sought to fashion himself as a reformer. During the first year of his administration, he cooperated with the GGA on a number of fronts, in particular by opposing amendments to the city charter that would have reestablished district representation on the City Council. He also hired former Boston Finance Commission head John A. Sullivan—a man he once called a "pool shark"—as his corporation counsel. Sullivan had an impeccable reputation, and the move gave Curley a measure of instant credibility in reform circles. These steps shocked many observers; when Curley attended a private dinner with GGA leaders arranged by Sullivan to discuss coordinating resistance to Martin Lomasney's efforts to change the city charter in 1914, the *Boston Journal* marveled that Curley "was not assassinated."[28]

Surprising though it was, Curley's defense of the new city charter had two purposes. It preserved institutional arrangements that weakened his rivals in the Democratic Party, and it gave him further credibility as a reformer. The Charter Association, launched by GGA leaders to prevent any tinkering with the reforms instituted in 1909, circulated a cartoon, "The Charge of the Boss Brigade," that dramatized the charter contest with martial imagery. "The Mayor" was arrayed with the Finance Commission, the United Improvement Association, the Chamber of Commerce, labor, and the Real Estate Exchange as defenders of the new charter. Such was the company Curley kept on this issue. Those preparing for the assault were led by the unmistakable figure of Martin Lomasney, flanked by several of the city's leading party politicians. Another flier, a "Charter Catechism for Boston Voters"—evidently aimed at a Catholic audience—condemned the proposed changes as the work of "reactionaries" beholden to "the local boss." Curley's opposition weighed heavily in the defeat of the amendment and placed him on the Progressive side of city politics.[29]

Accolades followed from unexpected sources. The GGA labeled Curley's early activities "indications of a policy entitled to the highest praise." Curley had "proved himself an attentive student of municipal affairs, eager to do his duty as he saw it, in the troublous conditions in which he was fallen," declared the staunchly Republican *Boston Herald* after he came out in opposition to Lomasney's charter amendments. A year later the strongly proreform *Journal* was still commending Curley for coming "closer to giving the city a genuine business administration" than any mayor since the early 1890s. Even observers outside Boston noted Curley's success as a reformer. The GGA remained friendly as well, and Curley made no attempt to cross it during his first year in office. He called the GGA election report for the December 1914 election "a little more charitable than usual," adding with gentle irony, "after all, what the GGA as an Association says about the candidate is only what each one of us as individuals would say of our friends or enemies."[30]

Curley subtly mocked the GGA's motives to remind his supporters that he may have been cooperating with the GGA leaders, but he was not one of them. When he pledged himself to "the welfare of the entire community" over "the wishes and welfare of a particular element of the community," he had specific interpretations of these phrases in mind. Even as he courted the GGA and its allies, Curley sent clear signals that he was pursuing a brand of reform with different social connotations. At the start of his term, he ordered a hike in tax assessments on downtown real estate with attendant fanfare. When the Real Estate Exchange dispatched a delegation to protest, the new mayor made sure his private response became public: "You people are entitled to no more consideration in the matter of assessments than is any other individual, and I propose that you get none." In another instance, he proudly trumpeted his rejection of a bribe from a businessman seeking a favorable settlement of his dispute with the city, a move designed to highlight the supposed corruption and hypocrisy of the city's economic elite.[31]

In Curley's formulation of Progressivism, the efficient and economical operation of city government would benefit the city's least powerful citizens. A self-styled "Mayor of the Poor," he remained a staunch advocate of generous social welfare policies. He supported aggressive city planning; built a hospital, playgrounds, bathhouses, and parks; and sought greater streetcar service with lower fares. That such projects often expanded his patronage base, allowing him to take credit for creating jobs, only enhanced his reputation among the city's working-class population. He also endorsed the creation of a public market, the restriction of child labor, pasteurizing the city's milk supply, and establishing mothers' pensions, all staples of Progressive social reform. He even supported woman suffrage, echoing the claims of social feminists that women voters would support the more generous welfare policies he proposed.[32]

Curley's zeal for improving the urban environment suited his political circumstances well. He lavished most of his attention and most of the city's money on working-class, ethnic neighborhoods. In the absence of stable, powerful party organizations, the distribution of collective benefits—policies that affected broad groups of people rather than individuals—became more important than ever as a tool of political mobilization. And since the mayor was responsible for initiating the municipal budget, he could make his presence felt on the neighborhood level, where charter reform had created a political vacuum. In immigrant wards, where the number and influence of locally elected officials had diminished sharply, Curley became a principal local advocate at city hall. His claim that he was closer than any previous mayor to delivering one hundred cents on the dollar rang especially true in these areas of the city.[33]

Curley used several strategies to make sure his presence was felt locally. In keeping with his reform persona, he worked closely with the local civic groups that were now the main connective tissue between city hall and the neighborhood, even though many had supported Kenny in 1914. In most cases they had close ties to the local press, and publicity was an important part of their work. Curley cultivated alliances with organizations such as the Italian-run North End Improvement Association, the South Boston Trade Association, and the Char-

lestown Improvement Association. In winning their loyalty, he gar-
nered positive appraisals from the leading voices of local civic life.[34]

Curley also used neighborhood and ethnic newspapers to connect
with voters. He maintained close relationships with the reform-
minded John Toomey of the *South Boston Gazette* and James Maguire
of the *East Boston Free Press,* receiving positive coverage in return. He
appointed James Donnaruma, editor of the *Gazzetta del Massachusetts,* to a part-time city post, thus assuring himself access to the columns of the city's only Italian newspaper. Curley often took advantage
of these connections to make sure he received credit for his efforts.
Without any organization to rely on, Curley understood that coverage
in local newspapers was an important way to establish himself as a
reformer working in the interests of the residents of Boston's working-
class ethnic neighborhoods.[35]

Many of his spending proposals targeted these districts. He campaigned fiercely for a subway tunnel stretching to East Boston and
later for a new park in the North End. Citing the neglect of the neighborhood by previous administrations, he promised four major improvements for Irish South Boston. Later in his term he pledged his
support for further improvements in East Boston, South Boston, Charlestown, Dorchester, West Roxbury, and Hyde Park—all districts with
significant ethnic populations.[36]

In sections of the city where Curley votes were less plentiful, city-
sponsored improvements were correspondingly scarce. Middle-class
Yankee suburbs and the organizations that represented them received
little attention and less money. During his first term Brighton secured
only one significant improvement. Measures such as the long-sought
widening of Faneuil Street were rejected in favor of plans for other
neighborhoods, a policy that angered the WASP-dominated Faneuil
Improvement Association. Similar resentment percolated in other suburban enclaves, galvanizing opposition to Curley among the native-
stock middle class.[37]

Besides pursuing the support of civic leaders in ethnic districts, Curley sought the support of labor leaders. His opposition to the policy of
docking the pay of outdoor workers when weather conditions prevented them from working, his advocacy of vacations for municipal
workers and union wages for all city mechanics, and his support of
other prolabor measures early in his career had already earned Curley
the backing of most Boston unions. As mayor, his struggle for a one-

day-off-in-three (instead of five) policy for firemen against the opposition of the GGA, the Finance Commission, and their City Council allies; his willingness to allow city workers to join AFL unions; and his refusal to fire older city workers—a proposal from the Massachusetts Real Estate Exchange—won him accolades from the Boston Central Labor Union, which by now had long abandoned its policy of political neutrality. The Irish-dominated BCLU proudly declared Curley a "friend of labor," and it backed him vociferously in his reelection bid in 1917.[38]

In sum, Curley aimed to win the support of those most isolated by charter reform. The neighborhoods where he tried to spend the bulk of city monies were the neighborhoods with the least pull in the CML and the UIA. His social policies and position on labor issues won the allegiance of precisely the people who did not participate in local civic associations. These constituencies would become his electoral base, making him mayor three more times, and sending him to the governor's office and another term in Congress over the next three decades.

"Urban liberalism" is an inadequate description of Curley's reform activism. Certainly he and other ethnic urban politicians pursued reforms that foreshadowed the evolution of the modern welfare state. But they did more than simply support innovative public policies. By casting himself as the representative of an aggrieved ethnic Boston, Curley imbued his version of Progressive reform with a specific social meaning. When he raised wages for city workers, launched construction of Boston City Hospital, or secured city funds for a new park, he was striking a blow for the city's blue-collar immigrant majority in its long-running battle against a hostile Yankee elite.[39]

The social significance of Curley's Progressivism arose from the backdrop of ethnic conflict that he forcefully emphasized. He linked reform with ethnic and class appeals designed to define Boston's Brahmin elite and its political arm, the GGA, as "special interests" corrupting city government and blocking progress. But Curley also mocked symbols of the Anglo-Protestant tradition that reached back to the city's (and the nation's) origins, where his predecessor Fitzgerald had been careful to distinguish between contemporary Yankee Boston and the ideals of its founders.

As part of this campaign, Curley used his sharp wit to belittle historical landmarks and revise local legend. The day after he was elected, Curley proposed the sale of the city's beloved Public Gardens, an idea that elicited apoplectic responses from wealthy Yankees and even earned Fitzgerald's scorn. He won similar reactions when he proposed the demolition of the Shirley-Eustis Mansion, a colonial-era landmark, because it did not conform to "modern building standards." Curley also claimed that Myles Standish was an Irish mercenary hired by the Pilgrims "to do their fighting for them" and that Samuel Adams and his raiding party had prepared to dump tea in Boston Harbor by consuming ale at an Irishman's saloon. Though humorous, these gestures were significant. They undermined popular respect for the city's storied past and set the stage for a rewriting of the city's history that would stress conflict over cooperation.[40]

Curley often grabbed center stage in these semicomic episodes, offering himself as a representative figure for Boston's immigrants and particularly its Irish residents. He built a mansion in the suburban Jamaica Plain district financed largely with graft during his first term. To distract public attention from the illicit funding of the project, Curley orchestrated an ethnic controversy. He planted a phony letter in the *Boston Post,* the leading paper among the city's Irish working class, supposedly from an indignant Yankee neighbor complaining about the shamrocks Curley had carved into the shutters of his new home. The pretense allowed Curley to engage in more Yankee bashing. At a Roxbury rally he declared that "the shamrocks are here to stay" and that the neighbor could "close his shutters" or "wear a blindfold" if he didn't want to see them. He added that he had begun construction of the house on St. Patrick's Day "and didn't do it by accident either." Although this manufactured incident was exposed a few days later, it allowed Curley to portray himself as the embodiment of an Irish Boston proudly fighting the slurs and deprecations of elite Yankees. It also insulated him from charges that his house had been built with city money by turning it into a symbol of Irish pride.[41]

All of Curley's actions—his corrupt practices and his calls for reform—took their meaning from this context. His role as ethnic flag-bearer inoculated him from charges of dishonesty because his actions, legal or not, became part of Boston's ongoing ethnic struggle. More importantly, the reforms Curley proposed drew their meaning from the social narrative he crafted. Progressive reform, in his hands, became the culmination of the century-long struggle in Boston for Irish legitimacy—and for the legitimacy of immigrants in general.

Curley's self-fashioning as the representative of unjustly blocked

Irish ambition in Boston did more than make him a folk hero. It contributed substantially to the redefinition of what it meant to be Irish in Boston. Curley was not simply tapping into long-held resentments that had always governed the city's public life. Only a decade before, Patrick Collins and his generation had evoked a sharply different symbolic universe that did not portray Boston as an inherently hostile place for Irish Catholics. Even John Fitzgerald, a few years earlier, did not present so stark a picture. Of course ethnic and religious grievances existed before the Progressive Era and played a role in city politics. But the vision of Boston, past and present, as a fundamentally anti-immigrant, anti-Irish community finally disintegrating in the face of Irish aggression did not become a dominant perception until Curley rewrote the ethnic Progressive narrative in these terms.

Broader cultural developments also contributed to the willingness of ethnic Boston to accept Curley's representation of the city's social character. Anti-immigrant, anti-Catholic feeling grew steadily throughout the country during Curley's four-year term. Efforts already under way to prohibit the sale of alcohol, to restrict the flow of immigrants, and to Americanize newcomers fueled anxiety in ethnic America. By 1917 cultural and economic tensions arising from the onset of World War I could be felt as well. But political developments were the most important factors driving the propensity of Boston's immigrants to see themselves as victims of Yankee oppression. The structural reforms of the Progressive Era gave the mayor unparalleled power in shaping popular perceptions, and the language and imagery of Progressivism proved a tremendously effective tool for doing so.

Curley's aggressive pursuit of policies that reflected his particular Progressivism exposed the different meanings operating within the shared rhetoric of reform. As a result, the tenuous Progressive coalition of wealthy businessmen and civic leaders, middle-class suburbanites, and substantial portions of various working-class ethnic voters that had twice endorsed charter reform began to unravel, a process well under way before World War I.

The same fate eventually befell Progressivism throughout the country. As a political movement it could no longer reconcile the multiple visions it had given birth to, and reform alliances began to dissolve. The coalition that backed New York fusion mayor John Purroy Mitchel in 1914 had disintegrated by 1917. His promise of an efficient municipal government had different meanings for the different groups supporting him. Businessmen wanted a streamlined, economical administration and lower taxes. Working-class ethnics sought more municipal services and expenditures. Mitchel was unable to meet these incompatible expectations. Even Wisconsin's Progressivism proved to be several Progressivisms united for a time by Robert LaFollette's political skills. But the state's Scandinavian voters developed expectations for reform that differed both from their German counterparts in Milwaukee and from the ideas of the Anglo middle class. As differences among these alternative Progressivisms grew sharper in the 1910s, LaFollette's coalition dissolved. The demise of Progressivism throughout the country stemmed more from its local, internal contradictions than from the cultural controversies that emerged with the onset of World War I.[42]

Clashes over city finances catalyzed this process in Boston. Although the mayor's fiscal power was greater under the new charter, he still did not possess the authority to increase municipal revenues. The power to raise property taxes, the city's primary source of income, rested with the state legislature. And while borrowing proposals originated in the mayor's office, they were subject to the approval of the City Council. Neither the legislature, with its Republican majority, nor the City Council, which was controlled by members with GGA and CML endorsements, supported Curley's efforts to expand his fiscal resources. His requests for tax hikes in 1915 and 1916 were blocked at the State House, in large part due to the lobbying efforts of the GGA. The City Council rejected his loan orders during the same years and, relying on figures supplied by the Boston Finance Commission, forced him to cut the city budget in 1915. These restrictions limited Curley's ability to expand his patronage base and to distribute the collective benefits so vital to voter mobilization in this new era of city politics.[43]

These disputes fractured the fragile entente between Curley and elite reform forces, prompting angry exchanges in which each side trotted out its favorite Progressive themes. After Curley called for a $500,000 loan for street repairs and a tax increase to pay for "progressive municipal work" in 1915, the GGA and others began to attack him as a corrupt boss whose efforts to build a patronage empire had blocked the delivery of necessary street improvements and threatened to bankrupt the city. "Mr. Curley and his predecessors skinned the streets in order to put money into the payroll," declared a GGA-orchestrated statement from a group of "representative citizens" that included the president of the City Council and members of the Chamber of Commerce, the Boston Real Estate Exchange, and the Charter Association. When state legislators rejected a bill authorizing money for street repairs in 1916, Curley blamed this on a conspiracy of "powerful influences," among them the GGA, the Finance Commission, the Massachusetts and Boston Real Estate Exchanges, and members of the City Council. He warned that in order to make the necessary repairs, the city would have to fire longtime employees, reduce services to the poor, and limit improvements throughout the city. In one instance he threatened to cut off power to the Brahmin Back Bay if the City Council did not authorize additional funds.[44]

Curley focused on the City Council as the source of his problems. The nine-member body was dominated by Citizens' Municipal League endorsees, who consistently voted against Curley's spending initiatives. During his first year in office, while he was still cooperating with the GGA, he made no effort to influence the results of Council elections. But in his second year, when his relations with elite reformers had soured, Curley organized a slate of Democratic candidates, despite the city charter's prohibition of partisan labels in city politics. Though the four office seekers would not be identified as Democrats on the ballot, they would run openly as partisan candidates.[45]

Curley's move did not signal the resurrection of grassroots party activism in Boston politics. What he revived was a party label, not an organization. At Curley's behest, the Democratic City Committee did stage a well-publicized meeting where, with attendant fanfare, the GGA-sponsored Council candidates were "read out of the Democratic Party." The meeting also featured "rancorous partisanship and clamorous appeals to simon pure Democracy," according to one observer. But the gathering was little more than a publicity stunt; it failed to reinvigorate the inert Democratic ward organizations across the city. Even the claim of the party's "publicity manager"—whose very existence underscored the changing shape of urban politics—that five hundred people attended the meeting was greeted with skepticism by the press.[46]

The evolution of Boston's Democratic Party reflected a larger pattern of American political development during this period. Parties did not dissolve but rather transformed themselves from grassroots organizations to publicity-based, candidate-centered operations. The process was gradual, extending into the second half of the twentieth century, and in many eastern and midwestern cities the local party apparatus continued to wield significant power. But in most settings, the party was becoming an extension of the politician, rather than vice versa.[47]

In Boston, Curley reshaped the Democratic Party in the context of his ethnic Progressivism. He justified his creation of a Democratic slate as a necessary response to the GGA and its supporters on the City Council. Their "chief object," Curley declared, "is to play politics and put the administration in as bad a light as possible in order to promote their own interests." During the campaign he attacked the GGA as a "political machine representing wealth, refinement, and corruption," renamed it the "Boston Tax Dodgers Association," and declared that "most of those who own and control the Good Government Association live in the suburbs." He labeled James J. Storrow, former mayoral aspirant and GGA-backed candidate for the City Council in 1915, a "millionaire" and "notorious boss." The contest became, in Curley's words, a battle pitting "the classes against the masses."[48]

In this context, the revival of partisanship was not a rejection of reform. The four Curley-backed Council candidates insisted that the GGA had already acted in a partisan fashion and that their use of the Democratic label was "following . . . not making precedent." The GGA, their campaign ads charged, "maintained and still maintains a political machine for nominating candidates and ignoring utterly the purpose of the charter revisionists, which was to have a non-political choice of city elective officers." Its candidates represented the selfish interests of a few, while "the nominees indorsed [sic] by the Democratic city organization represent the progressive movement in municipal politics. Their aim will be to do something for Boston; and not to nullify the constructive energies of others."[49]

This clash temporarily renewed popular interest in city affairs, which had been flagging since charter reform. One measure was the rate of voter participation. Table 8 shows that after several years of steady decline following charter reform, voting in nonmayoral city elections rose suddenly in 1915 and increased again in 1916, precisely when Curley began waging his battle for control of the City Council. This rise was evenly distributed among lower-, middle-, and upper-class districts, suggesting that Curley's aggressive campaign and the

Table 8. Voter Turnout in Municipal Elections, 1911–1916

Year	Percent registered[a]	Percent voting[b]
1911	54	52
1912	53	45
1913	52	42
1914	50	45
1915	50	69
1916	55	72

a. Percentage of adult males registered to vote.
b. Percentage of registered voters casting ballots in municipal election.
Sources: Boston Board of Election Commissioners, *Annual Reports for 1911–1916* (Boston, 1912–1917).

GGA's counterattack had intensified attitudes on both sides of the developing political divide.

Curley's rhetoric targeted a broad segment of the city's population. At one point he linked the GGA with banks that failed to report mortgage sales and pay city taxes on them. This cost the city $70,000, he charged, an amount "equal to the value of the ten houses in South Boston, Dorchester, and East Boston." Rich bankers needed "to pay their taxes honestly into the treasury of the city as does every little homeowner." Curley's selection of distinctly ethnic neighborhoods mattered, as did his use of the term "homeowner." While much of his rhetoric and many of his policies targeted the ethnic working class, he also sought to draw middle-class immigrants into the politics of resentment and reform.

Although Curley's candidates for the City Council lost in 1915, the campaign helped bring the contradictions within Boston's Progressivism into sharper relief. This was most evident at the local level, where Curley's rhetoric fueled simmering suspicions about the Brahmin elite until they boiled over into outright hostility. Middle-class civic leaders in ethnic neighborhoods, who proudly trumpeted their devotion to good government, readily accepted his representation of public life in Boston. They echoed Curley's charge that the GGA and a handful of its wealthy allies were conspiring to deprive the majority of economic and political representation. Even the revival of the Democratic Party became acceptable in this context, as a response to the illicit manipulations of the city's Yankee aristocracy. The words of one Irish editor summed up the prevailing view in ethnic Boston: "the Mayor is at the head of the forces of the mass of voters against a selected few individuals who feel that it is their special function to govern the city at all times."[50]

Nowhere was the emergence of this perception more clear than among the civic leaders of Irish South Boston. Curley spent lavishly on the district, capturing the allegiance of the local improvement groups that had established themselves as the nonpartisan representatives of the neighborhood after charter reform. John Toomey, editor of the *South Boston Gazette,* a key figure in the South Boston Citizens Association and the South Boston Trade Association, and a longtime advocate of municipal reform, defended Curley on the eve of a 1915 recall vote mandated by the city charter. Using the Progressive terms that Curley had set forth, Toomey insisted the mayor was "chafing in the GGA harness," frustrated by the reform group's efforts "to throw the leader of the people, chosen by them, from his seat, in the selfish hope of securing the same seat at the next election." Another local commentator urged voters to "put men in office . . . who will cooperate with the mayor in his efforts for the people." From the South Boston perspective, Curley was a reformer doing battle on behalf of "the people" against a conspiracy of rich Yankees seeking to control city government.[51]

Curley's view of Boston's public life was warmly endorsed in other ethnic neighborhoods as well. He won strong support in East Boston through his willingness to spend money for street repairs and other improvements and particularly through his aggressive efforts to repeal the toll charge for use of the tunnel connecting the district to downtown Boston. When he charged the GGA and its allies with obstructionism, the *East Boston Free Press*—whose editor and publisher, Irish Democrat James Maguire, had political ambitions of his own—backed him up. The paper described Boston's elite reformers as a "few self-appointed self seekers posing as apostles of political light and cleanliness" who were "the greatest menace to free representative government in the city." They were "moral and political hypocrites," a quality they demonstrated by rejecting Curley, despite his cooperation with them over the first year of his administration. "The Mayor's ticket is the real people's ticket," the *Free Press* concluded, in a fashion that made clear that support for Curley and for reform were far from antithetical.[52]

Curley's success in framing the issues of debate highlighted the differences between Boston's divergent strains of Progressive reform. As a result, the facade of political unity based on reform rhetoric began to crumble. The United Improvement Association, the coordinating body for neighborhood organizations throughout the city, split over Curley's campaign to borrow money for street repairs. While the Association's leadership sided with the GGA in opposition to the loan, several of its constituent bodies from ethnic districts broke ranks. When Curley attacked both the UIA and the GGA, he was endorsed by ten neighborhood civic groups, including the UIA-affiliated Charlestown Improvement Association and South Boston Trade Association. This split marked the beginning of a period of decline for the UIA. Although it would remain on the scene for another decade, it came to be regarded as just another tool of Brahmin conspirators, and its influence in public affairs steadily diminished.[53]

The Citizens' Municipal League's fortunes followed a similar trajectory. Despite the CML's success in nominating City Council candidates, the GGA dismantled its creation after 1914 because it had failed to back a winning mayoral candidate. Both Fitzgerald and Curley succeeded in portraying their CML-sponsored opponents as the tools of wealthy Brahmin interests, an impression reinforced when the CML's secretary was accused of illegally collecting nominating signatures after the 1914 election. Fearing that future CML endorsees would appear to be the "handpicked" candidates of an elite few, the GGA withdrew its support for the group, which quickly disintegrated.[54]

Sensing the shifting winds of public opinion, politicians who had once sought support from the CML and the GGA now abandoned them. Although GGA-backed candidates swept the 1915 elections and controlled the Council, the Association's influence rapidly diminished. Those Irish city councilmen who had been elected with the reform group's support soon found themselves forced to abandon the GGA. Daniel J. McDonald of Charlestown, who owed his election to the endorsements of the CML and the GGA, began to oppose GGA positions in 1915. Running for reelection in 1916, he bragged that he had "incurred the wrath of the Good Government Association" and promised to oppose it at all times. Other Irish councilmen also succumbed to popular pressure. Even Thomas Kenny of South Boston, Curley's CML- and GGA-backed opponent in the 1914 mayoral race, broke with the GGA. By 1916 the Association had only four sure votes on the Council on key fiscal issues, despite having endorsed all nine members. A year later, with seven endorsees still in office, it could rely on just two of them to buck public opinion and remain loyal.[55]

In engineering this transformation in popular perceptions, Curley broadened his Progressive representation of a struggle between public and private interests into an enduring clash of cultures. The gentle, tongue-in-cheek character of his anti-Yankee pronouncements early in his term gradually gave way to a more venomous brand of humor. The pretext for one of Curley's fiercest diatribes against Yankees was a 1916 speech by elite reformer John F. Moors to the New England Women's Department of the National Civic Federation, lamenting the dominance of the Irish and the corresponding absence of the Brahmin elite in city politics. Describing the original Irish immigrants as "mostly peasants" whose descendants now ruled the city, Moors complained that "not a rich man's son under forty years of age today is taking an important part in the political life of this city." Curley's response revealed the next stage in the development of his ethnic Progressivism.[56]

The rejoinder began with a Darwinian critique of Brahmin Boston. Moors, a Brahmin banker who served on the Finance Commission, was a member of both the GGA and the Immigration Restriction League: a perfect representative of the Anglo elites trying to defy the Irish quest for power and legitimacy. Where John Fitzgerald had seen just a few Yankee conspirators in 1910, Curley envisioned an entire social group in 1916. Moors was "a pathetic figure of a perishing people who seek by dollars and denunciations to evade the inexorable and inevitable law of the survival of the fittest"; a member of "a strange and stupid race, the Anglo-Saxon beaten in a fair, stand-up fight, he seeks by political chicanery and hypocrisy to gain the ends he lost in battle, and this temperamental peculiarity he calls fair play."[57]

Curley saw duplicity of this sort as a long-standing part of the city's Anglo-Protestant tradition. In his formulation Boston's past became a time "when the traders in rum, salt cod and slaves were engaged with the New England Historical Genealogical Society in fabricating family histories." From his perspective, the rise of the immigrant Irish was Boston's redemption, a democratic tide that washed away the city's hierarchical, hypocritical past. Paraphrasing Boston Archbishop William Cardinal O'Connell, Curley proclaimed: "the Puritan is passed; the Anglo Saxon is a joke; a newer and better America is here." While O'Connell and others certainly contributed to the growing Irish-Catholic militancy in early-twentieth-century Boston, Curley, using the power of the mayor's office, did more than any other leader to encourage it and give it meaning.[58]

In distinguishing between the efforts of Boston's Irish to improve the city and the work of their Yankee counterparts, Curley employed gendered imagery as well. The masculinization of reform during the Progressive Era allowed him to associate Irish reformism with practical, masculine efforts to improve the city, while attacking elite Yankee reform as effeminate and ineffective. "No country is ever ruined by a virile, God fearing people like the Irish," Curley insisted. Conversely, "no land was ever saved by clubs of female faddists, old gentlemen with disordered livers, or pessimists croaking over imaginary good old days and ignoring the sunlit present," he declared. "What we need in this part of the world is men and mothers of men," Curley concluded, "not gabbing spinsters and dog-raising matrons in federation assembled."[59]

With this rhetorical tour de force, Curley offered his fullest expression of the narrative that defined his version of Progressivism. For a century or more, Boston's immigrants—especially the Irish—had suffered from the discrimination and hostility of selfish, prejudiced, effeminate Brahmins. Now a majority, ethnic Boston would wrest power from their hands. Progressive reform would be the instrument of that transformation, by bringing fair, democratic, and effective government working in the interest of ordinary citizens. The continued resistance of the Anglo-Protestant elite and the GGA to these changes only reinforced the perception that Yankee Boston was a selfish, corrupt force working against the common good.

It is important to remember that this understanding was new and was largely the product of Curley's manipulation of Progressivism. It had not been the dominant conception even among ethnic Bostonians a dozen years earlier, when the eminently respectable and respectful Patrick Collins served as mayor. Even John Fitzgerald, who had taken great pains to distinguish present-day reformers from their colonial ancestors, accused Curley of "inverted APAism."[60] Only when Curley turned Progressivism from an argument for Irish legitimacy into an indictment of Puritan Boston did the representation of Boston as a city defined by ethnic conflict fully take hold. The roots of modern Boston's ethnic polarization—and especially of blue-collar Irish Boston's clannish hostility—are not as deep as many believe; they rest mostly in the topsoil of the Progressive Era rather than in the deeper layers of the city's Anglo-Saxon past.

Boston's 1917 mayoral election foreshadowed the ways in which the centrifugal pattern created by Progressivism would accelerate in coming years.[61] Curley ran for reelection while the GGA endorsed Yankee Democrat and former Congressman Andrew Peters of Jamaica Plain. Both sides pursued their favorite reform themes: the GGA equated "Curleyism" with "Tammanyism" and called for the end of "old machine rule"; Curley portrayed himself as a reformer battling "bosses" with "unlimited resources." But these charges were leveled in a new context. America's entry into World War I, a "war to make the world safe for democracy," gave Progressive rhetoric an added power. The wartime drive for unity, and the cultural controversies that followed, fed the conflicts already fermenting in the political culture of Progressivism.[62]

Wartime urgency heightened the abrasive tone of elite reform rhetoric. "Our men have gone to fight for democracy," the GGA announced in its endorsement of Peters's candidacy; "when they return it should be to a city that has not failed to practice the ideals for which it sent them forth to fight." Peters framed the contest in these terms: "if democracy is worth fighting for assuredly it is worth practicing; . . . the coming election puts us to the test." He made "wise expenditures" a key component of his platform by placing it in a wartime context, insisting that "every dollar wasted puts us so far behind in our backing of the war." The implication that Curley and his supporters were traitors only fanned the flames of group hatred in Boston.[63]

In turn, the ethnic appeals of Curley and his allies became even blunter. The editor of the Irish weekly *The Hibernian,* a close ally of Curley, issued the most forceful statement during the campaign. The paper declared the election "a fight between the Irish and anti-Irish forces" and urged "every red-blooded son of the race" to back Curley. "A vote for Peters is a vote for the anti-Catholic, anti-Irish combination," *The Hibernian* declared. The chief force within this conspiracy was the GGA, which had "done more to keep alive the race and religious issue in this city than any other organization, not excepting the A.P.A." Although Peters was a Democrat, party affiliation now mattered less than ethnic ties; and as a Yankee, he would be loyal to the GGA first and foremost. This vision of Boston public life had been developing for more than a decade, but it had never been presented so starkly. As the issues surrounding the war stoked ethnic consciousness, such overt expressions of group antagonism would become the norm in Boston public life.[64]

The perils of multicandidate, nonpartisan elections cost Curley his reelection bid. James A. Gallivan, a popular South Boston politician who inherited Curley's congressional seat, also ran for mayor in 1917. His appeal paralleled Curley's in many ways. He presented himself as a reform candidate opposed by bosses ranging from Martin Lomasney to the "Andrew Peters–State Street Gang." Like Curley, he had staunchly opposed immigration restriction measures while in Congress. Gallivan cut into Curley's vote, especially in South Boston. In all he captured 19,427 votes to Curley's 28,848. Peters received 37,923, enough to win but well below the combined total of Gallivan and Curley supporters.[65]

Gallivan's success in attracting Irish voters taught Curley a lesson. In the absence of a formal political organization that controlled nominations, he would need to define himself even more emphatically as the voice of ethnic Boston. During ensuing municipal campaigns, in which Curley invariably faced Irish opposition, he worked even more aggressively to define himself as the representative of an aggrieved immigrant community. As a result, his rhetoric grew even harsher, and the fading possibility of ethnic accommodation grew even more remote.

The tone of the campaign that preceded the 1917 election and what this foretold of Boston politics to come were more important than the result. In subsequent years, elite reformers continued to pursue the concept of a single public interest with the certainty that they knew what that was, a vision reinforced by the rhetoric of wartime unity. At the same time, the intensification of ethnic nationalism, and especially the question of home rule in Ireland, would fuel the issue of Irish civic legitimacy in Boston already formulated during the Progressive Era. The development of these and other cultural issues after the war would bring to fruition the seeds of group antagonism planted by the emergence of Progressive-style politics.

CHAPTER SIX

Ethnic Progressivism Triumphant: Boston Public Life in the 1920s

James Michael Curley's return to the mayoralty in late 1921 seemed to sound the death knell for Progressivism in Boston. His campaign was an unrelenting attack on the reformers who had worked closely with Andrew Peters's administration. "Four years of Goo-Goo reform" was the stock theme of his stump speeches. "The public is discovering that four years of reform administration in Boston is [*sic*] more destructive to everyone and everything than a plague," Curley declared. John R. Murphy, his chief opponent, had been the chairman of the Boston Finance Commission and was endorsed by the GGA, attributes that made him especially vulnerable to these attacks.[1]

Curley's victory was but one of many signals throughout the country that the era of Progressive reform had apparently come to an end. The presidential triumph of Warren Harding and his call for "normalcy" in 1920, the shattering of the Wilson coalition, the election of antireform mayors in New York and Chicago, a growing intolerance of political and ethnic differences during and after the war, and the rise of the Ku Klux Klan and other antimodern movements contributed to a perceived backlash against political and social innovation that left intellectuals and reformers disillusioned.[2]

Historians tend to share this interpretation of public life after World War I. While some note the continuities between the Progressive Era and the twenties, most historians depict the decade as an "entr'acte" separating two great reform movements, Progressivism and the New

Deal. Indeed, a caricature of the twenties, featuring cultural conflicts, the unrestrained pursuit of profit, and a loosening of moral standards, has served as a useful foil for portraying the Progressive Era as a period of idealistic liberal reform. A few scholars have detected fragments of reform persisting through the 1920s, but most place the end of Progressivism—and the end of their analyses—between 1917 and 1920.[3]

A solid grasp of what Progressivism was and was not is needed to unravel the connections between public life before and after World War I. When conceived of as a political language and style instead of a coherent ideology or even a constellation of ideologies, Progressivism's persistence beyond 1920 becomes evident. Boston's sociopolitical divisions during the 1920s were not between those who favored and those who opposed Progressive reform, but between different versions of Progressivism. Curley's supposedly anti-Progressive 1921 mayoral campaign is instructive on this point. While he attacked "reformers," he did so in terms drawn directly from the language of political-business corruption that infused Progressivism. He characterized the GGA as an organization "hedged with unlimited money, furnished by millionaire real estate trustees and lawyers who represent unscrupulous promoters seeking city contracts." In his battle against these corrupt forces, the former mayor sought the support of "all those who wish to see Boston freed of the unseen influence of privileged interests and back again in the hands of the people." He linked the GGA to "the Morgan interests in New York" and catalogued his opponents as ward bosses (especially Martin Lomasney), "Goo-Goos," and "Real Estate Trusts." While there were obvious class dimensions to this rhetoric, the ethnic connotations embedded in these terms were also well established by the 1920s in Boston.[4]

The other key component of Curley's Progressivism, a commitment to activist government, remained intact as well. He campaigned aggressively in the city's ethnic neighborhoods, citing the numerous improvements he had made during his first term and promising more if given a second. A Curley circular listing ten campaign promises fit the traditional definition of a social reformer. He advocated a reduction in streetcar fares, a street and sewer construction program, a new committee on public health, a revival of the port and of business generally, and "a return to humane treatment of all requests at City Hall for Executive assistance." He promised that he would replace the "official lethargy" of the Peters administration with "official activity."[5]

The ethnic dimensions of Curley's Progressivism were even sharper by 1921, fueled by the divisive issues that emerged after World War I. When Curley attacked the GGA and Murphy, he linked them not only to insidious financial interests but to anti-Catholic, anti-immigrant, and even anti-Irish movements, despite Murphy's Irish-Catholic lineage. "If there is any real difference between the Goo-Goos and Ku Klux Klan I cannot see it," Curley declared, in what became a common theme of his anti-GGA rhetoric. He connected Murphy and the GGA with the Loyal Coalition, a local organization of prominent Yankees established after World War I to oppose Ireland's independence from England. For Irish Bostonians, the drive for home rule in Ireland was a powerful issue, with clear parallels to their own efforts to secure political leadership in the city. When the Loyal Coalition formally endorsed Murphy as the only candidate who could "help Boston to emerge from the un-American path in which the city now finds itself," Curley seized the opportunity to sharpen his old theme of a Brahmin conspiracy working against the well-being of immigrant Bostonians. The Loyal Coalition was an "aristocratic and selfish body of men," Curley shot back with characteristic flair, that "would crush the poor and lowly of their community between the millstone of aristocracy and caste and the netherstone of cant and hypocrisy." The mingling of this rhetoric with a Progressive-style attack on Yankee Boston would have powerful political appeal through the 1920s and beyond.[6]

Progressivism did not disappear in Boston in the 1920s; rather its divergent meanings reached full flower, intensifying social conflict. The different definitions of the shape and character of the city's public life residing within the language of Progressivism now hardened, and their disparate social meanings became more explicit. The immigrant/Irish reading of Progressivism articulated by Curley and many neighborhood political and civic leaders—and, if election results are any measure, shared by a large portion of ethnic Boston—dominated the city's public life in the twenties, clashing with the businessmen's Progressivism of the GGA and its allies usually thought to be the one and only "true" Progressivism. Other Progressivisms rooted in ethnic, gender, and class identities persisted as well. But the vision of the city as a battleground between a predominantly Irish "people" and a small set of Brahmin "interests," with an activist government seen as a weapon in the contest, came to define public life in Boston.

Two developments buttressed ethnic Progressivism's triumph. The first of these was the growth of suburbs. Beginning in the late nineteenth century and accelerating after World War I, middle-class Yankees and then better-off ethnics moved from the city center to the rapidly developing suburban areas. This precursor of post–World War II suburban flight strengthened the lower-class character of inner-city districts such as the North End and even more peripheral neighborhoods such as South Boston and Charlestown. The remaining residents were primarily those most isolated from the kinds of political action encouraged by charter reform. Not surprisingly, the mass mobilization strategies used by Curley and other politicians were most effective in these districts.

The second factor perpetuating Progressive Era political patterns was the rise of culturally contentious issues in the wake of World War I. Concerns over the resurgence of the Ku Klux Klan, the fate of Ireland after the war, Prohibition, immigration restriction, and the Red Scare intensified and politicized ethnic identities. As a result these issues became effective tools of group mobilization, even if they were not directly related to municipal affairs. They reinforced the narrative of Irish-Yankee conflict that had become the defining feature of Boston's twentieth-century public life, even after the possibility of Brahmin rule had become absurdly remote.

The dominance of this perspective prevented the cross-ethnic cooperation that had marked an earlier era of Boston's public life. A decade earlier the broad and vague language of Progressivism allowed for varied interpretations of charter reform. But by the 1920s the different definitions of "the people" and "the interests" blocked the construction of similar voting coalitions. It was in this atmosphere that the first large-scale efforts to mobilize women as voters took place, with predictable results. Suffragist efforts to create a single, organized female voting bloc based on shared feminine interests ran aground on the shoals of the politics of ethnic Progressivism. The Good Government Association also remained active, but the power it had once wielded declined, until its endorsement became a near guarantee of electoral defeat and many of its structural reforms had been dismantled.

The ground-level workings of urban politics in the 1920s remain largely unexplored. Stereotypes about machine politics suffice for this period, much as they do for the Progressive Era. Studies purporting to trace or measure the persistence of machine politics into the 1920s and

1930s often rely on secondary works that are themselves flawed by their consistent reliance on the biased reports of Progressive Era social workers and journalists. They assume that city politics continued unchanged, operating the same way in 1890 as it did in 1940. In fact, ground-level politics in Boston during the 1920s still operated along the lines marked out by its 1909 charter reform; no reversion to decentralized machine-style partisan politics occurred. Citywide elections continued to be based on mass appeals designed to mobilize voters collectively, rather than in the ward-centered fashion of party organizations. James Michael Curley remained the unchallenged master of this political environment.[7]

Curley reentered office at a ripe moment for his brand of politics. The postwar economic downturn weakened the city government's ability to deliver services. Although the state legislature had seen fit to raise Boston's property tax rate several times with a respectable Yankee in the mayor's office, much of that money was devoted to suburban street improvements rather than the kinds of social spending that won Curley popularity in ethnic districts. These developments only heightened popular suspicion that a handful of Yankee businessmen and their political allies sought to deprive immigrant Boston of economic and political resources.

This perception of neglect fueled resentment in ethnic neighborhoods. When the Peters administration provided the South Boston Citizens Association with less money than it had requested to stage its annual Evacuation Day celebration, the *South Boston Gazette* angrily attacked the mayor's motives. "It is surprising but not entirely unexpected the meager appropriation that the mayor has given this district," the paper declared. "Geographically South Boston isn't situated right. If it lay out around Commonwealth Avenue or Stuart Street" (a reference to two Brahmin Back Bay thoroughfares), then "undoubtedly the citizens could then get any amount of money they desired." From this perspective, Curley was "the one who has done the most for this district" and remained the true reformer; his return to office constituted the defeat of the "money interests."[8]

Curley worked aggressively to meet these expectations, enacting numerous large-scale social reform measures that contrasted with the parsimony of the Peters administration. He created a new City Planning Board, spent $11 million to improve Boston City Hospital, destroyed more than two thousand tenements, built a dozen new parks, extended three subway lines, worked for a reduction in streetcar fares, cleared mudflats for bathhouses and beaches, rebuilt bridges and repaired streets, pushed for a universal old-age pension, and established a Municipal Employment Bureau to assist unemployed soldiers caught in the postwar economic slide. This frenzy of activity expanded his patronage resources and gave credence to his populist rhetoric.[9]

The institutional arrangements of Boston politics also helped Curley reestablish himself as the dominant presence in the public life of ethnic neighborhoods. A patronage-based grassroots organization remained ineffective within the nonpartisan, at-large election system set up by the 1909 city charter. Of course Curley still used patronage and remained as corrupt as ever in his dealings with friendly contractors. But these tactics were as insufficient for the task of mass mobilization in the 1920s as they had been a decade earlier. As Curley himself observed to an audience of his supporters, "if there was no civil service regulation applying, and . . . if every man in the city employ under civil service were turned out tomorrow it would be an utter impossibility to provide for all those now seeking an opportunity." Curley relied on his public relations skills, the cooperation of still powerful neighborhood civic associations, and the rhetoric of reform to reinforce his image as a municipal benefactor for Boston's working-class ethnics.[10]

Curley's struggle against Martin Lomasney for the loyalty of Italian voters showed how these tactics worked. After the 1916 redistricting, the North End became part of ward five, a territory that included Martin Lomasney's West End. Lomasney dominated ward five much as he had ward eight before 1916. The electoral inactivity of many Italians and other new immigrant residents of the district, a circumstance that was only gradually beginning to change during the early 1920s, made that possible. Lomasney had opposed Curley in 1917 and 1921, costing Curley support in the largest immigrant district in the city. In response, Curley devoted significant time and attention to the North End in an effort to mobilize the large number of the district's nonvoting Italians, emphasizing a shared political identity based on both ethnicity and neighborhood.[11]

Curley lavished money and attention on the North End, making sure that he received credit for the benefits that followed. He ordered loans to clean and pave local streets, build a playground and bathhouse, and improve sewer and water services. In each case, the mayor made a great show of consulting "representative North End citizens," usually leaders of local civic and reform organizations such as the North End Improvement Association and the North End Union settlement; these consultations served to enhance Curley's antimachine, proreform persona. After the *Italian News* complained about the condition of North End parks, Curley personally inspected them and ordered the Parks Department to remedy the problem. When the Boston Elevated cut trolley service to the neighborhood in 1922, Curley publicly negotiated with the company to replace the lost trolley routes with bus lines. He supplemented official measures of this sort with personal gestures, such as a $25 donation to the Home for Italian Children.[12]

These efforts won Curley warm praise in Italian Boston, and his stature as an advocate of "the Italian people" increased. The *Italian News,* a new English-language paper based in the North End, enthusiastically greeted his promise to make the district "a paradise." "Since assuming office again," the paper gushed, "[Curley] has done more for the North End and for the race in general than any other Chief executive of Boston." The Mazzini-Garibaldi Republican Club echoed these sentiments, noting that he had "appropriated for the good of the Italian people of this city over $500,000 to be expended on playgrounds in health betterment and in general for the benefit of the Italian people." Over the course of the twenties, as second-generation Italian Americans began to vote in large numbers, North End resistance to Lomasney's dictates gradually increased. Curley finally received a majority of the district's votes in his third bid for the mayoralty in 1929. Combining a careful eye for publicity with liberal municipal spending, Curley was able to make himself a powerful presence in the public life of the North End.[13]

While Curley became the most popular public figure in Boston's working-class Italian enclave, his persona was an overwhelming one in the city's Irish districts. The absence of an effective municipal party organization in neighborhoods like South Boston kept the process of political mobilization wide open. Curley's delivery of collective benefits and his knack for publicity made him the center of political attention in that community. Soon after his election in 1921, he delivered on his campaign promise to complete work on the Strandway, the district's waterfront boulevard, which had been started during his first term but was neglected while Andrew Peters was mayor. This was followed by an onslaught of improvements: new ambulances, a new bathhouse, a new municipal building, and a host of other measures that pleased the South Boston Citizens Association and other local spokespersons. "The many things done for South Boston by James M. Curley as Mayor, if enumerated, would require six columns," the *South Boston Inquirer* declared in 1923. The Association was even satisfied with Curley's appropriation of $5,000 for the celebration of Evacuation Day, although it was less than they had requested.[14]

South Boston's elected leaders employed Curley's beneficent image to their own advantage. They regularly published letters to the mayor in the local press requesting improvements for their districts. Perennial local candidate Robert Bigney frequently wrote to Curley asking for street repairs, more lifeguards at local beaches, and other improvements. When Joseph F. Daly decided to run for state representative in 1922, he launched his campaign by asking Curley for a bathhouse for South Boston. State Senator (and future Speaker of the U.S. House of Representatives) John McCormack, a close Curley ally; State Representative Leo J. Halloran; and several others made the public letter to Curley a staple of South Boston politics in the 1920s. Entreaties of this sort established the local politico's devotion to his constituents and underscored the central place that Curley now occupied in the city's political firmament, at least as it was viewed from South Boston.[15]

Maintaining that role required a steady expansion of the city treasury, something Curley's political opponents sought to prevent. The state legislature, encouraged by the result of an investigation into Curley's first term sponsored by Martin Lomasney and backed by the opinions of the GGA and the Finance Commission, refused to grant the property tax increases demanded by Curley. In the last year of his term, the legislature actually reduced the tax rate, thereby strangling Curley's primary source of revenue and forcing him to borrow to fund his projects. Though a now more pliable City Council made the approval of loan orders more likely, Curley found the prospect of deficit spending politically unattractive, because it gave additional ammunition to those who insisted he was a fiscally profligate boss.[16]

When he came under attack, Curley fought fire with fire, usually coming out ahead. Angered at a Finance Commission accusation that he had installed the floor in his Jamaica Plain home at city expense, Curley attacked the investigative body as "the servile catspaw of the dominant party on Beacon Hill, which in turn was bossed and directed by the GGA whose authority was vested in a little camerilla of financial politicians." Another time he dismissed the GGA as "a robust organization of Pharisees" that sought only to "keep down the tax rate by a spurious economy, which expresses itself in money unspent for the upkeep of the city, resulting in neglected streets and parks, undermanned departments, scrimping of health and hospitalization work, postponement of necessary public improvements, the result of which must inevitably be reflected by municipal stagnation."[17]

Neither this rhetoric nor the circumstances that led to it represented a sharp break from Progressive Era political conflict. Despite World War I and the controversies that followed, the prewar patterns of Boston public life grew stronger in the 1920s. Politics and policy continued to revolve around mass mobilization and the shaping of public opinion, and the rhetorical terms in which this contest played out remained largely the same.

Suburbanization sharpened the politics of ethnic conflict in Boston by placing an even greater premium on mass mobilization techniques. The steady movement of middle-class urbanites from city center to outlying communities strengthened the working-class character of neighborhoods near the city center. Relatively few of the remaining residents in these districts participated in the civic group politics ushered in by the 1909 charter reform. If they were to be mobilized politically in a period of weakening grassroots party organization, it would be through the mass-mediated ethnic appeals that had become the basic building blocks of electoral majorities in Boston politics during the Progressive Era.

The seemingly constant social geography and relatively static population of Boston masked a steady turnover. A key aspect of this process, with important implications for early-twentieth-century urban politics, was the rise of suburbs, particularly after World War I. Communities surrounding major cities experienced a sudden spurt of growth during the 1920s, a surge fueled by the burgeoning popularity of the automobile. Between 1920 and 1930, the districts adjacent to the ninety-six largest cities in the country grew twice as fast as the cities themselves.[18]

Metropolitan Boston's social geography displayed this pattern earlier than did most major cities. Suburbs such as Cambridge and Somerville, encouraged by early rail lines, had begun to develop around the city even before the Civil War. Other "streetcar suburbs" soon followed. Some were incorporated into the city during the annexation boom of the 1860s and 1870s; the rest remained independent, tied to Boston only by the short railway commutes their residents made each day. The rapid expansion of the city's mass transportation network fostered the steady growth of these communities during the late nineteenth and early twentieth centuries, allowing many middle-class Bostonians to move farther away from the city center.[19]

Suburbanization accelerated after World War I. Boston, which had averaged a 20 percent population increase per decade since 1880, added 33,128 people to its 748,060 total between 1920 and 1930, an increase of just 4 percent. During the same years, the number of residents of the twelve cities and towns immediately adjacent to Boston grew from 503,676 to 615,555, an 18.2 percent jump. From 1900 to 1930, Boston's population grew by 33 percent, while the surrounding communities expanded by 86.8 percent. Former city dwellers undoubtedly represented a large chunk of suburban population growth.[20]

The shift from city center to outlying sections occurred within municipal lines as well. The Boston Council of Social Agencies reported that the health and welfare areas "clustered in the center of the city" decreased in population between 1920 and 1930. The average population drop for Boston's three inner-city immigrant neighborhoods was 20 percent; in the surrounding areas that the South End House called the Zone of Emergence, the decline was 4.7 percent. But the number of people living in the city's six suburban neighborhoods increased rapidly during this period, growing by an average of 32 percent. By the end of the decade, much of middle- and upper-class Boston had fled the city center.[21]

A significant portion of this outflow came from immigrant stock. Newcomers to Boston's adjacent towns with at least one foreign-born parent accounted for 69 percent of the population increase there. Another measure was the rapid growth in the number of Roman Catholic parishes—one of the institutional bulwarks of Irish and Italian communities—in these suburban neighborhoods. Between 1890 and 1930, thirty-eight new Catholic parishes opened in the twelve cities and towns contiguous with Boston. By 1930 predominantly upper-middle-class Newton had seven Catholic parishes, reflecting the steady rise of second- and third-generation ethnics within its borders. The same pattern was at work in the city, as nineteen new parishes opened during that period in the middle-class residential sections located several miles from the city center.[22]

The continuing geographic separation of Bostonians by class had clear political implications. As suburban towns grew, they lured away many of the middle-class civic leaders who had dominated neighborhood public life and had served as intermediaries between neighborhoods and local government. George Nutter of the GGA complained of the "constant emigration from the city into the neighboring towns of by far the better type of citizen . . . We are rather left with a dairy product of which the cream has been skimmed off." This development had its most substantial effect on Boston's lower-middle-class and working-class districts. Those left behind had fewer institutional connections to public life and were thus the most susceptible to the techniques of mass mobilization practiced by Curley and other urban politicians.[23]

The fate of the Charlestown Improvement Association illustrates this process. Under the leadership of Augustus A. Fales, the Association was Charlestown's dominant political voice after 1909. But by 1920 it had disbanded, in part because a large portion of its membership had moved away. Of the 258 members on the Association's roster in 1914, when it was at the peak of its influence, only 48 were still listed as Charlestown residents in the city directory in 1928. A significant portion of this decline appears to have resulted from suburban flight (along with death). The *Charlestown News* lamented the departure of "hundreds of old-time residents [who] have left the district and are now living in the various suburbs of the greater city" during the 1920s.[24]

Of the seventy-nine officers representing the seventeen neighborhood improvement groups that belonged to the United Improvement Association in 1911, only twenty-nine still lived in the same district in 1928. The pattern was even more pronounced among the leaders of organizations in neighborhoods near downtown. Only five of the thirty-one officers serving these groups remained in the same district in 1928; the rest were either dead or had moved. In the North and West Ends, none of the eight men and women, mostly settlement workers, who had run the two local improvement societies in 1911 still lived there seventeen years later. Though new leaders emerged to take the place of those who departed, and these organizations remained important, there were fewer "representative citizens" of the sort that post–charter reform city politics had placed at the center of local public life.[25]

Curley and his politics of group antagonism were the great beneficiaries of these demographic changes. His constant, well-publicized efforts on behalf of these neighborhoods gave him enormous stature among their lower-class residents, who had little access to the principal corridors of power determined by charter reform. A vision of nativist Brahmin bankers and corrupt ward bosses blocking Curley's efforts to help ordinary Bostonians came to be their accepted interpretation of the facts of municipal public life. The absence of any significant alternative forms of political mobilization made these claims all the more powerful.

The onset of World War I, and the culturally contentious issues that arose in its wake, also buttressed the position of ethnic conflict at the center of Boston's public life. The accelerated drive for Americanization during the war; the questions of national self-determination that arose at Versailles; and the controversies surrounding Prohibition, immigration restriction, the Red Scare, and the rise of the Ku Klux Klan sharpened ethnic sensibilities and increased ethnic consciousness in the city and throughout the nation. As seen from Boston's ethnic communities, a nation that was supposed to be culturally open and tolerant appeared ready to cut off immigrants and their children from the fruits of American society. Local politicians, led by James Michael Curley, easily grafted these perceptions—already framed by the conspiratorial theme in American reform rhetoric—onto the stalk of ethnic Progressivism.[26]

Though many of the cultural controversies of the 1920s were not altogether new, the rise of mass communications gave them an unprecedented immediacy. Negotiations at Versailles, the Palmer raids, speakeasies, gangster wars, and real and imagined Ku Klux Klan activities found their way into the increasingly sensation-minded urban daily press and, as the decade progressed, onto radio airwaves. While the Ku Klux Klan (KKK) made little headway in or near Boston, pictures of hooded Klansmen and "investigations" of Klan operations in Massachusetts nevertheless filled daily papers. Local radio covered the 1924 Democratic convention, which became embroiled in controversy over the formal condemnation of the KKK. These broadcasts included a description of the efforts of Charlestown delegate Thomas Green to wrest the state banner out of the hands of McAdoo backers and hold it for a procession supporting Irish hero Al Smith. Green's actions were greeted ecstatically in his home district not simply because he helped Smith but because a Charlestown man—and by extension, Charlestown itself—was playing an important role in national affairs. Such was the ability of the mass media to make distant controversies real at the local level.[27]

In other cases, national issues took on specifically local dimensions that reinforced existing perceptions of ethnic conflict. The Immigration Restriction League, an organization that spearheaded the drive for limitations on immigration that culminated in the 1920s, had originated in the 1890s with a small group of Boston Brahmins, including several figures active in municipal reform circles. The formation of the Loyal Coalition in 1920 by a group of old-stock civic leaders opposed to Irish independence helped make that issue even less distant for Irish Bostonians. Even the fear of radicals that broke out during 1919 had its own local manifestation, the Boston police strike. The strike, which unleashed several days of rioting in downtown Boston that required the mobilization of the National Guard to quell, pitted an Irish-dominated police force seeking affiliation with the AFL against the police commissioner, the mayor, and Governor Calvin Coolidge, all of whom were Yankees. Native-stock domination of the National Guard—the "Yankee Division"—and the temporary police force used to maintain order fueled the image of the strike as at least in part an ethnic conflict. The incident had several legacies, not the least of which was bringing Coolidge to national attention. It also confirmed the belief of many Anglo Americans that immigrants could never become law-abiding citizens, and highlighted the social and cultural hatred that was to course through the city's public life in the coming years.[28]

Charges that newer Americans were unfit for citizenship provoked angry, defensive responses from ethnic spokesmen in Boston. When one commentator suggested that the Irish were "incapable of assimilation," the editors of the *Charlestown News* responded forcefully, declaring of Irish Americans, "those we know seem to have assimilated all of the virtues and comparatively few of the vices of colonial New England." All Americans were pilgrims, the paper insisted, "whether we came here in 1620 or 1920." The *Jewish Advocate* editorialized repeatedly against immigration restriction and other Americanizing measures, arguing that "Jews have contributed immeasurably to the wealth, honor, and prestige of the United States." The *Italian News* made similar arguments, which it summed up by declaring: "there is considerable talk nowadays of 'Americanizing' the foreigner. WE think there is equal need of Americanizing some Americans."[29]

While historians have noted the connections between Progressive thought and the Americanizing drives of the 1920s, they have ignored the Progressive tone of the ethnic responses to these campaigns. Just as leaders of Boston's Irish and other ethnic communities saw their support for reform as a demonstration of their "civic patriotism," so did they vigorously assert their identity as loyal Americans during the debate over Americanization precipitated by the war and its aftermath. They often perceived the forces opposing their claims to full status as Americans in the same Progressive terms in which they viewed opponents of their claims to municipal leadership: as illegitimate interests conspiring against the people. The *Charlestown News* described the Anti-Saloon League, the driving force behind the passage and enforcement of Prohibition, as an "invisible government . . ., the most tremendous political machine ever known in the History of American Government . . . the purpose of which was and is to overawe and control Legislatures, Congress, public officials, and voting committees." The *Italian News* blamed Prohibition on the same "clique" that backed immigration restriction.[30]

The concordance between ethnic responses to the cultural controversies of the 1920s and ethnic Progressivism made these issues attractive political tools. As before, no local politician was better able to use national developments to local advantage than James Michael Curley. Although there was little evidence of its presence in and around Boston, Curley constantly invoked the specter of the Ku Klux Klan, that "monstrous spawn of ignorance, bigotry, greed, and deception." City papers filled with verbal sparring between Curley and Eugene Farnsworth, King Kleagle of the Maine Klan (apparently a more local foil was not available). At one point rumors spread that a Klan plot to kidnap the Curley children was afoot. During his unsuccessful 1924 gubernatorial bid, in the midst of the uproar at the national Democratic convention over the issue of condemning the KKK, he made the Klan issue a centerpiece of his campaign. He reputedly went so far as to stage a cross burning near a campaign stop to capitalize on the issue. He also launched frequent verbal attacks on the Loyal Coalition, linking its opposition to Irish independence with the Klan's agenda, and he continuously campaigned in Jewish and Italian neighborhoods against the passage of the immigration restriction laws.[31]

Curley wove these issues into the fabric of his attacks against his political opposition. He explicitly linked the members of the Boston Finance Commission, still outspoken critics of his administration, with the KKK: they were "pious humbugs, humorless hypocrites, fellows with Ku Klux Klan principles and yellow dog courage, patriots who obey orders and believe that servility is service and that the terms of democracy and depravity, Irish and iniquity are synonymous." He saved his harshest invective for the GGA. It was a "robust organization of pharisees" whose "sole concern [was] to keep down the tax rate by a spurious economy." Its only hope of success, "like that of the Ku Klux Klan," rested "in its ability to foment dissension, create quarrels, and divide the people of Boston." Curley used the Klan to foster the perception that Boston's politicized ethnic tensions were part of a larger, national cultural conflict. He also turned the GGA's principal criticism of him—that his politics were divisive—back at the Association's leaders, implying that he actually represented the cause of unity in city affairs while they were a cadre of nativists conspiring against the city's ethnic majority.[32]

Other politicians followed suit, none more noticeably than former district attorney Joseph Pelletier. A Catholic of Irish and French extraction, Pelletier had been among the most popular politicians in Boston since his election as district attorney in 1909. He was a leading figure in the local and national arms of the Knights of Columbus and other Catholic organizations, and the pope made him a knight of St. Gregory in 1920. His continual reelection was a foregone conclusion for more than a decade until the Watch and Ward Society, a Brahmin-tinged body dedicated to the regulation of public morals, accused Pelletier and Nathan Tufts, district attorney of neighboring Middlesex County, of taking bribes in exchange for halting prosecutions. After an investigation by the Boston Bar Association—another organization viewed as an elite enclave—the state's Supreme Judicial Court removed Pelletier from office and disbarred him in 1922. He vigorously countered the charges, using an abbreviated mayoral bid in

1921 and then staging an aggressive campaign to return to the district attorney's office. The terms in which Pelletier conducted those campaigns, and the level of support he received, testified to the continued power of political appeals combining ethnic antagonism and Progressive themes.[33]

Like Curley, Pelletier attacked "reformers" during his 1921 mayoral bid; but he did so in terms drawn from the language of ethnic Progressivism. He described his accusers as part of an "interlocking reform trust" that encompassed the Bar Association, the Good Government Association, the Union Club, and the Loyal Coalition—organizations dominated by members of Boston's Anglo elite. In one other instance he included the Ku Klux Klan in this cabal. The leaders of these groups, he warned, were "plotting to secure control of the political power of this city, in which many of them do not reside." At stake was the issue of "whether the classes or the masses shall rule." To be sure nobody missed the ethnic dimensions of these attacks, Pelletier declared the upcoming election a battle of the "new bloods" against the "blue bloods." Here was a full statement of the more aggressive strain of ethnic Progressivism that emerged in 1920s Boston: a charge that a small collection of elite Brahmin financiers and civic figures, many of whom had moved to the suburbs, had combined with nativist forces to undermine the political, civic, and cultural legitimacy of the "people" of Boston, defined in both class and ethnic terms. The threat was all the more alarming because it represented the local dimension of a national offensive against immigrant Americans.[34]

One measure of the power of this description was the strength of Pelletier's electoral support. He withdrew from the mayoral race in 1921 and endorsed Curley, leading to speculation that he was a stalking horse for the former mayor. Pelletier's long record of support for Curley lends credence to the theory, though no proof of it exists. His return to the stump in 1922 in a bid to regain the district attorney's office after his removal and disbarment testified to the power of his appeal, even in the face of strong evidence of his guilt. Citing the nativism and anti-Catholicism of his critics, a claim echoed by the Knights of Columbus, Pelletier continued to depict himself as the victim of a Brahmin conspiracy. Although the GGA and the Republican Party backed another Irish Democrat, Thomas C. O'Brien, partly to divide the Irish vote, Pelletier won more than 76,000 of the 177,000 votes cast. The large size of his vote—judged to be chiefly Irish Catholic—illustrated the political power of his Progressive-style appeal.[35]

Statistical analysis underscores how effectively both Pelletier and Curley used ethnic Progressivism to forge an Irish voting bloc. Table 9 presents the results of a regression equation measuring the relationship between voting levels for both men and the size of the Irish-stock and working-class populations in a ward. The high (and statistically significant) coefficients for the Irish variable indicate that both candidates attracted strong followings in Irish wards. Pelletier also appears to have attracted strong support in working-class districts. There is no evidence that Curley earned the same backing in those sections, probably because two of his three leading opponents came from Charlestown and South Boston, both neighborhoods with large blue-collar populations, and because Martin Lomasney's opposition cut into Curley's vote in ward five, the poorest section of the city.

These results are even more impressive because of the opposition the two men faced. Neither was simply the "Irish candidate." Two of Curley's three main rivals in 1921 were Irish Catholic, as was Pelletier's 1922 opponent. Nonetheless, Curley and Pelletier managed to unite Boston's Irish behind their candidacies by establishing themselves as spokesmen for a community victimized by a Brahmin conspiracy. It was the persuasiveness of the ethnic narrative they pre-

Table 9. Linear Regression Analysis of Irish and Working-Class Vote for Curley and Pelletier, 1921 and 1922

Election	Percent Irish	Percent working class	R^2
1921 Curley vote (mayor)	.61 (.17)[a]	.13 (.19)	.45
1922 Pelletier vote (district attorney)	.68 (.18)[a]	.63 (.20)[a]	.66

Standard error in parentheses.

a. Significant at $P < .05$ or better.

Sources: A sample drawn from the U.S. census manuscript, 1920, by James Connolly and Philip Ethington; Boston Board of Election Commissioners, *Annual Reports for 1921, 1922* (Boston, 1922, 1923).

Model: percentage 1921 mayoral vote for James Michael Curley = intercept + percent Irish stock + percent working class. Model statistics: intercept = .24; N = 26.

Model: percentage 1922 district attorney vote for Pelletier = intercept + percent Irish stock + percent working class. Model statistics: intercept =.01; N = 26.

Note: See Statistical Appendix for a discussion of the construction of variables.

sented, not simply the knee-jerk loyalty of Irish voters to one of their own, that earned them such strong support.

Informed by Progressivism and reinforced by the growth of national cultural issues, a vision of ethnic conflict now defined Boston's public life. Its power rendered impotent political action based on the premise of a civic unity that encompassed the whole city. Organizations such as the Citizens' Municipal League and the United Improvement Association either disbanded or lost much of the power and persuasiveness they had wielded before the war. The inability of women's groups to create an effective, gender-based politics after suffrage and the gradual faltering of the GGA reflected the diminishing possibilities for political movements cutting across lines of class and ethnicity. Not only were these efforts untenable, they became counterproductive in the conflict-laden political atmosphere of 1920s Boston.

One indication of the enduring power of ethnic Progressivism was the failure of suffragists to construct an effective, unified women's political organization after 1920. Though gender-based public activism never fully overcame ethnic and class boundaries in Progressive Era Boston, the drive for woman suffrage did win support from both middle-class Yankee women's groups and some working-class ethnic voices. But after the Nineteenth Amendment passed and efforts to secure the vote changed into attempts to use it, political action based on the assumption of a shared definition of the public interest among women proved ineffective.

Boston's leading proponent of united political action by women was the League of Women Voters (LWV), an outgrowth of the Boston Equal Suffrage Association for Good Government. The idea that women had a shared set of interests animated the League, much as it did other women's reform bodies during the Progressive Era. "The great majority of women desire such things as proper care and education of all children, the protection of women in industry, the promotion of social hygiene, and the removal of legal discriminations on account of sex," an early LWV report declared. Its political activism would be centered on (although not limited to) the pursuit of these goals and justified by the argument that it represented the nonpartisan voice of the city's women in the electoral arena.[36]

In attempting to establish itself as a nonpartisan force for reform, the Boston LWV followed the lead of the national League of Women

Voters, organizational heir to the National American Woman Suffrage Association. Hewing to the counsel of suffragist Carrie Chapman Catt, the national LWV worked to avoid controversial issues and concentrated on lobbying for reforms that would unite women. It also established a stance of strict nonpartisanship, in the hopes of winning support from a broad cross section of the new female electorate and establishing itself as the voice of women in politics.[37]

Although cautious at the start, the Boston LWV quickly injected itself into many aspects of local affairs. As a self-declared reform group, it staunchly opposed a 1920 effort to revamp the city charter by restoring "the old district method of electing members of the City Council" as well as a measure to legalize 2.75 percent beer. The following year the LWV dispatched a delegation to observe a City Council session, to better acquaint itself with the workings of city government. It also submitted questionnaires to each municipal candidate. Many of the questions focused on moral and social reform issues, ranging from workers' pensions to the regulation of dance halls. The League also called for improvements in municipal budgeting, an open bidding process for city contracts, and the retention of competent city employees. In supporting these measures, it strove to define Boston's women voters as a strong force for all aspects of reform and to establish itself as their organizational embodiment.[38]

When the League decided to endorse candidates, it did so warily, careful not to jeopardize its standing as the nonpartisan voice of Boston women. In its first year of existence, it refused to officially support any candidates at all. But the following year the League decided that it could express its views on city elections, since they were nonpartisan affairs. Even then, the League would only offer its endorsement to those candidates who had earned at least two-thirds of the votes of the ninety-member Municipal Affairs Committee, which included delegates from every ward (as well as a handful from outside the city).[39]

After several weeks of intense lobbying by Curley and John R. Murphy, the two leading candidates, the League's Municipal Affairs Committee chose the GGA-backed Murphy. Committee members based their decision on reform principles. The issue, a League statement announced, was "clean, decent city government and the return of the spoilsmen to office." In this context, their choice was clear. Murphy represented clean politics and good government, Curley embodied corruption. Electing Murphy would make Boston's city government "our pride instead of our shame."[40]

The League stressed that its choice represented the will of Boston women as a whole. It billed its endorsement of Murphy as "the official support of the Hub's feminine electorate." Confident of that assertion, Hilda Quirk, a member of both the League and the GGA, declared shortly before the election that "women are lined up against Mr. Curley in the ratio of five to one."[41]

Curley's long record of support for many of the social reforms advocated by women reformers and for woman suffrage made the decision to oppose him politically risky. During his first term he had endorsed mothers' pensions and the restriction of child labor, reforms strongly backed by many women's reform groups. He also cooperated with the Women's Municipal League in their municipal housekeeping endeavors, winning praise from that middle-class body for his assistance. And when a nonbinding referendum on the question of woman suffrage appeared on the Massachusetts ballot in 1915, Curley aggressively supported it, borrowing from women activists the argument that female voters would more strongly support the welfare policies he advocated.[42]

The presence of Curley in the race and his record of support for women's causes made it impossible to maintain the facade of feminine unity constructed by the League. Several Irish members, led by Carrie F. Sheehan, a self-described suffragist from Charlestown, bolted when the decision to back Murphy was made. In a public letter Sheehan attacked the League's selection process, pointing to the presence of women from upper-middle-class suburbs such as Brookline, Cambridge, Newton, Milton, and Winthrop on the Municipal Affairs Committee. She also decried the participation of John R. Murphy's wife, who voted to endorse her husband in what Sheehan claimed was her first-ever "suffragette meeting." Sheehan held that the LWV's decision was even more indefensible in light of Curley's record in support of woman suffrage. Boston women had been told, in effect, "we must forget the man who did more than any other man in the state for us, and as Mayor of Boston, spoke for us on every occasion where we needed help."[43]

Curley and his supporters also linked the League with the GGA, which by now was widely considered the tool of Boston's Brahmin elite. The presence of Hilda Quirk on the executive committees of both organizations heightened these suspicions. (She was appointed to the GGA board in 1921.) Carrie Sheehan gave credence to these accusations when she revealed that the League had relied on GGA research in making its decision. The GGA, she charged, was "most unfair and [was] raising a campaign fund for John R. Murphy," and she accused the LWV of allowing the Association to make the League's decision instead of democratically consulting the women of Boston.[44]

These accusations gave politicians ammunition to mobilize women along ethnic lines. Joseph Pelletier used the issue of the League's ties to the GGA before withdrawing from the mayoral race. He angered the League by posting a "Pelletier's Women's Voter League" sign outside his headquarters. When the League of Women Voters complained that this was misleading, he shot back, "I would no sooner think of trying to give the impression that I had secured the indorsement [*sic*] of the Boston League of Women Voters than I would that of the Good Government Association, of which your organization is generally recognized as an auxiliary." Leaving such blunt attacks to Pelletier, Curley aimed his appeals at Irish women. While his wife asked for the support of women voters on the basis of her husband's warmheartedness, Curley urged "Irish-American women" to register and vote to counteract the forty thousand women registered by the GGA. His appeal was a direct challenge to the LWV's claim for the political commonality of Boston women, regardless of social background.[45]

In the wake of Curley's 1921 victory, the League's credibility diminished. While the city did not keep records of how women voted, it seems clear that neither Curley nor Murphy won over a large majority of the female electorate.[46] More significantly, the LWV's claim that it spoke for Boston women collapsed. In the years following 1921, its political power in Boston was sharply limited by the popular perception that it worked solely in the interests of the city's wealthy Brahmin elite. It would remain on the scene but tread much more cautiously. The restructured social character of the city's public life, with an organizing theme of ethnic conflict, precluded the mobilization of women on the basis of their supposedly shared interests. This was not the only reason for the failure of the LWV to create a women's politics in Boston, but it was an essential one.[47]

The same circumstances that crippled the League of Women Voters' vision of gender solidarity limited the efficacy of nonelectoral political action by women's groups. The Women's Municipal League, the prime exponent of municipal housekeeping in Boston, also had little success navigating the shoals of Boston's ethnic politics. The exigencies of wartime had momentarily enhanced its prestige, as the WML took the lead in endeavors to conserve food and Americanize immigrants. But in the wake of the war, economic hardship and the unraveling of the Progressive fiction of a single public interest made implausible its status as a representative of all of Boston's women. Its membership drives fizzled, and its headquarters closed in the early 1920s; by 1922 it had begun "a policy of retrenchment." It remained a far more significant presence in suburban neighborhoods such as Jamaica Plain than in the ethnic neighborhoods of South Boston and Charlestown. Although the WML continued to be part of Boston's public scene for several decades, it became the politically insignificant preserve of a handful of upper-middle-class, mostly suburban, women.[48]

The inability of the Women's Municipal League and the League of Women Voters to overcome ethnic and class boundaries did not mean that immigrant-stock women were politically inert. Throughout the city, they engaged in political action that combined gender roles with neighborhood and ethnic identities. The women of East Boston's ward one formed a Women's Improvement Association in 1921 to lobby on behalf of their district. When the Boston Elevated threatened to shut down a streetcar line to East Boston in 1923, five hundred women from the neighborhood organized a mass protest and marched to the offices of the Elevated trustees, where they demanded (and obtained) a continuance of the service. Angered by the imminent passage of immigration restriction laws, a dozen Italian women's groups combined to form the "Circoli Femminili," devoted to opposing such legislation. Jewish women also developed numerous organizations, many of which were affiliated with the Council of Jewish Women, an umbrella group belonging to the General Federation of Women's Clubs.[49]

Irish-Catholic women also engaged in political activism. The League of Catholic Women continued to operate along separate but parallel lines from the WML, pursuing various social reforms designed to extend women's roles into public life. By 1920 it had committees devoted to immigration, legislation, charities, civic welfare, social welfare, the Red Cross, girls' clubs, and home economics. During World War I its members participated in preparedness and Americanization campaigns, often in conjunction with secular groups. Although its ecclesiastical ties limited some of its efforts, the League supported restrictions on child labor, even in the face of William Cardinal O'Connell's demand that Catholics oppose such a measure—a stand that even Curley was afraid to take.[50]

Underlying these efforts was a continued emphasis on female solidarity that echoed the ideals of the Women's Municipal League and other municipal housekeeping organizations. A 1920 account of the LCW described it as "the material expression of an ever deepening movement among our women for unity," language that could easily have been found in the literature of any number of secular groups. But the phrase "our women" meant Boston Catholics, which in practice usually meant Irish Catholics. The rhetoric of unity that suffused women's activism in Progressive Era Boston persisted, but with multiple meanings in the postwar context.[51]

Unlike the WML, the LCW's frankly group-oriented version of women's activism made it increasingly popular during the 1920s. Its membership rose above ten thousand, and the number of local societies affiliated with it increased to more than eighty. Its affiliates included clubs and parish guilds throughout the city and surrounding communities, including several active groups in Charlestown and South Boston. It purchased new headquarters in downtown Boston, its lectures attracted standing-room-only crowds, and it soon began producing radio broadcasts. The League's membership would continue to grow, reaching over more than forty thousand by the 1940s.[52]

With numbers came influence. "Our organization is recognized as the leading moral force in the community," a history of the League's first fifteen years bragged. "There is not a committee of importance in the city or state for which the services of the President of our League are not sought officially by the Governor or Mayor." Though hyperbolic, boasts of this sort had some truth. By the mid-1920s the LCW's president was a member of fourteen commissions and committees "doing public service for the people of the city and the state," and the League had become a force to be reckoned with on such legislative issues as child labor, health reform, and prison policy.[53]

The LCW's popularity, the WML's decline, and the LWV's troubles together reflect the character of public life in post–World War I Boston. Institutions predicated solely on female unity failed, while institutions that allowed women to act as members of ethnic and religious groups and neighborhoods prospered. In a political culture based increasingly on ethnic identification and conflict, this was only to be expected.

The most obvious measure of the changed nature of Boston's public sphere was the fate of the GGA. The vision of a single public interest remained the cornerstone of its political faith through the 1920s. It continued to endorse candidates for the City Council and for mayor based on the issues of fiscal responsibility and public honesty that had shaped its activities since 1903. "In all its work, the association has recognized as a fundamental principle that the citizens must not be divided into groups, but there must be unity of citizenship," it declared in a statement welcoming women members after the passage of the Nineteenth Amendment. "The association steadily opposed any appeal either to race or to religion. It now seeks the application of the same fundamental principle to the question of sex." But the efficacy of this ideal, so powerful in the prewar years, faded in the 1920s and with it went what was left of the GGA's public prestige.[54]

The Association's power declined because it lost the battle to define the city in its terms. Instead, the vision of ethnic conflict articulated by its opponents, particularly James Michael Curley, governed Boston politics. The effectiveness with which Curley and other politicians used Progressivism to frame popular perceptions of the city's public life as a contest between Yankee and immigrant, and especially between Yankee and Irish, fixed the GGA on one side of that divide. "Presumably the GGA connotes in too many Boston minds the Back Bay, evening dress, Rolls Royces and 'the interests,'" the *New York Times* observed perceptively after Curley's 1921 victory over the Association-backed Murphy. "If the Irishmen get together on this proposition of electing a mayor," the *South Boston Gazette* declared just before the same election, "the GGA will be snowed under as usual." Such statements reflected the new perception of the city's politics: the Irish on one side, the Brahmin-run GGA on the other.[55]

The *Gazette* continued to see "the GGA's ideas" conflicting with "the people's interests." The Association and its leaders remained the tool of "the selfish interests that are successful in controlling a certain number of votes in the city." This illicit power translated into electoral victories, which meant that "the people of the whole city suffer while those selfish interests are carefully guarded in the years to follow." The continued prevalence of this Progressive discourse of public versus private interests, its ethnic connotations, and the popular response to it handcuffed the GGA and eroded its political power.[56]

In one instance the Association was compelled to deny charges that it was connected with the Ku Klux Klan. The GGA vigorously rebutted the charge, insisting that it had "no sympathy" with the Klan or any other organization "based upon racial and religious bigotry which attempt to substitute private vengeance and terrorism for the operation of public opinion." Although such accusations were preposterous and it is unlikely that many voters believed them, they had symbolic force. The GGA found it necessary to counter them publicly, an indication of how effectively Curley, Pelletier, and others portrayed the elite reform body as an antiethnic organization.[57]

By the early 1920s, the GGA clearly recognized the effect of the attacks against it. When it resumed publishing *City Affairs* in 1922 after a hiatus prompted by World War I, the Association's rhetoric had grown more defensive. "At the outset we want to re-state the purposes of our organization, for we have attained the enviable position of being bitterly and persistently misrepresented," the first issue complained. Repeated charges that its leaders were wealthy suburbanites—a claim with ethnic connotations itself—forced the GGA to insist that all of its members were "bona fide legal residents of Boston." By this time the GGA admitted that its governing ideal of civic unity was not easily achieved: "It is very hard in a great cosmopolitan community such as this for men and women to forget race, religion, party, the distinction of wealth, social position, and geographical situation of residence."[58]

GGA head George Nutter was even blunter in private, acknowledging that the Association had lost the battle for public opinion. "The psychological argument that we are a small body has been . . . dwelt on for all these years and has produced an effect," Nutter noted after John R. Murphy's failure in 1921. "It was not Murphy endorsed by the GGA; it was the GGA running Murphy." The solid defeat of two of its three candidates for City Council in the fall of 1922 only further underscored the hostile public climate in which the GGA was now operating. If it was to remain a viable political force, the Association would have to rehabilitate its image enough to attract a larger share of the city's ethnic vote, something it had been able to do before the war.[59]

As a step in this direction, the Association moved to diversify the makeup of its executive committee. It added two women to the committee after the enactment of woman suffrage. One was Mrs. Robert Homan, the former Abigail Adams, sister of Charles F. and Henry Adams and a descendant of two presidents. The Association chose her to represent the "Back Bay element." To balance this quintessentially Brahmin selection, the GGA also chose Hilda H. Quirk, an active suffragist and the wife of a prominent Irish-American lawyer. But Quirk now resided in the suburbs (as did many GGA officials by this time, despite the Association's claims to the contrary). Though anxious to appear inclusive, the Association apparently was unable to find a suitable Irish woman residing within Boston's city limits.[60]

As popular disapproval of the GGA became more evident, Association leaders also began to recruit ethnic men for the executive committee. In 1923 they induced Jewish civic leader Abraham Pinanski to sign on, and after a long search they finally found two acceptable Irishmen, Theodore Kelley and Dr. Thomas Giblin, who were willing to work with the GGA. The hope was that the announcement of these additions to the executive committee would have "a dramatic effect" in restoring the Association's credibility. The diversification strategy did give the GGA some rhetorical ammunition. When it was accused of cavorting with the Ku Klux Klan, the Association pointed to the presence of representatives of "each of the three leading religious groups in Boston as well as several different races" on its executive committee as proof of its broad-mindedness. But there were limits to how far GGA leaders would go in accommodating public opinion. A 1923 proposal that all but the three most recent appointees resign and turn over control of the organization to its new ethnic leaders was emphatically rejected. "To hand the GGA over to a young, unknown man, that man an Irishman, would be to commit political suicide," an agitated George Nutter declared after the meeting at which the idea was discussed.[61]

Instead of suicide, the GGA opted for a slow death. Their limited attempt to broaden the ethnic composition of the executive committee fell victim—and with it the Association itself—to the ethnic polarization of city politics. In 1925 the Association refused to back any of the three Irish candidates and instead endorsed Yankee Republican Malcolm Nichols. Its two Irish leaders resigned, claiming that the issue had been "decided from the beginning" and that no Irish candidate was even considered. The resignation of Kelley and Giblin and their public statements confirmed the popular perception that the Association was the tool of a handful of Brahmins and was implacably hostile to Irish Boston. Although it persisted into the 1930s and even endorsed an Irish candidate for mayor in 1929, the GGA thereafter wielded relatively little influence on city affairs.[62]

Another measure of the declining power of the GGA and its ideals was a drive to amend the city charter. In 1923 the state legislature appointed a committee to reconsider the arrangements for electing the City Council, in response to complaints from groups and locales that had been unable to earn representation under the at-large system. The committee presented a choice to the public in 1924 in the form of a referendum: either a return to a ward-based system, or a borough plan in which the city would be divided into five boroughs, each allotted three seats in the City Council.[63]

The ward-based plan, which the Charter Association warned would "restore power once more to the local bosses and invisible government," won by nearly 5,000 votes out of 107,864 cast. The key to its success was the overwhelming support it received in central city districts, where it captured more than 64 percent of the vote. The borough plan won in middle-class suburban wards, but not by enough to offset the large margins favoring the ward-based system downtown and in such ethnic districts as Charlestown and South Boston. Perhaps even more significantly, more than half the voters left their ballots blank on this question. In 1909 only 7.4 percent of the electorate failed to cast a vote for or against charter reform; when the issue arose again in 1914, less than 11 percent of those voting took no position. Structural reform no longer sparked the same popular fervor in the postwar period.[64]

Even the GGA's alternative proposal implicitly abandoned the reform ideals that had informed its activities for almost a quarter of a century. George Nutter, who served on the state-appointed committee that reconsidered the city's governmental arrangements, and other GGA members advocated a proportional representation scheme. This allowed voters to cast more than one vote for a single candidate, thus increasing the chances of minority groups to win representation. That process, as Nutter privately admitted, would give the GGA a better chance of electing its endorsees to the City Council. Though rejected, the significance of this plan lay in what it said about its GGA proponents. By presenting a proposal designed to ensure minority representation, the GGA was directly acknowledging that such groups existed in the municipal body politic, a dramatic change from its traditional contention that only one uniform public interest existed within the city. The GGA was even forced to admit, if only privately, that it represented one of those minority groups. That recognition reflected the triumph of the ethnic Progressive vision over the GGA's interpretation of reform.

In truth, there was little the GGA could have done to save itself or its reform vision. It was less the victim of its own actions than of the rhetorical tour de force achieved by James Michael Curley and the local politicians who followed in his footsteps. They succeeded in creating and then solidifying a representation of the city's public life as ethnic conflict. Ironically, they did so through the language of Progressivism—the same vocabulary the GGA itself used. But while the GGA saw a handful of greedy Irish politicians conspiring to wrest control of the city from its essentially honest, though deceived, citizenry, Curley described a handful of Brahmin financiers clinging to power and scheming against the interests of the city's ethnic majority. Curley's depiction, aided by cultural and demographic trends, triumphed. Even when all but a small remnant of Yankee Boston had fled to the suburbs, and Boston politics was almost entirely an intra-Irish struggle, the image of a Brahmin elite striving to limit the authority of immigrants and their descendants would remain a powerful rhetorical device in the city's politics.

The sense of group conflict that shaped public life in 1920s Boston was unprecedented. Ethnic tension itself was of course not new. And hostility to the politically dominant Irish from other immigrant groups was certainly present. But the view that a handful of Brahmins controlled power in the city at the expense of the immigrant majority, of which the Irish were the principal element, now defined public life as never before. Every form of political action, from voting to organizing an interest group, derived its meaning in that context, whether the protagonists wished it to or not. Even purportedly apolitical organizations like the Boston Bar Association could not avoid ethnic labels when they ventured into public affairs.[65] The pretense of a unified community, which had shaped the character of the city's public life for three-quarters of a century, no longer prevailed.

Ironically, the triumph of ethnic conflict in Boston represented the culmination of Progressivism, not a reaction against it. More specifically, it marked the victory of a particular reform vision: ethnic Progressivism's portrayal of Boston as a battleground between elite Brahmin business interests and an immigrant people. To be sure, social practices, demographic patterns, and cultural differences also fueled ethnic antagonism in Boston. But it was the institutional changes and innovations in public discourse of the Progressive Era that made intergroup hostility the defining element in Bostonians' understanding of themselves and their city.

Viewed in these terms, as a source of the pluralism that has defined so much of modern urban politics, the historical significance of Progressivism merits reconsideration. We think of the Progressive Era as the starting point for much of our modern public life: mass mobilization, interest group politics, partisan decline, an expanding state. This transformation is presumed to have eclipsed an older, more tribal and localistic political order. But at least in the case of Boston, modern politics, ushered in by Progressivism, redefined and intensified ethnic identification and antagonism. By simultaneously providing a language of group identity and communal unity, and by creating an institutional environment in which that rhetoric flourished, the drive to consolidate social and political power multiplied the bases of political action. In Boston, it made ethnicity the keystone of local public life.

Epilogue

The legacies of Boston's ethnic Progressivism stretched well into the twentieth century. Institutional arrangements forged during the Progressive Era changed little after 1925, and a narrative of cultural conflict continued to define group identities within local public life. The political reconstruction of the city's social history had broader repercussions as well. Representations of Boston as a city where twentieth-century conflicts grew out of nineteenth-century social changes became a cornerstone in the foundation of urban political history. Thus a reconception of Boston's ethnic past challenges the prevailing scholarly understanding of public life in modern American cities.

Politics in 1920s Boston more clearly resembled late-twentieth-century American political culture than the partisan world of the 1890s. The demise of ward organizations and the rise of new kinds of campaigning left some observers longing for the past. "Charlestown has always been a hotbed of politics, yet somehow or other the old enthusiasm, the red fire, the torchlight parades of other days are strangely missing," lamented the *Charlestown News* in 1926. "The old ward room" had become "a lonely relic of other times and other customs." In place of those traditions, new forms had arisen: "Politics today is a business proposition," the paper declared; "it has been caught up in the rush of the times. Advertising, propaganda, radio, the house-to-house canvass, and the entrance of women in the political arena have changed all those things that intrigued the old timer and have stamped the aspect of modern efficiency upon politics as it is played today."[1]

Unlike the turn of the century, candidates now mattered more than parties. "The only political organizations in Boston," the *News* noted in 1927, "are one-man organizations without a semblance of party responsibility." In South Boston, the *Gazette* described the "building up" of organizations by prospective candidates before the 1924 primaries, each devoted to the fortunes of a single office seeker rather than the party as a whole. Unlike the factions competing for control of ward committees a generation earlier, these candidate-centered groups did not battle over party resources. They sought only to promote the fortunes of one man in one election and usually disbanded after the votes were counted.[2]

Local ward organization became increasingly irrelevant amid this atomistic politics. When local Democratic Party leaders issued a call to "hundreds of prominent South Boston citizens" to organize a registration drive in 1923, only forty people bothered to show up, and there were never more than eighteen in the room at any one time. "The meeting was a sad pathetic failure," the *South Boston Gazette* reported. The only person pleased by the low turnout was the municipal building janitor, who noted that Democratic Party meetings had once added greatly to his labors but now barely inconvenienced him. In 1928, the year Al Smith's presidential campaign raised political enthusiasm in Boston to an unprecedented pitch, only nine of Boston's twenty-two wards featured contests to control the Democratic ward committee.[3]

Nowhere were the changes in grassroots politics more evident than in the response of the Boston Democracy to Smith's White House bid. No other city—not even New York—greeted his candidacy as enthusiastically as Boston did. The aspirations that Smith embodied on the national level precisely paralleled the civic hopes that Boston's ethnic Progressivism expressed. The son of immigrants, product of Tammany Hall, and Progressive governor of New York, Smith represented the best that immigrant America—especially its Irish element— could offer. If he were to win the presidency in the face of vehement anti-Catholic, anti-immigrant opposition, it would mark the full acceptance of immigrants generally, and the Irish particularly, into American society. Smith's candidacy, James Michael Curley declared, was "an acid test of our right to the title American citizen."[4]

Politicians anxious to associate themselves with Smith's historic bid rushed to support him, setting off a scramble that underscored the absence of a cohesive Democratic organization in Boston. When state party leaders excluded him from the "Boston Smith Campaign Executive Committee," Curley announced the formation of his own "Smith volunteers." He rented a headquarters in a downtown hotel, where he staged noontime rallies each day, distributed Smith literature, and registered voters. When Smith came to Boston in October, Curley was at his side for nearly all of the forty-eight-hour visit, basking in the reflected glory of the first Irish Catholic to be nominated for president by a major party. Not to be outdone, Curley rival Theodore Glynn created a third campaign organization, the "Smith Flying Wedge," while former Mayor Andrew Peters headed a fourth Democratic group, the "Smith Campaign Advisory Committee."[5]

In the absence of a coherent partisan movement for Smith, alternative categories of political mobilization became more important. Instead of pursuing the votes of Democrats through a Democratic organization, Smith's Massachusetts backers sought the support of various immigrant groups and neighborhoods. The official campaign organization in the North End was an "Italians for Smith" club, not the local Democratic ward committee. Enterprising civic and political leaders formed similar bodies throughout the city, based on ethnic and neighborhood loyalties rather than party allegiances. The leaders of these organizations saw Smith's campaign as a vehicle for the recognition of their constituency and for themselves as spokesmen for that group.[6]

The institutional character of Boston politics changed little over the next half century. Charter reforms in 1924 and 1949 failed to restore party organizations to the preeminent place they once held in local public life. The 1924 revision provided for ward-based elections but kept them nonpartisan. It also reduced the number of signatures required for a place on the ballot to one hundred, a clause that encouraged large numbers of candidacies while making elaborate grassroots organizations even less necessary. Voters approved a return to a nine-member, at-large City Council in 1949 while maintaining the nonpartisan clause first introduced in 1909, a system that left no room for a cohesive party apparatus at the municipal level.[7]

Nor did national political developments during the mid–twentieth century alter Boston public life dramatically. The depression and the

New Deal did not create a shift to political divisions predicated on ideology or social class. Federal programs and policies were implemented by local leaders, who directed benefits to their own constituencies while depriving others. James Michael Curley was prescient enough to endorse Roosevelt's presidential candidacy while the rest of the state's Democratic leaders were still backing Smith, thus earning him control of a large share of New Deal patronage. Curley also capitalized on his reputation as a friend to the poor during the depression to win reelection to the mayor's office in 1929 and to capture the governor's office in 1934, where he advocated New Deal–style welfare programs. But while he pushed for relief, he continued to frame the delivery of social services in the context of ethnic conflict.[8]

The international issues of the 1930s and 1940s also reinforced the proclivity of the Boston Irish to see themselves as an embattled minority. Reports on the oppression of Catholics in Mexico and Spain, the anticommunist, anti-Semitic rhetoric of the enormously popular radio priest Charles Coughlin, and an Anglophobic isolationism contributed to the perception that Catholics throughout the world were being persecuted in ways that paralleled the fate of Boston's Irish. Local politicians drew regularly on this material (the Boston City Council often seemed to be a forum for discussing the fate of Catholics around the globe), using it as a tool to reinforce the siege mentality that Progressivism had encouraged in Irish Boston.[9]

Continuing political cultivation of ethnic grievances had clear consequences for race relations in the city during the second half of the twentieth century. When the migration of large numbers of African Americans to Boston after World War II pushed the question of racial discrimination to the fore, the city's Irish leaders refused to address it. South Boston City Councilman Michael Kinsella summed up the prevailing view in 1943 when he insisted that the Irish rather than blacks were the true "minority race" in Boston. This perception would persist, blinding the city's Irish majority to the racial difficulties that emerged in the postwar era. When tensions finally boiled over a generation later, the inability of Irish Boston to imagine the issue of school desegregation as anything but a challenge to its social and political power contributed significantly to the violence that broke out.[10]

The ethnic mythology forged in Progressive Era Boston especially flourished during the 1950s. To nobody's surprise, an aging James Michael Curley played a central role in cultivating the legend. In his ghostwritten autobiography, *I'd Do It Again,* Curley summed up Boston's ethnic history and his place within it. He was "the tribal chieftain who led the invading Irish" in their battle against "State Street carpetbaggers and Boston Bourbons"—"Brahmins" for short. They were "the Back Bay and Beacon Hill Hatfields who, around the turn of the century, became embroiled in a picturesque struggle with the Irish McCoys." Boston's Brahmins, Curley went on to explain triumphantly, "were and are . . . the top, homogenized members of the Yankee overlords who, after repelling the British twice, during the Revolution and the War of 1812, were conquered by a horde of invading Irish." The author, of course, took credit for the victory.[11]

Curley wrote his autobiography to cash in on the popularity of a fictional portrayal of Boston politics. Edwin O'Connor's 1956 novel *The Last Hurrah,* the story of the final campaign of Frank Skeffington (a character modeled on Curley) in a city (clearly Boston) where long-standing Irish-Yankee hatred defined the public landscape, offered a romanticized, nostalgic view of urban politics. The plot centered around the observations of Skeffington's naive nephew, who spends the campaign traveling around the city with his uncle, where he enjoys a firsthand view of a fading political era of backroom deals, Irish wakes, and ethnic feuding. The popularity of the novel, followed by a movie version directed by John Ford and starring Spencer Tracy, enshrined both the image of Boston as a city torn by tribal hatreds and the caricature of ethnic politicians as benevolent rogues in American popular culture.

O'Connor's version of city politics neatly paralleled academic writing on the subject during the 1950s. *The Last Hurrah's* explanation of Frank Skeffington's demise even earned "thesis" status among scholars analyzing the rise and fall of machine politics. The novel explained the declining political popularity of Skeffington as the by-product of an increasingly active welfare state, which provided many of the services once delivered by local politicians. O'Connor's plot device soon earned scholarly adherents, who shared both its assumptions about urban public life in the early twentieth century and its view of the relationship between machine politics and Franklin Roosevelt's New Deal. Even critics of the "*Last Hurrah* thesis" have usually accepted the notion that urban politicians prospered during the early twentieth century because they provided needed help to their immigrant constituents.[12]

As in so many cases, scholars wrote this history to suit a particular intellectual agenda. In the midst of the cold war and in the wake of World War II, many writers and academics sought to distinguish American public life from both communism and fascism. Criticizing what they saw as overly ideological, irrational protest movements—a category that included Populism, Progressivism, and especially McCarthyism—they identified moderation and pragmatism as the defining characteristics of American politics. The New Deal, from their perspective, embodied these qualities and represented the best of American politics.[13]

For this interpretation to work, Roosevelt and his policies had to be uncoupled from earlier reform movements. Most accounts of the time made the New Deal the culmination of a reform tradition that began with Populism and continued through Progressivism. In order to divorce Roosevelt and his program from this history, a new one needed to be created. A number of historians began to invent a more usable past, as Terrence McDonald has persuasively shown, by making an argument similar to the one O'Connor's novel made: that the New Deal had grown out of the political practices of urban bosses. In the process of making this argument, these historians offered a reinterpretation of big-city politics that became the dominant view for at least two generations of scholarship.

At the center of this revisionist thrust was Richard Hofstadter, whose *The Age of Reform* provided the framework for the recasting of modern American political history. Published in 1956 (the same year as *The Last Hurrah*), Hofstadter's book offered a sweeping account of American reform movements from the 1890s through the 1930s. While carefully differentiating between Populism, which he saw as the last gasp of an agrarian tradition, and Progressivism, which he presented as the movement of a middle class worried about its declining status, Hofstadter nevertheless linked them together. Both represented irrational, impractical responses to the emergence of a modern, industrial society.[14]

An essential part of this reinterpretation considered the nature of urban politics during the Progressive Era. Hofstadter turned the prevailing view of the time, which depicted corrupt bosses battling honest, public-spirited reformers, on its head. Following the lead of sociologist Robert Merton, who argued that ward bosses prospered because they performed "latent functions," Hofstadter presented the machine politician as a modern version of the feudal lord, earning the political fealty of an urban peasantry by delivering much-needed assistance in a humane, personal manner. Urban progressive reformers, on the other hand, emerged from the pages of *The Age of Reform* as overly moralistic, intolerant middle-class Yankees seeking to impose their beliefs on reluctant immigrants. Progressive Era urban politics thus became, at bottom, a clash of cultures.[15]

Defining Progressivism as the expression of a particular social group obscured its connections to ethnic activism. As products of a "peasant environment," immigrants and their offspring were inherently hostile to the Yankee middle-class ideology of Progressive reform, according to Hofstadter. Citing their "loyalty to the bosses," he described urban ethnics as "a potent mass that limited the range and achievements of Progressivism." The cultural gap between the two was just too large to overcome. "The typical immigrant and the typical Progressive were immensely different," Hofstadter proclaimed, in a sentence that made "immigrant" a virtual antonym for "Progressive."[16]

Hofstadter's version of early-twentieth-century city politics prevailed, accepted even by those who dissented from his broader interpretation of American political history. The linkage of Progressive reform and a native-born middle class became an accepted fact, running through a wide range of historical writing. Even those who reject the dichotomy made popular by Hofstadter remain reluctant to acknowledge the explicitly ethnic dimensions of Progressivism, choosing labels such as "urban liberalism" or "municipal populism" to differentiate the reform activism of immigrant groups from honest-to-goodness Progressivism.[17]

The roots of this perspective reach partially into earlier scholarship on Boston. Hofstadter's conception of immigrant politics drew explicitly from Oscar Handlin's synthesis of American immigration history, *The Uprooted,* as Terrence McDonald has noted. In many respects, *The Uprooted* represented a broader, vaguer statement of the arguments advanced in *Boston's Immigrants,* Handlin's earlier, more concrete study of the immigration process in one city. The chiefly Irish immigrants who came to Boston in the nineteenth century were peasants torn from a premodern society, according to Handlin. Their arrival disrupted and reshaped the city's social and political development. Even when a degree of cooperation and harmony emerged late in the century, it represented only an "appearance of group stability" that masked the deeper "underlying conflicts" between immigrant and Yankee that would inevitably reemerge. Handlin's depiction of nineteenth- and twentieth-century urban public life astride an ethnic fault line, incorporated into Hofstadter's work, thus seeped into the broader scholarship on urban politics.[18]

This characterization is inadequate, both for Boston and for city politics in the Progressive Era more generally. As this study has shown, the reduction of urban public life to a cultural clash between a "boss-immigrant-machine complex" and an Anglo-middle-class Progressive ethos conceals far more than it illuminates. Progressivism was far too open and complex a phenomenon to be pigeonholed as the expression of a specific group, and the nature of ethnic identity is much too malleable to accept it simply as a fixed source of political action. A full urban political history of the twentieth-century United States must examine the interplay among Progressive rhetoric, narratives of social identity, and the institutional environment in which they operated.

A more dynamic approach to urban political history can also shed new light on the ethnic and racial clashes that have dominated big-city public culture in recent decades. Instead of assuming that all urban politics was nonideological machine politics, historians and political scientists need to reconstruct the institutions, languages, and practices through which past public action took place. Putting politics, broadly but precisely conceived, at the heart of studies of group formation and conflict allows scholars to escape the determinism that has sometimes blinded past scholarship to the social consequences of political development. From this angle of vision, considerable variation will emerge among cities. But a fuller understanding of these differences is required before a clearer picture of the common processes that defined the social and political life of urban America in the twentieth century can emerge.

Boston's experience may not have been representative, but the patterns that emerged there were not entirely unique either. The growth of a politics that emphasized group identification in place of partisanship has occurred in almost every urban setting over the course of the twentieth century. Declining voter turnout, weaker partisanship, a proliferation of ethnic- and community-based interest groups, candidate-centered elections, and an emphasis on racial and ethnic conflict have become staples of municipal public life in the United States. The manner in which this process has unfolded in various communities has had a powerful effect on the shape and character of group relations in those settings.

Chicago's experience offers a useful comparison. Its political development unfolded much differently than Boston's, with distinctive social consequences. Unlike Boston, the various interpretations of Progressivism active in Chicago never coalesced enough to alter the city's institutional structure. Charter reform failed when ethnic interest groups, under the auspices of the United Societies for Local Self-Government, balked at provisions in the new city charter designed to limit liquor licenses, while women reformers rebelled against the absence of a woman suffrage clause. The proreform coalition fractured before significant institutional alterations could be made in the city's government and politics.[19]

As a result, Chicago maintained a ward-based, partisan-dominated politics long after Boston's political culture had changed dramatically. Instead of an ethnically charged public life dominated by the charismatic James Michael Curley, Chicagoans got the Cook County Democratic machine and the bureaucratic boss Richard Daley. Intergroup tensions persisted in Chicago, but the cooperation necessary to maintain organizational effectiveness encouraged a degree of ethnic and racial cooperation—if not social justice—that benefited many, including some leaders of the steadily expanding African American community in Chicago.[20]

When the Cook County machine began to give way to new forms of political action based on group grievances, intergroup cooperation diminished as well. Inspired by the civil rights movement and angered by the racial inequities of the city, many African Americans abandoned the Democratic organization for extrapartisan communal groups that aimed to reshape the city's social and political character. Many whites responded by organizing similar groups to defend themselves and their communities against what they saw as threats to their interests. No longer channeled into partisan categories, political action increasingly revolved around racial and neighborhood identities, a process that made group conflict a greater force in the city's politics.[21]

Changes in public life deserve attention when considering the racial politics of New York City as well. The city's public life has featured cycles of reform and "machine" regimes through much of the twentieth century. African-American political activism has run along similar lines. Some black politicians have operated through a locally based political club system with links to the remnants of the Tammany organization, while others have adopted an insurgent political style. The differences between the two approaches extend beyond technique. Communal activists created a history of race relations in the city emphasizing an implacable white racism that demanded militant African-American solidarity. Those more closely linked to the Democratic Party organization continued to recognize the possibility of interracial cooperation. As parties weakened and extrapartisan activism intensified during and after the 1960s, racial identities and race relations changed as well.[22]

Of course political development does not explain everything. Other factors, including the physical features, the economic character, and the ethnic, racial, and class compositions of cities, have helped shape urban social relations. The numerical dominance of the Irish in Boston, where they constituted more than half the city's population during the early part of the twentieth century; the late and relatively small influx of African-American migrants; and the ease with which middle-class Bostonians could retreat outside the city proper made the ethnic appeals of Curley and others especially effective. Likewise the larger influx of African-American migrants and the more varied collection of European immigrants in Chicago and New York shaped political and social outcomes in those cities. But fuller histories of these and other communities require an understanding of the interaction between social and political development, a step that cannot be taken until we abandon the stereotypes that have pervaded urban political history for the past half century.

Reconceiving past city politics offers more than just an opportunity to write better community studies. The waves of migration and immigration that have reshaped modern America crested in cities. These newcomers entered into a changing political culture that has increasingly made social group identities rather than party allegiance the basis of political mobilization. The institutions, languages, and practices through which this collective politicization takes place have played a powerful role in determining ethnic experiences in the twentieth-century United States. We know less than we should about this process because of a reliance on shopworn clichés about bosses, reformers, and the connections between ethnicity and political behavior. At the very least, the immigrant-reform dichotomy has obscured the agency of immigrant leaders who made Progressivism a language of ethnic activism and a tool of political insurgency.

Attention to the development of urban political culture can help us understand other parts of our most recent social history. We now spend so much energy considering the historical origins of the group identities that infuse contemporary public life that we risk missing the ways in which the evolution of public life itself has helped define those identities and has made their expression a central source of political mobilization. The institutional changes and rhetorical innovations that began during the Progressive Era helped produce a public culture in which ethnic tension was a defining feature of Boston's social history, and have played a vital role in shaping the social conflicts that pervade modern urban America. Any effort to overcome the suspicion and anger that pervade present-day ethnic and racial relations must recognize this fact and move beyond the politics of group antagonism that fuels these hatreds.

Statistical Appendix

Studies comparing past electoral patterns and social statistics in large cities have been impeded by the absence of reliable ward-level voting data. Ethnic profiles of electoral districts in cities obtained through published census reports are forced to rely on categories determined by the census takers, measurements that do not always allow the necessary degree of analytical precision. The number of "foreign born" in a district, for instance, yields a much fuzzier portrait than does a count of the number of people of Irish parentage, Italian parentage, and so on. Classifications of social class are even more elusive. Official reports did not include employment breakdowns or income levels, forcing scholars to rely on such proxy variables as literacy or median rental rates. As a result, few urban political histories can make confident assertions about the class and ethnic bases of voting behavior in the cities they examine.

This study has sought to overcome some of these limitations through the use of individual-level datasets derived from the U.S. census. Some of this material is available through public use samples. The remainder was drawn from U.S. census manuscripts. Records drawn from both sources included the place of birth of parents, employment and employment status (wage-earning employee, self-employed, or employer), and a variety of other information. Together, the two samples offer sufficient information on enough people to overcome many of the obstacles presented by reliance on published reports, including the creation of ethnic stock and socioeconomic class variables.

The regression equation reported in Table 1 used data from a sample of the U.S. census drawn from the *Integrated Public Use Microdata Series, 1995* (IPUMS) and a sample of the 1900 U.S. census manuscript drawn by James Connolly and Philip Ethington. The IPUMS sample was assembled under the direction of Steven Ruggles at the University of Minnesota.[1] The combined dataset yielded a 2,856-person sample for Boston, or an average of 114 people per ward.

Census data used for analysis in Chapters 2 through 4 came from a "public use sample" collected from the 1910 census manuscript by the Inter-University Consortium for Political and Social Research (ICPSR) that provides data on individuals. The ICPSR compiled the public use dataset by recording the census entries of one out of every 250 people, yielding a 2,765-person sample for Boston, or an average of 111 people in each of the city's 25 wards.[2]

Table 9 uses a sample of the 1920 U.S. census manuscript drawn by James Connolly and Philip Ethington. This dataset was compiled using random-sampling techniques, recording basic demographic information about each individual sampled. It incorporates the records of 2,326 people in Boston, or an average of 89 per ward.

Despite the advances these samples represent, historians cannot duplicate contemporary survey techniques that compare a person's voting behavior with his or her social profile. The individual-level information now available from census data does not include reports on how those people actually voted. Instead, historians turn to statistical techniques designed to compare the voting behavior and social profiles of aggregate units. From these results, we infer how most individuals sharing particular characteristics voted. The principal technique used for this purpose is linear regression, a statistical procedure that measures the strength and significance of the relationship between one or several independent variables and a dependent variable. In the case of this study, the independent variables were the social characteristics of the wards—the percentage of working-class residents or people of Irish stock in the district, for instance. The dependent variables were the vote shares for the candidate or proposal under consideration. The size of the regression coefficient (from 0 to 1.0) indicates the strength of the relationship between each independent variable and the dependent variable. The closer to 1.0, the stronger it is.[3]

The results of the regression equations presented in this study include two statistics designed to measure their statistical significance. The p-value, ranging from 0 to 1.0, indicates the likelihood that the reported coefficient is simply a random result (or not statistically different from 0). The closer to 0 the p-value is, the greater the odds that the relationship described by the coefficient is accurate. A p-value of .05 or less is generally considered statistically significant. The R-squared (R^2) value, also ranging from 0 to 1.0, measures the strength of the entire regression model. Unlike the p-value, the closer to 1.0 the R^2 value is, the greater the explanatory power of the regression model being tested. In the equations performed for this study, which compare two separate aggregate datasets (voting results and social statistics), R^2 results as low as .30 can still indicate a reasonably powerful model.[4]

Statistical analysis of voting behavior in a single city faces an additional limitation. In the linear regression technique used throughout the book, the number of observations in the analysis determines the degrees of freedom, or the number of independent variables that can be used. Boston's twenty-five wards provided twenty-five observations, a total that limited the number of social characteristics employed as independent variables to just two, or at most three. Faced with this restriction, I chose the two most common variables in electoral analysis, social class and ethnicity. In one instance (Table 3), I supplemented this total with a variable measuring the degree of suburbanization. In each equation, I selected the social characteristics that provided the best test for the validity of my assertions or the historical interpretations under consideration.[5]

I derived variables representing social class from occupational data provided in the census sample. I coded the job listed for each employed individual according to the standard ten-stratum scale used by Alba Edwards and Stephan Thernstrom. Coding decisions were also influenced by the census description of each entry's status as either self-employed, an employer, or a wage-earning employee. Since ten categories were too large a number for a single-city analysis, I reduced the classifications to working class (semiskilled and unskilled workers) and white-collar (proprietors, professionals, and clerical and sales workers). I did not include the most highly skilled and self-employed blue-collar workers in the working-class variable as a way of making it a sharper, more definitive measurement.[6]

I created three variables measuring ethnicity. The first, Irish stock, measures the number of people in a district who either were born in Ireland themselves or had a mother who was. The decision to use maternal stock was arbitrary. It was designed to account for a portion of the people with mixed parentage, based on the reasoning that some but not all members of that group would associate themselves with that heritage. Since the Irish were the dominant immigrant group in Boston, and a large part of this study examines their political activity, I use this variable most frequently. In one case, presented in Table 7, I measured the size of the foreign stock in each ward. This variable includes all people born in another country as well as those whose mothers were born outside the United States. The U.S.-stock variable included in the regression equation reported in Table 3 represents people whose families (at least on their mother's side) had lived in the United States for two generations or more.

Table 3 presents the results of an equation that uses a third variable, suburbanization. This variable served to distinguish between inner-city, suburban, and semisuburban wards. It is a rough measurement, following approximately the descriptions laid out by social worker Robert Woods and his South End House colleagues. The inner wards received a value of 0, the middle-range districts were assigned a value of 0.5, while the most suburban sections of the city were valued at 1.0. Although the South End House categories have come under some fire, numerous urban historians have employed them in their work. Since I was testing this prevailing set of historical assumptions about the role of suburbanization in Progressive Era politics, I employed the same classifications.[7]

Voting rates reported in all tables were based on the share of the total votes received by the candidate or referendum in question. It would be more desirable to measure the portion of eligible voters who supported a candidate or ballot initiative, but these figures are not consistently available. While the number of eligible voters can be derived from decennial census data, it does not exist for the intervening years. (Boston's Board of Election Commissioners only recorded the number of residents in each district, not the number of citizens allowed to vote.) The high rate of migration in and out of Boston made it inadvisable to use totals derived from the 1910 census for elections that took place several years before or after that vote. In the interest of consistency, I chose not to use eligibility figures for the elections that took place during the same year that census counts were taken.

The regression results reported in Chapter 6, note 46 used one other variable. The variable used in those equations to represent the percentage of women voters mobilized in each ward was determined by dividing the number of eligible women voters into the number who voted in the 1921 municipal election. Eligibility totals were derived from the 1920 census, by adding native-born and naturalized adult women. Unfortunately, no breakdown of the women's vote for each candidate exists for the 1921 mayoral election.

Tests for collinearity were completed for each multiple regression to make sure that no independent variables were too closely related. In no case did the R^2 values of the test equations exceed .31, well within the acceptable limits specified in M. S. Lewis-Beck's *Applied Regression: An Introduction*.[8]

Selected Primary Sources

Manuscript Collections

Chancery Correspondence, Archives, Archdiocese of Boston, Brighton, Mass.

Elizabeth Lowell Putnam Papers, Schlesinger Library, Radcliffe College, Cambridge, Mass.

George Read Nutter Diaries, 1905–1936, Massachusetts Historical Society, Boston, Mass.

James Michael Curley Scrapbooks [microfilm], Boston Public Library, Boston, Mass.

League of Catholic Women Papers, Archives, Archdiocese of Boston, Brighton, Mass.

Martin Lomasney Scrapbook [microfilm], Massachussetts Historical Society, Boston, Mass.

Maude Wood Park Papers, Women's Rights Collection, Schlesinger Library, Radcliffe College, Cambridge, Mass.

Nathan Matthews Jr. Political Papers, Littauer Library, Littauer Center, Harvard University, Cambridge, Mass.

Parish Census Files, Archives, Archdiocese of Boston, Brighton, Mass.

Patrick Collins Memorial Scrapbook, Rare Books Department, Boston Public Library, Boston, Mass.

Records of the Good Government Association, Massachusetts Historical Society, Boston, Mass.

Records of the Boston Central Labor Union, Massachusetts Historical Society, Boston, Mass.

Wenona Osborne Pinkham Papers, Women's Rights Collection, Radcliffe College, Cambridge, Mass.

Newspapers and Periodicals

Boston Daily Globe, 1900–1928.
Boston Evening Globe, 1900–1928.
Boston Evening Transcript, 1900–1928.
Boston Herald, 1900–1928.
Boston Post, 1900–1928.
Charlestown Enterprise, 1900–1920.
Charlestown News, 1924, 1926–1928.
City Affairs, 1905–1928.
East Boston Argus-Advocate, 1916–1917, 1921–1923.
East Boston Free Press, 1915–1918, 1921–1923, 1926–1927.
La Gazzetta del Massachusetts, 1903, 1907–1911, 1915–1928.
Italian News, 1922–1928.
The Item (Brighton), 1900–1928.
Jamaica Plain News, 1900–1912.
Jewish Advocate, 1905–1928.
The Pilot, 1888–1900.
The Republic, 1900, 1904, 1906–1907, 1909–1910, 1914–1925.
Roxbury Gazette and South End News, 1900–1911, 1913–1922, 1924–1926.
South Boston Gazette, 1905–1917.
United Improvement Association Bulletin, 1910–1912.
Women's Municipal League Bulletin, 1909–1922.

Public Documents

Boston Board of Election Commissioners, *Annual Reports for 1900–1925* (Boston, 1901–1926).

Boston City Council, *Proceedings of the City Council of Boston, 1922–1926* (Boston, 1923–1927).

Boston Council of Social Agencies, Bureau of Research and Studies, *Social Statistics by Census Tracts in Boston: A Neighborhood Study* (Boston: Boston Council of Social Agencies, 1933).

Boston Finance Commission, *Reports of the Boston Finance Commission*, vols. 1, 2, and Final Report (Boston, 1909).

Boston School Committee, *Proceedings of the Boston School Committee, 1905* (Boston, 1906)

Massachusetts Bureau of Statistics and Labor, *Census of the Commonwealth of Massachusetts: 1885*, vol. 1, *Population and Social Statistics* (Boston: Wright and Potter, 1887).

Massachusetts Bureau of Statistics and Labor, *Census of the Commonwealth of Massachusetts: 1905*, vol. 1, *Population and Social Statistics* (Boston: Wright and Potter, 1909).

Massachusetts Bureau of Statistics and Labor, *Census of the Commonwealth of*

Massachusetts: 1915, vols. 1 and 2, *Population and Social Statistics* (Boston: Wright and Potter, 1917).

United States Bureau of the Census, "Manuscript Schedule, Fourteenth Annual Census of the United States, 1920" [microfilm].

United States Bureau of the Census, *Thirteenth Annual Census of the United States: Population Schedule* (Washington, D.C., 1910).

United States Bureau of the Census, *Twelfth Annual Census of the United States: Population Schedule* (Washington, D.C., 1900).

United States Congress, *Congressional Record,* 62nd Congress, 2nd session, 1912 (Washington, D.C., 1913).

Statistical Databases

Samuel H. Preston, "United States Census Data, 1910: Public Use Sample" (Ann Arbor: Inter-University Consortium for Political and Social Research, 1989; ICPSR 9166).

Steven Ruggles and Matthew Sobek, *Integrated Public Use Microdata Series, IPUMS-95, Version 1.0* (Minneapolis: Social History Research Laboratory, Department of History, University of Minnesota, 1995).

Notes

Abbreviations

BCLU   Records of the Boston Central Labor Union, Massachusetts Historical Society, Boston, Mass.

GGA   Records of the Good Government Association, Massachusetts Historical Society, Boston, Mass.

LCWP   League of Catholic Women Papers, Archives, Archdiocese of Boston, Brighton, Mass.

JMCS   James Michael Curley Scrapbook [microfilm], Boston Public Library, Boston, Mass.

MLS   Martin Lomasney Scrapbook, Massachusetts Historical Society, Boston, Mass.

NMPP   Nathan Matthews Jr. Political Papers, Littauer Library, Littauer Center, Harvard University, Cambridge, Mass.

WMLB   *Women's Municipal League Bulletin,* Boston Public Library, Boston, Mass.

WRC   Women's Rights Collection, Schlesinger Library, Radcliffe College, Cambridge, Mass.

Introduction

1. For a full account of the conflict and its background, see Ronald P. Formisano, *Boston Against Busing: Race, Class, and Ethnicity in the 1960s and 1970s* (Chapel Hill: University of North Carolina Press, 1990).

2. Ibid., pp. 8–9, 42.

3. This perspective on Boston's ethnic history received its fullest statement recently in Thomas H. O'Connor, *The Boston Irish: A Political History* (Boston: Northeastern University Press, 1995).

212 · *Notes to Page 5*

4. The new emphasis on political history itself and on the effects of politics on social relations has many dimensions, some stressing institutions and policies, others more concerned with language and culture. For a few recent statements on these approaches, see the following: Theda Skocpol, *Protecting Soldiers and Mothers: The Political Origins of Social Policy in the United States* (Cambridge: Harvard University Press, 1992), pp. 47–54; idem, "Bringing the State Back In: Strategies of Analysis in Current Research," in P. B. Evans, D. Reuschemeyer, and T. Skocpol, *Bringing the State Back In* (New York: Cambridge University Press, 1985), pp. 3–37; Richard L. McCormick, "The Social Analysis of American Politics—After Twenty Years," in Richard L. McCormick, *The Party Period and Public Policy: American Politics from the Age of Jackson to the Progressive Era* (New York: Oxford University Press, 1986), pp. 137–140; Richard Oestreicher, "Urban Working Class Political Behavior and Theories of American Electoral Politics, 1870–1940," *Journal of American History* 74 (1988): 1257–1286; Terrence J. McDonald, *The Parameters of Urban Fiscal Policy: Socioeconomic Change and Political Culture in San Francisco, 1860–1906* (Berkeley: University of California Press, 1986); Philip J. Ethington, "Recasting Urban Political History: Gender, the Public Household, and Political Participation in Boston and San Francisco during the Progressive Era," *Social Science History* 16 (1992): 301–333. Several scholars have emphasized politics as a factor in social group formation, including Ira Katznelson, *City Trenches: Urban Politics and the Patterning of Class in the United States* (Chicago: University of Chicago Press, 1981), and Amy Bridges, "Becoming American: The Working Classes in the United States Before the Civil War," in Ira Katznelson and Aristide Zolberg, *Working Class Formation: Nineteenth-Century Patterns in Western Europe and the United States* (Princeton: Princeton University Press), pp. 157–196.

5. Skocpol, "Bringing the State Back In," p. 20. The concept of orientation is derived from Peter L. Berger and Thomas Luckmann, *The Social Construction of Reality: A Treatise on the Sociology of Knowledge* (New York: Anchor Books, 1966), p. 42. See also Keith Michael Baker's discussion of political culture in Keith Michael Baker, ed., *The Political Culture of the Old Regime* (Oxford: Pergamon Press, 1987), pp. xi–xiii.

6. Stuart Hall, "Cultural Identity and Diaspora," in Jonathan Rutherford, ed., *Identity, Culture, and Difference* (London: Lawrence and Wishart, 1990), p. 225. George Steinmetz, "Reflections on the Role of Social Narratives in Working Class Formation: Narrative Theory in the Social Sciences," *Social Science History* 16 (1992): 489–491. See also Werner Sollors, ed., *The Invention of Ethnicity* (New York: Oxford University Press, 1989), pp. ix–xx; Wsevol W. Isajiw, "Definitions of Ethnicity: New Approaches," *Ethnic Forum* 14 (1994): 9–17; Richard Jenkins, "Rethinking Ethnicity: Identity, Categorization, and Power," *Ethnic and Racial Studies* 17 (1994): 197–223.

7. Steinmetz, "Reflections on the Role of Social Narratives in Working Class Formation," p. 491.

8. Werner Sollors, "Introduction: The Invention of Ethnicity," in Sollors, ed., *The Invention of Ethnicity,* pp. xii–xiii. Sollors points especially to the arguments in Eric Hobsbawm and Terence Ranger, eds., *The Invention of Tradition* (Cambridge: Cambridge University Press, 1983). On the development of nationalism, see Benedict Anderson, *Imagined Communities: Reflections on the Origin and Spread of Nationalism* (London: Verso, 1985).

9. The great migration that brought a large African presence to many Northern cities during and after World War I had a relatively limited impact on Boston's population. The city's 11,591 blacks accounted for just 2.1 percent of its population in 1900. By 1930 there were 20,574 blacks, but they still accounted for only 2.6 percent of the city's expanding population. Not until the 1960s did Boston's African-American community constitute even 10 percent of the city's total number of inhabitants. See Elizabeth Haflin Pleck, *Black Migration and Poverty: Boston, 1865–1900* (New York: Academic Press, 1979), p. 209. On the political life of Boston's Progressive Era black community, including its support for reform, see John Daniels, *In Freedom's Birthplace* (New York: Arno Press, 1969), pp. 266–307.

10. On the development of the ward boss image, see Terrence J. McDonald, "Introduction," in William J. Riordan, *Plunkitt of Tammany Hall,* edited with an Introduction by Terrence J. McDonald (Boston: Bedford Books, 1993), pp. 20–25. A diverse array of scholars accepted this explanation of how ward politics worked. See for example such distinctly different works as Katznelson, *City Trenches;* John D. Buenker, *Urban Liberalism and Progressive Reform* (New York: W. W. Norton, 1973), especially pp. 4–6; Robert Dahl, *Who Governs: Democracy and Power in an American City* (New Haven: Yale University Press, 1961); Herbert G. Gutman, "Work, Culture, and Society in Industrializing America, 1815–1919," in Herbert G. Gutman, *Work, Culture, and Society in Industrializing America: Essays in American Working Class History* (New York: Vintage Books, 1977), p. 57; John Bodnar, *The Transplanted: A History of Immigrants in Urban America* (Bloomington: Indiana University Press, 1985), pp. 202–204.

11. Terrence J. McDonald, "The Problem of the Political in Recent American Urban History: Liberal Pluralism and the Rise of Functionalism," *Social History* 10 (1985): 330–342. As McDonald notes, this account made its way into the historical writings of Richard Hofstadter, Oscar Handlin, and Samuel Hays, and it informed the idea of latent functionalism developed by Robert Merton. Several studies have demonstrated that nineteenth-century party machines did not serve as informal welfare agencies, including Robin L. Einhorn, *Property Rules: Political Economy in Chicago, 1833–1872* (Chicago: University of Chicago Press, 1991), and McDonald, *The Parameters of Urban Fiscal Policy.* For other critiques of the machine model, see David Thelen, "Urban Politics Beyond Bosses and Reformers," *Reviews in American History* 7 (1979): 406–412; Jon Teaford, "*Finis* for Tweed and Steffens: Rewriting the History of Urban Rule," *Reviews in American History* 10 (1982): 133–149; Bruce M. Stave et al., "A Reassessment of the Urban Political Boss: An Ex-

change of Views," *History Teacher* 21 (1988): 293–312; Alan DiGaetano, "The Rise and Development of Urban Political Machines: An Alternative to Merton's Functional Analysis," *Urban Affairs Quarterly* 24 (1988): 242–267.

12. McDonald, "The Problem of the Political," p. 345.

13. The key statements in the debate over Progressivism include Peter Filene, "An Obituary for the Progressive Movement," *American Quarterly* 22 (1970): 20–34; Daniel T. Rodgers, "In Search of Progressivism," *Reviews in American History* 10 (1982): 113–132; Richard L. McCormick, "The Discovery that Business Corrupts Politics," in McCormick, *The Party Period and Public Policy,* pp. 311–356. For a recent discussion of Progressivism that treats it as a coherent body of ideas, see Eldon Eisenach, *The Lost Promise of Progressivism* (Lawrence: Kansas University Press, 1994).

14. Daniel T. Rodgers made an impressive effort to bring some kind of analytical coherence to the study of this topic in his review essay "In Search of Progressivism," *Reviews in American History* 10 (1982): 113–132. He divided Progressive reform into three "languages"—antimonopoly, social unity, and efficiency. These strains were not exclusive, he argued, and reformers mixed them together in various and even contradictory ways. The distinct advantage of Rodgers's approach is its flexibility. The different languages became activated in different ways according to historical circumstance, thus preserving the complexity of Progressivism. But this approach still overlooks the common theme that unites all dimensions of Progressive reform. As Rodgers notes, all three of his languages "tended to focus . . . discontent on arbitrary, unregulated individual power" (p. 123). While this concern was not new to American public life, the enormous outburst of popular concern, and the accompanying rise in nonpartisan political action it triggered, were. The unprecedented clamor and the volume of this new sort of activity defined Progressivism. For an intriguing and generally persuasive explanation of the sudden origins of Progressivism, see McCormick, "The Discovery that Business Corrupts Politics." See also Daniel T. Rodgers, *Contested Truths: Keywords in American Politics Since Independence* (New York: Basic Books, 1987), pp. 176–211.

15. See Richard L. McCormick, "Antiparty Thought in the Gilded Age," in McCormick, *The Party Period and Public Policy,* pp. 228–259, for the roots of this notion and Thomas R. Pegram, *Partisans and Progressives: Private Interest and Public Policy in Illinois, 1870–1922* (Chicago: University of Illinois Press, 1992), for an analysis of the tensions between Progressivism and partisanship.

16. As Morton Keller has pointed out, the analytical utility of the term "middle class" for the Progressive Era is doubtful. It usually referred to a category of people so broad that it encompassed a large part of the American public. See Morton Keller, *Regulating a New Society: Public Policy and Social Change in America, 1900–1933* (Cambridge: Harvard University Press, 1994), p. 3.

17. Richard Abrams, in *Conservatism in a Progressive Era* (Cambridge: Harvard University Press, 1964), argued that Massachusetts did not experience Progressivism as other states did because it had already enacted most of the reforms demanded by Progressives elsewhere. His argument rests on an interpretation of Progressivism as a campaign on behalf of specific measures and ideas. The present study rejects that definition and thus the contention that Progressivism did not arise in Massachusetts. The "discovery that business corrupts politics" described by Richard McCormick occurred in Boston as much as it did in any other city or state. See McCormick, "The Discovery that Business Corrupts Politics." On muckraking, see Peter Hansen, "Muckraking," in James T. Kloppenberg and Richard Wrightman Fox, eds., *A Companion to American Thought* (Cambridge, Mass.: Blackwell, 1995), pp. 471–474, and Thomas C. Leonard, "The Civics and Anti-Civics of Muckraking," in *The Power of the Press: The Birth of American Political Reporting* (New York: Oxford University Press, 1986), pp. 193–221.

18. See Amy Bridges, "Creating Cultures of Reform," *Studies in American Political Development* 8 (1994): 4–7; Martin J. Schiesl, *The Politics of Efficiency: Municipal Administration and Reform in America, 1800–1920* (Berkeley: University of California Press, 1977), pp. 6–24; Kenneth Fox, *Better City Government: Innovation in American Urban Politics, 1850–1937* (Philadelphia: Temple University Press, 1977), pp. 3–22.

19. Quotation from Richard Hofstadter, *Anti-Intellectualism in American Life* (New York: Vintage, 1963), p. 190. See also Alan Trachtenberg, *The Incorporation of America: Culture and Society in the Gilded Age* (New York: Hill and Wang, 1982), pp. 163–165; Paula Baker, "The Domestication of Politics: Women and American Political Society, 1780–1920," *American Historical Review* 89 (1984): 620–664, n. 27.

20. Lincoln Steffens, *The Shame of the Cities* (New York: Hill and Wang, 1957), p. 167.

21. Baker, "The Domestication of Politics," pp. 620–647. For broader overviews that place women's activism during the Progressive Era in context, see Karen J. Blair, *The Clubwoman as Feminist: True Womanhood Redefined* (New York: Holmes and Meier, 1980), and Anne Firor Scott, *Natural Allies: Women's Associations in American History* (Urbana: University of Illinois Press, 1991).

22. On republicanism, see Daniel T. Rodgers, "Republicanism: The Career of a Concept," *Journal of American History* 79 (1992): 11–38, and James T. Kloppenberg, "Republicanism in American History and Historiography," *Tocqueville Review* XIII, no. 1 (1992): 119–136. For explications of some of the connections between republicanism and Progressivism, see John Patrick Diggins, "Republicanism and Progressivism," *American Quarterly* 37 (1985): 572–598; James A. Morone, *The Democratic Wish: Popular Participation and the Limits of American Government* (New York: Basic Books,

1990), pp. 97–128; McCormick, "The Discovery that Business Corrupts Politics," pp. 319–326.

23. Exponents of these many and varied interpretations of Progressivism include Richard Hofstadter, *The Age of Reform: From Bryan to F.D.R.* (New York: Vintage Books, 1955); George Mowry, *The California Progressives* (Berkeley: University of California Press, 1951); Samuel Hays, "The Politics of Reform of Municipal Government in the Progressive Era," *Pacific Northwest Quarterly* 55 (1964): 157–169; Robert Weibe, *The Search for Order, 1877–1920* (New York: Hill and Wang, 1967), p. 153; Michael P. Rogin and John L. Shover, *Political Change in California: Critical Elections and Social Movements, 1890–1966* (Westport, Conn.: Greenwood Press, 1970); Gabriel Kolko, *The Triumph of Conservatism: A Reinterpretation of American History, 1900–1916* (New York: Free Press, 1963); James Weinstein, *The Corporate Ideal in the Liberal State, 1900–1918* (Boston: Beacon Press, 1968); Martin J. Sklar, *"The Corporate Reconstruction of American Capitalism, 1890–1916: The Market, Law and Politics,"* (New York: Cambridge University Press, 1988); Estelle Freedman, "Separatism as Strategy: Female Institution Building and American Feminism, 1870–1930," *Feminist Studies* 5 (1979): 512–529; Paula Baker, "The Domestication of Politics"; Noralee Frankel and Nancy S. Dye, eds., *Gender, Class, Race, and Reform in the Progressive Era* (Lexington: University of Kentucky Press, 1991); Buenker, *Urban Liberalism and Progressive Reform*; J. Joseph Huthmacher, "Urban Liberalism and the Age of Reform," *Mississippi Valley Historical Review* 44 (1962): 231–241; Robert M. Crunden, *Ministers of Reform: The Progressives' Achievement in American Civilization, 1889–1920* (New York: Basic Books, 1982).

24. Several studies of urban reform during the Progressive Era have begun to sketch a broader picture than old-fashioned boss-reformer dichotomies allow. See Philip J. Ethington, "Urban Constituencies, Regimes, and Policy Innovation in the Progressive Era: An Analysis of Boston, Chicago, New York City, and San Francisco," *Studies in American Political Development* 7 (1993): 275–315; Kenneth Finegold, *Experts and Politicians: Reform Challenges to Machine Politics in New York, Cleveland, Chicago* (Princeton: Princeton University Press, 1995); Maureen Flanagan, *Charter Reform in Chicago* (Carbondale: Southern Illinois University Press, 1987).

25. The two main statements of the urban liberalism thesis are Huthmacher, "Urban Liberalism and the Age of Reform," and Buenker, *Urban Liberalism and Progressive Reform*.

26. One of the best ways to get a sense of the diversity of Progressivism is to read the articles in Frankel and Dye, eds., *Gender, Class, Race, and Reform in the Progressive Era*. See also Douglas Flamming, "African-Americans and the Politics of Race in Progressive-Era Los Angeles," in William Deverell and Tom Sitton, eds., *California Progressivism Revisited* (Berkeley: University of California Press, 1994), pp. 203–228; George Sanchez, *Becoming Mexican-*

American: *Ethnicity, Culture, and Identity in Chicano Los Angeles, 1900–1945* (New York: Oxford University Press), pp. 108–125; Herbert F. Margulies, *The Decline of the Progressive Movement in Wisconsin, 1890–1920* (Madison: State Historical Society of Wisconsin, 1968), pp. 91–92, 283–285.

1. Politics and Society at the End of the Nineteenth Century

1. Oscar Handlin, *Boston's Immigrants: A Study in Acculturation,* rev. ed. (Cambridge: Harvard University Press, 1979), pp. 187–189, 198–206, 219–220.

2. Richard L. McCormick, *The Party Period and Public Policy: American Politics from the Age of Jackson to the Progressive Era* (New York: Oxford University Press, 1986), p. 3. The major works that make up the "ethnocultural school" include Lee Benson, *The Concept of Jacksonian Democracy: New York as a Test Case* (Princeton: Princeton University Press, 1961); Ronald P. Formisano, *The Birth of Mass Political Parties: Michigan, 1827–1861* (Princeton: Princeton University Press, 1971); Richard Jensen, *The Winning of the Midwest: Social and Political Conflict, 1888–1896* (Chicago: University of Chicago Press, 1971); Paul Kleppner, *The Cross of Culture: A Social Analysis of Midwestern Politics, 1850–1900* (New York: The Free Press, 1970); and Samuel T. McSeveny, *The Politics of Depression: Political Behavior in the Northeast, 1893–1896* (New York: Oxford University Press, 1972). For a critique of the oversimplification and misinterpretation that has been built up around this body of literature, see Ronald P. Formisano, "The Invention of the Ethnocultural Interpretation," *American Historical Review* 99 (1994): 453–477.

3. Jean H. Baker, *Affairs of Party: The Political Culture of Northern Democrats in the Mid-Nineteenth Century* (Ithaca: Cornell University Press, 1983), pp. 261–316; see also Michael E. McGerr, *The Decline of Popular Politics: The American North, 1865–1928* (New York: Oxford University Press, 1986), pp. 12–41. McGerr notes the waning of "spectacular politics" in the late nineteenth century, but the process was gradual and alternatives to party identity emerged slowly.

4. For the British-American influx, see Handlin, *Boston's Immigrants,* p. 264, Table XXXIII, and David Ward, "Nineteenth-Century Boston: A Study in the Role of Antecedent and Adjacent Conditions in the Spatial Aspects of Urban Growth" (Ph.D. diss., University of Wisconsin, 1963), p. 178. By 1885, Irish immigrants and their children numbered 162,979 out of a total population of 390,393 (41.7 percent). This figure does not account for third- and fourth-generation Irish Americans, who, by the 1880s and 1890s, would likely increase this total significantly. Over the ensuing twenty years, the percentage of first- and second-generation Irish in Boston would remain roughly the same (42.5 percent in 1905), although the number of third- and fourth-generation Irish—many of whom undoubtedly considered themselves Irish—probably

increased over time. Carroll D. Wright, *Census of the Commonwealth of Massachusetts: 1885* (Boston: Wright and Potter Printing Company, 1887), p. 550, and Massachusetts Bureau of Statistics and Labor, *Census of the Commonwealth of Massachusetts: 1905,* vol. I, *Population and Social Statistics* (Boston: Wright and Potter Printing Company, 1909), p. 368.

5. Sam Bass Warner, *Streetcar Suburbs: The Process of Growth, 1870–1900,* 2nd ed. (Cambridge: Harvard University Press, 1978), p. 79. Robert A. Woods and Albert K. Kennedy, eds., *The Zone of Emergence: Observations of Lower, Middle, and Upper Working Class Communities in Boston, 1905–1914* (Cambridge: M.I.T. Press, 1962). David Ward has sharply criticized the zone theory employed by Woods and his colleagues and later developed more fully by University of Chicago sociologists. See David Ward, *Cities and Immigrants: A Geography of Change in Nineteenth-Century America* (New York: Oxford University Press, 1971), pp. 126–127, and idem, "Nineteenth-Century Boston," pp. xi–xv.

6. Handlin, *Boston's Immigrants,* p. 210. Peter K. Eisinger, "Ethnic Political Transition in Boston, 1884–1933: Some Lessons for Contemporary Cities," *Political Science Quarterly* 93 (1978): 221. Geoffrey Blodgett, "Yankee Leadership in a Divided City: Boston, 1860–1910," *Journal of Urban History* 8 (1982): 372–373. Barbara Miller Solomon, *Ancestors and Immigrants: A Changing New England Tradition* (Boston: Northeastern University Press, 1989), pp. 43–58.

7. Geoffrey Blodgett, *The Gentle Reformers: Massachusetts Democrats in the Cleveland Era* (Cambridge: Harvard University Press, 1966), p. 150. Lois Bannister Merk, "Boston's Historic Public School Crisis," *New England Quarterly* 31 (1958): 179–180. James Benjamin, "The School Question in Massachusetts, 1870–1890: Its Background and Influences on Public Education" (Ph.D. diss., University of Missouri, 1970), pp. 178–190. Robert Lord, John Sexton, and Edward T. Harrington, *History of the Archdiocese of Boston in the Various Stages of Its Development,* vol. 3 (New York: Sheed and Ward, 1944), pp. 110–111.

8. Merk, "Boston's Historic Public School Crisis," p. 180. Benjamin, "The School Question in Massachusetts," pp. 191–193.

9. John T. Galvin, "Patrick Maguire: Boston's Last Democratic Boss," *New England Quarterly* 55 (1982): 401. Merk, "Boston's Historic Public School Crisis," pp. 187–190. Benjamin, "The School Question in Massachusetts," pp. 199–202.

10. Merk, "Boston's Historic Public School Crisis," pp. 178–179. Blodgett, *The Gentle Reformers,* p. 150.

11. Blodgett, *The Gentle Reformers,* pp. 153–158. Lawrence W. Kennedy, "Power and Prejudice; Boston Political Conflict, 1885–1895" (Ph.D. diss., Boston College, 1987), pp. 316–317, 230. James J. Keneally, "Catholicism and Woman Suffrage in Massachusetts," *The Catholic Historical Review* 53 (1967): 43–59.

12. Merk, "Boston's Historic Public School Crisis," pp. 179–180. Solomon, *Ancestors and Immigrants*, pp. 49–54. Blodgett "Yankee Leadership in a Divided City," p. 382. Blodgett, *The Gentle Reformers*, p. 153. Handlin, *Boston's Immigrants*, p. 189. Matthews played a particularly important role in defeating the 1888 inspection bill and in removing the teeth from the 1889 bill. See Nathan Matthews to Dr. Thomas Dwight, March 6, 1889, NMPP, vol. 2; Matthews to Hon. Patrick Maguire, June 6, 1889, NMPP, vol. 2.

13. *Boston Globe*, March 18, 1891, clipping, NMPP, vol. 3, p. 49. Nathan Matthews, Speech to Boston College Commencement, June 30, 1890 [typescript], NMPP, vol. 3, p. 56.

14. On O'Reilly's career, see Francis G. McManamin, *The American Years of John Boyle O'Reilly* (New York: Arno Press, 1976); Francis R. Walsh, "John Boyle O'Reilly, *The Pilot,* and Irish-American Assimilation, 1870–1890," in Jack Tager and John W. Ifkovic, *Massachusetts in the Gilded Age: Selected Essays* (Amherst: University of Massachusetts Press, 1985), pp. 148–163; and Arthur Mann, *Yankee Reformers in an Urban Age: Social Reform in Boston, 1880–1900* (New York: Harper and Row, 1954), pp. 24–44. O'Reilly's connection and influence with Yankee Democrats can be glimpsed in Nathan Matthews to J. B. O'Reilly, February 1, 1888, NMPP, vol. 1. On Maguire, see John T. Galvin, "Patrick Maguire: Boston's Last Democratic Boss," *Massachusetts Historical Society Proceedings* 89 (1977): 88–111.

15. *The Pilot,* July 28, September 8, 1888. *Boston Republic,* April 19, 1890, quoted in Blodgett, *The Gentle Reformers,* p. 153.

16. *Donahoe's Magazine,* August 1888. Merk, "Boston's Historic Public School Crisis," pp. 189–190. See also Keneally, "Catholicism and Woman Suffrage in Massachusetts," p. 43.

17. *The Republic,* September 21, 1895. *The Pilot,* November 22, 1888.

18. *The Pilot,* October 13, 1888. *The Republic,* quoted in *The Sacred Heart Review,* December 29, 1888. See also Walsh, "John Boyle O'Reilly," pp. 155–156, for examples of his confident emphasis on Boston's demographics.

19. *Boston Daily Globe,* July 5, 1895. Donald L. Kinzer, *An Episode in Anti-Catholicism: The American Protective Association* (Seattle: University of Washington Press, 1964), pp. 186–187. Thomas H. O'Connor, *The Boston Irish: A Political History* (Boston: Northeastern University Press, 1995), pp. 154–156.

20. *The Republic,* July 13, 1895.

21. *The Republic,* July 20, 1895. *The Pilot,* July, 13, 1895.

22. *Donahoe's Magazine,* May 1889. *The Sacred Heart Review,* January 12, 1889.

23. Paul Kleppner, "From Party to Faction?: The Dissolution of Boston's Majority Party, 1876–1908," in Ronald Formisano and Constance Burns, eds., *Boston: 1700–1980: The Evolution of Urban Politics* (Westport, Conn.: Greenwood Press, 1984), pp. 111–132. Kleppner's otherwise intriguing thesis is marred by his reliance on the ward boss model for ground-level politics. He

concludes that Boston's Democratic politics disintegrated into battles among entrenched ward bosses. In fact, intraward factionalism was common throughout Boston. The "dissolution" of Boston's Democratic Party extended all the way to the ward level, eventually allowing ambitious citywide politicians to circumvent party organizations and mobilize voters along alternative lines. The mistaken assumption that every ethnic ward was controlled by a boss obscures this process.

24. James Sanders, "Catholics and the School Question in Boston: The Cardinal O'Connell Years," in Robert E. Sullivan and James M. O'Toole, eds., *Catholic Boston: Studies in Religion and Community, 1870–1980* (Boston: The Archbishop of Boston, 1985), p. 121.

25. *Boston Globe,* December 14, 1905, clipping, Patrick A. Collins Memorial Scrapbook, Rare Books Department, Boston Public Library. Thomas Mason, "Reform Politics in Boston" (Ph.D. diss., Harvard University, 1963), pp. 63–68. Blodgett, *The Gentle Reformers,* pp. 53–55. See also Michael Curran, *Life of Patrick Collins* (Norwood, Mass.: Norwood Press, 1906).

26. Curran, *Life of Patrick Collins,* pp. 132, 136–140.

27. Boston Board of Election Commissioners, *Annual Report for 1903* (Boston, 1903), p. 192.

28. Richard Abrams, *Conservatism in a Progressive Era* (Cambridge: Harvard University Press, 1964), p. 135. Constance Burns, "The Irony of Progressive Reform: Boston 1898–1910," in Formisano and Burns, eds., *Boston: 1700–1980,* pp. 134–135. On Quincy, see Geoffrey Blodgett, "Josiah Quincy, Brahmin Democrat," *New England Quarterly* 38 (1965): 435–445.

29. *Boston Post,* May 10, 1902. Collins quoted in Burns, "The Irony of Progressive Reform," p. 145. See also National Municipal League, *Proceedings of the Boston Conference on Good City Government, 1902* (Philadelphia: National Municipal League, 1902), p. 6.

30. *The Republic,* September 23, 1905, Patrick A. Collins Memorial Scrapbook. *The Republic* was now published by John F. Fitzgerald.

31. Blodgett, "Yankee Leadership in a Divided City." See also John T. Galvin, "The Dark Ages of Boston Politics," *Massachusetts Historical Society Proceedings* 89 (1977): 88–111; O'Connor, *The Boston Irish,* pp. 164–165; and Roger Lane, *Policing the City: Boston, 1822–1885* (Cambridge: Harvard University Press, 1967). Martin Shefter notes that similar alliances between urban elites and party organizations helped solidify party power in eastern cities in this period. See Martin Shefter, *Political Parties and the State: The American Historical Experience* (Princeton: Princeton University Press, 1994), p. 176. Urban party organizations without access to state-level resources often had difficulties maintaining party discipline. See Steven Erie, *Rainbow's End: Irish Americans and the Dilemmas of Urban Machine Politics, 1840–1985* (Berkeley: University of California Press, 1985), p. 30.

32. On Maguire, see Galvin, "Boston's Last Democratic Boss."

33. Blodgett, *The Gentle Reformers,* pp. 159–165. Robert A. Silverman,

"Nathan Matthews: Politics of Reform in Boston, 1890–1910," *New England Quarterly* 50 (1977): 628. Blodgett, "Josiah Quincy, Brahmin Democrat," pp. 435–455.

34. Blodgett, *The Gentle Reformers,* pp. 151–153. Quotation from O'Connor, *The Boston Irish,* p. 118. *Boston Post,* December 1, 1888, clipping, NMPP, vol. 1.

35. *Boston Herald,* December 1, 1888, clipping, NMPP, vol. 1. *Boston Post,* December 1, 1888, clipping, NMPP, vol. 1.

36. Both Geoffrey Blodgett ("Yankee Leadership in a Divided City") and Paul Kleppner ("The Dissolution of Boston's Majority Party") point to growing factionalism as the source of the Democratic Party's declining ability to organize public life in Boston. Aside from my quarrel with their assumption that each ethnic ward was governed by a ward boss, this interpretation fails to recognize the continuing preeminence of partisanship as the only effective basis for political action in Boston. The city's Democrats may not have cooperated in the late 1890s, but they did not abandon their party. Rather they battled for control of it. It was not until the Progressive Era that parties lost their privileged place in Boston's public life.

37. See James J. Connolly, "Boston's Other Irish Wards: Democratic Ward Politics Without Bosses, 1895–1905" (M.A. thesis, University of Massachusetts–Boston, 1989).

38. Galvin, "The Dark Ages of Boston Politics," pp. 98–102. Herbert Zolot, "The Issue of Good Government: James Michael Curley and the Boston Scene, 1897–1918" (Ph.D. diss., State University of New York at Stonybrook, 1975), p. 169.

39. *Brighton Item,* September 24, 1900.

40. Blodgett, *The Gentle Reformers,* pp. 230–231. McKinley defeated Bryan in Boston, an unprecedented Republican victory in the city. While the McKinley triumph can be seen as a rejection of Bryan's ideological appeal, it can also be interpreted as fidelity to the local Democratic organization, which supported Bryan lukewarmly at best and opposed the efforts of Williams and the Massachusetts Bryanites to gain control of the party.

41. Blodgett, "Josiah Quincy, Brahmin Democrat," pp. 435–445.

42. Blodgett, *The Gentle Reformers,* pp. 256, 258. *Boston Post,* November 9, 11, December 1, 1897; November 13, December 15, 1898.

43. *Boston Post,* November 3, 16, December 4, 6, 13, 1899.

44. Material in this paragraph and the following is drawn from Leslie Ainley, *Boston Mahatma: Martin Lomasney* (Boston: Humphries, 1949), pp. 86–90, and *Boston Herald,* October 21, 1898; December 12, 1925.

45. *Charlestown Enterprise,* September 30, 1899. See also Connolly, "Boston's Other Irish Wards," and Maurice Baskin, "Ward Boss Politics in Boston, 1896–1921" (senior honors thesis, Harvard University, 1975).

46. *Roxbury Gazette and South End Advertiser,* December 8, 1900.

47. BCLU, vol. 5, p. 237.

48. BCLU, vol. 5, pp. 357–360. *Boston Globe,* December 9, 1899. These techniques were becoming increasingly popular among all kinds of political activists in the late nineteenth century. See McGerr, *The Decline of Popular Politics,* pp. 69–106.

49. See McGerr, *The Decline of Popular Politics,* pp. 42–68, for a discussion of the development of this trend. Burns, "The Irony of Progressive Reform," p. 139. Abrams, *Conservatism in a Progressive Era,* p. 59. "First Report of the Boston Equal Suffrage Association for Good Government, 1901–1903," MWP, folder 95. Allen F. Davis, *Spearheads for Reform: Social Settlements and the Progressive Movement, 1890–1914* (New York: Oxford University Press, 1967), p. 150.

50. Nathan Matthews, *Boston City Government* (Boston, 1895), p. 179.

2. The Dimensions of Progressivism

1. Lincoln Steffens, *The Autobiography of Lincoln Steffens* (New York: Harcourt Brace Jovanovich, 1931), p. 631.

2. *Boston Herald,* October 31, November 2, 1909. See also Paul Kellog, "Boston's Level Best: The 1915 Movement and the Work of Civic Organizations for Which It Stands," *The Survey* 22 (June 5, 1909): 382–395.

3. *Boston Herald,* November 2, 1909. Thomas Mason, "Reform Politics in Boston" (Ph.D. diss., Harvard University, 1963), pp. 235–252.

4. Samuel Hays, "The Politics of Reform in Municipal Government in the Progressive Era," *Pacific Northwest Quarterly* 55 (1964): 157–169. James Weinstein, *The Corporate Ideal in the Liberal State: 1900–1918* (Boston: Beacon Press, 1968), pp. 92–116. See also Martin J. Schiesl, *The Politics of Efficiency: Municipal Administration and Reform in America, 1800–1920* (Berkeley: University of California Press, 1977).

5. George Read Nutter, "History of the Good Government Association" [typescript], GGA, p. 3. Good Government Association handbill, October 1903, GGA, Files and History, File: 1936.

6. Boston had a reputation as a well-governed city. See National Municipal League, *Proceedings of the Boston Conference on Good City Government, 1902* (Philadelphia: National Municipal League, 1902), p. 6, and the *Boston Post,* May 10, 1902; Richard Abrams, *Conservatism in a Progressive Era* (Cambridge: Harvard University Press, 1964), p. 135; Geoffrey Blodgett, *The Gentle Reformers: Massachusetts Democrats in the Cleveland Era* (Cambridge: Harvard University Press, 1966), p. 255; and Constance K. Burns, "The Irony of Progressive Reform: Boston, 1898–1910," in Ronald Formisano and Constance K. Burns, *Boston: 1700–1980: The Evolution of Urban Politics* (Westport, Conn.: Greenwood Press, 1984), pp. 134–135.

7. See Frederic Cople Jaher, *The Urban Establishment: Upper Strata in Boston, New York, Charleston, Chicago, and Los Angeles* (Urbana: University of Illinois Press, 1982), pp. 87–125, and E. D. Baltzell, *Puritan Boston and*

Quaker Philadelphia: Two Protestant Ethics and the Spirit of Class Authority and Leadership (New York: Free Press, 1979), pp. 375–383.

8. Profile compiled from *The Boston City Directory for 1903* [microfilm], Boston Public Library. Blodgett, *The Gentle Reformers*, p. 160. George Read Nutter Diaries, vol. 14, June 4, 1921.

9. Frank Grinnell, "George Read Nutter," *Proceedings of the Massachusetts Historical Society* 68 (1944–1947): 460–461. Nutter Diaries, vol. 15, July 13, 1922.

10. *Boston Transcript*, January 21, 1903. Richard L. McCormick, "The Discovery that Business Corrupts Politics: A Reappraisal of the Origins of Progressivism," in Richard C. McCormick, *The Party Period and Public Policy: American Politics from the Age of Jackson to the Progressive Era* (New York: Oxford University Press, 1986), pp. 340–341.

11. Burns, "The Irony of Progressive Reform," p. 146. Lincoln Steffens, *The Shame of the Cities* (New York: Hill and Wang, 1957), pp. 162–194, quotation from p. 1. GGA handbill, October 1903, GGA, Files and History, File: 1936.

12. GGA handbill, October 1903, GGA, Files and History, File: 1936.

13. Ibid.

14. Nutter Diaries, vol. 2, February 20, 1907. See Eldon J. Eisenach, *The Lost Promise of Progressivism* (Lawrence: University Press of Kansas, 1994), pp. 74–103, for a discussion of the shifting conception of public opinion in the Progressive Era.

15. GGA handbill, October 1903, GGA, Files and History, File: 1936. "Plan of Action Memo," November 1, 1905, GGA, Files and History, file 1. *Boston Transcript,* November 10, 1906.

16. Nutter, "History of the Good Government Association," Chapter 1, p. 9.

17. Ibid., Chapter 2, pp. 3–7.

18. *City Affairs,* vol. 1, no. 2 (April 1905). *City Affairs,* vol. 1, no. 3 (May 1905). Nutter, "History of the Good Government Association," Chapter 2, pp. 3–7.

19. Nutter Diaries, vol. 1, October 24, November 18, 1905. Nutter, "History of the Good Government Association," Chapter 2, pp. 7–8. Nutter pronounced himself pleased with the volume of press coverage of the controversy. On the GGA's desire for this publicity, see Nutter Diaries, vol. 1, October 19, 1905. See McCormick, "The Discovery that Business Corrupts Politics," pp. 332–339, on the wave of urban scandals between 1905 and 1907.

20. *City Affairs* vol. 2, no. 2 (December 1906).

21. The literature describing women's role in reform and in public life generally during the Progressive Era is now quite large. Some of the important works include Estelle Freedman, "Separatism as a Strategy: Female Institution Building and American Feminism, 1870–1930," *Feminist Studies* 5 (1979): 512–529; Paula Baker, "The Domestication of Politics: Women and American Political Society, 1780–1920," *American Historical Review* 89 (1984): 620–647; Kathryn Kish Sklar, "Hull House in the 1890s: A Community of Women

Reformers," *Signs* 10 (1985): 658–677; Maureen Flanagan, "Gender and Urban Political Reform: The City Club and the Women's City Club of Chicago in the Progressive Era," *American Historical Review* 95 (1990): 1032–1050; Theda Skocpol, *Protecting Soldiers and Mothers: The Political Origins of Social Policy in the United States* (Cambridge: Harvard University Press, 1992), pp. 47–54; Robyn Muncy, *Creating a Female Dominion in American Reform, 1890–1935* (New York: Oxford University Press, 1991).

22. Karen J. Blair, *The Clubwoman as Feminist: True Womanhood Redefined, 1868–1914* (New York: Holmes and Meier, 1980), pp. 73–85. Sarah Deutsch, "Learning to Talk More Like a Man: Boston Women's Class-Bridging Organizations, 1870–1940," *American Historical Review* 97 (1992): 388–402.

23. "First Report of the Boston Equal Suffrage Association for Good Government, 1901–1903," MWP, folder 95. Sharon Hartman Strong, "Leadership and Tactics in the American Woman Suffrage Movement: A New Perspective from Massachusetts," *Journal of American History* 62 (1975): 296–315.

24. Dorothy Worrell, *An Account of the Women's Municipal League of Boston as Given at the First Public Meeting, January 20, 1909* (Boston: Southgate Press, 1909), pp. 1–5.

25. Ibid., p. 2. *WMLB,* December 1909.

26. Worrell, *An Account of the Women's Municipal League,* p. 3. *WMLB,* December 1909.

27. *WMLB,* December 1909. See also *WMLB,* March 1910, for a sample of the lobbying activities by the Committee on Streets and Alleys, which included the investigation of waste disposal by the city, street cleaning, improvements for the North End slum district, and the backing of a bill empowering the police to arrest litterers.

28. *WMLB,* January 1918. *WMLB,* December 1915.

29. Worrell, *An Account of the Women's Municipal League,* p. 7. Mary B. Follett, "Report on Schoolhouses as Social Centres," in Worrell, *An Account of the Women's Municipal League,* pp. 14–16. *Boston Herald,* January 9, 1910.

30. *WMLB,* December 1909. *WMLB,* March 1910. *WMLB,* November 1910. Worrell, *An Account of the Women's Municipal League,* pp. 35–36.

31. Some studies locate the principal source of urban Progressivism in suburban neighborhoods. See Richard C. Wade, "Urbanization," in C. Vann Woodward, ed., *The Comparative Approach to American History* (New York: Basic Books, 1968), p. 196. See also Zane L. Miller, *Boss Cox's Cincinnati: Urban Politics in the Progressive Era* (New York: Oxford University Press, 1968), and Michael McCarthy, "The New Metropolis: Chicago, the Annexation Movement, and Progressive Reform," in Michael E. Ebner and Eugene M. Tobin, eds., *The Age of Urban Reform: New Perspectives on the Progressive Era* (Port Washington, N.Y.: Kennikat Press, 1977), pp. 43–54.

32. Sam Bass Warner, *Streetcar Suburbs: The Process of Growth in Boston, 1870–1900,* 2nd ed. (Cambridge: Harvard University Press, 1978), pp. 41–

42. Thomas H. O'Connor, *Bibles, Brahmins and Bosses: A Short History of Boston,* 2nd ed., rev. (Boston: Boston Public Library, 1984), p. 108.

33. Alexander von Hoffman, *Local Attachments: The Making of an American Urban Neighborhood, 1850–1920* (Baltimore: Johns Hopkins University Press, 1994), pp. 115–116.

34. Ibid., p. 36, 38, 147.

35. Ibid., pp. 116–117.

36. Charles K. Cheape, *Moving the Masses: Urban Public Transit in New York, Boston, and Philadelphia, 1880–1912* (Cambridge: Harvard University Press, 1983), pp. 109–114, 148.

37. Von Hoffman, *Local Attachments,* pp. 196–200.

38. Cheape, *Moving the Masses,* pp. 147–152. Abrams, *Conservatism in a Progressive Era,* pp. 64–68. On Whitney, see also Blodgett, *The Gentle Reformers,* pp. 109–113. On the resurrection of the old charges, see *Jamaica Plain News,* October 28, 1905.

39. *Jamaica Plain News,* July 1, November 4, 1905.

40. *Jamaica Plain News,* September 23, 1905.

41. *Jamaica Plain News,* October 21, November 11, 1905, March 10, October 27, November 3, 1906. Brackett became president of the JPCA in 1907 (*Jamaica Plain News,* April 20, 1907).

42. Von Hoffman, *Local Attachments,* pp. 142, 161–163. *WMLB,* May 1913.

43. *Jamaica Plain News,* November 13, 1906.

44. *Jamaica Plain News,* January 27, September 15, 1906.

45. *Jamaica Plain News,* September 8, 15, 1906.

46. *Brighton Item,* November 21, 1908. While no formal record of the UIA's official forming is available, the process can be pieced together from local newspaper accounts. See *Jamaica Plain News,* January 13, 1906; February 9, 1907; January 30, 1909; *Dorchester Beacon,* February 9, 1907; October 16, 1909. Part of the impetus also came from John Fitzgerald's decision to include a representative of local improvement associations when he formed the Boston Finance Commission in 1907 (see Chapter 3).

47. J. Joseph Huthmacher, "Urban Liberalism and the Age of Reform," *Mississippi Valley Historical Review* 44 (1962): 231–241. John D. Buenker's *Urban Liberalism and Progressive Reform* (New York: Charles Scribner and Sons, 1973) is the broadest statement of this perspective, and it focuses on the Progressive Era.

48. Robert A. Woods, ed., *Americans in Process: A Settlement Study by Residents and Associates of South End House* (Boston: Houghton-Mifflin, 1902), p. 24. Massachusetts Bureau of Statistics and Labor, *Census of the Commonwealth of Massachusetts: 1905,* vol. 1; *Population and Social Statistics* (Boston: Wright and Potter, 1909), p. xcvii. Census data taken from Samuel H. Preston, "United States Census Data, 1910: Public Use Sample" (Ann Arbor: Inter-University Consortium for Political and Social Research, 1989). See Statistical Appendix for construction of data set. See also Edwin Fenton, *Immi-*

grants and Unions, A Case Study: Italians and American Labor, 2nd ed. (New York: Arno Press, 1975), p. 219; Anna Maria Martellone, *Una Little Italy: Nell'Atene d'America: La Comunità Italiana di Boston del 1880 al 1920* (Napoli: Guida Editori, 1973), p. 579; and William M. DeMarco, *Ethnics and Enclaves: Boston's Italian North End* (Ann Arbor: UMI Research Press, 1981), pp. 72–74.

49. Frederick A. Bushee, *Ethnic Factors in the Population of Boston* (Boston: South End House, 1903), p. 132. Gustave R. Serino, "Italians in the Political Life of Boston: A Study of the Role of an Immigrant and Ethnic Group in the Political Life of an Urban Community" (Ph.D. diss., Harvard University, 1950), p. 34. See also Woods, *Americans in Process*, pp. 64–65 and De-Marco, *Ethnics and Enclaves*.

50. Fenton, *Immigrants and Unions*, pp. 221–233. *Gazzetta del Massachusetts*, November 5, 1904; September 23, 1905.

51. Fenton, *Immigrants and Unions*, pp. 221–223. Donnaruma and D'Alessandro eventually split over D'Alessandro's cooperation with the Boston Central Labor Union, which insisted that such *prominenti* as Donnaruma and Scigliano sever their connection with the Italian Laborers Union. D'Alessandro was eventually drawn into the Central Labor Union's orbit, and his role in purely local affairs diminished. See Fenton, *Immigrants and Unions*, p. 241.

52. Serino, "Italians in the Political Life of Boston," p. 39. *Il Moscone*, November 14, 1905, clipping, MLS, vol. 11. Ward 6 Democratic Party Flyer, MLS, vol. 15.

53. Woods, *Americans in Process*, pp. 163–170. Allen F. Davis, *Spearheads for Reform: The Social Settlements and the Progressive Movement, 1890–1914* (New York: Oxford University Press, 1967), p. 286, n. 4. Eleanor Woods, *Robert Woods, Champion of Democracy* (Boston: Houghton-Mifflin, 1929), p. 169. *Boston Post*, November 2, 1902, clipping, MLS, vol. 8.

54. Ward 6 Regular Democratic Club Flyer, MLS, vol. 11.

55. *Gazzetta del Massachusetts*, November 11, December 9, 1905. *Boston Post*, November 9, 1905, clipping, MLS, vol. 12.

56. *Gazzetta del Massachusetts*, September 21, November 9, 16, 1907. See the *Gazzetta* generally between 1905 and 1914 for fierce anti-Fitzgerald rhetoric.

57. *Gazzetta del Massachusetts*, September 5, October 31, 1908.

58. Maurice Baskin, "Ward Boss Politics in Boston, 1896–1921" (senior honors thesis, Harvard University, 1975), p. 48. Boston Board of Election Commissioners, *Annual Report for the Year 1908* (Boston, 1909), p. 128. *Boston Herald*, December 16, 1908. *Gazzetta del Massachusetts*, November 6, 1909. *Boston Globe*, November 4, 1909.

59. Jacob Neusner, "The Rise of the Jewish Community, 1890–1914" (Ph.D. diss., Harvard University), pp. iii, 6–14. See also Jacob Neusner, "The Impact of Immigration and Philanthropy upon the Boston Jewish Community (1880–1914)," *Publication of the American Jewish Historical Society* 146 (1956): 71–85.

60. Neusner, "The Rise of the Jewish Community," p. 115. See *Boston Advocate,* September 1, 8, 15, 1905, for biographies of Jewish politicians. See also Albert Ehrenfield, *A Chronicle of Boston Jewry from the Colonial Settlement to 1900* (Boston: Irving Bernstein, 1963), and Ellen Smith, "Israelites in Boston, 1840–1880," in Jonathan D. Sarna and Ellen Smith, eds., *The Jews of Boston: Essays on the Occasion of the Centenary (1895–1905) of the Combined Jewish Philanthropies of Greater Boston* (Boston: Combined Jewish Philanthropies of Greater Boston, 1995), pp. 49–67.

61. Neusner, "The Rise of the Jewish Community," p. 67. *Jewish Chronicle,* September 9, 1892, quoted in Neusner, "The Rise of the Jewish Community," p. 117.

62. The West End neighborhood, lying north and west of the Boston Common, is no longer a residential district. Urban redevelopment turned it into a district of high-rise apartment and office buildings during the 1960s.

63. *Jewish Advocate,* August 26, 1910. Massachusetts Bureau of Statistics and Labor, *Census of Massachusetts: 1905,* vol. 1, *Population and Social Statistics,* p. xciii. The figures are for Russians, a proxy that probably underestimates the total number of Jews. Census data taken from Preston, "United States Census Data, 1910: Public Use Sample." See Statistical Appendix for data set construction. Gerald H. Gamm, "In Search of Suburbs: Boston's Jewish Districts, 1843–1994," in Sarna and Smith, eds., *The Jews of Boston,* p. 139, puts the Jewish population of the West End at 24,000.

64. On the development of Jewish charity institutions, see Neusner, "The Impact of Immigration and Philanthropy upon the Boston Jewish Community." On politics, see William A. Braverman, "The Emergence of a Unified Community, 1880–1917," in Sarna and Smith, eds., *The Jews of Boston,* pp. 85–86.

65. For biographical information, see James R. Green and Hugh Carter Donahue, *Boston Workers: A Labor History* (Boston: The Trustees of the Public Library of the City of Boston, 1979), p. 75; Neusner, "The Rise of the Jewish Community," p. 78; Allon Gal, *Brandeis of Boston* (Cambridge: Harvard University Press, 1980); Neusner, "The Rise of the Jewish Community," pp. 94–95; Ehrenfield, *A Chronicle of Boston Jewry,* p. 639.

66. Woods, *Americans in Process,* pp. 183–189. Leslie G. Ainley, *Boston Mahatma* (Boston: Bruce Humphries, 1949), p. 45.

67. *Jewish Advocate,* September 29, 1905. *Proceedings of the Boston School Committee for 1905* (Boston: Municipal Printing Office, 1906), pp. 374–379, 401. *Jewish Advocate,* October 13, 1905. The Jewish leaders based their charges on the minority report, which singled out Lomasney for attempting to pressure the board. See also Braverman, "The Emergence of a Unified Community," p. 86.

68. See Gal, *Brandeis of Boston,* pp. 87–90, for a summary of the Silverman issue. *Proceedings of the School Committee for 1905,* p. 401. *Jewish Advocate,* December 5, October 6, 1905.

69. *Jewish Advocate,* October 27, December 8, 1905.

70. *Jewish Advocate,* February 22, 1906, quoted in Neusner, "The Rise of the Jewish Community," p. 118. *Jewish Advocate,* October 20, 1905. Gal, *Brandeis of Boston,* p. 93.

71. *Boston Post,* October 14, 1906, clipping, MLS, vol. 14. Levenson Campaign Flyer, MLS, vol. 14. *Boston Herald,* October 22, 1906, clipping, MLS, vol. 14.

72. *Jewish Advocate,* November 12, 1905.

73. *Jewish Advocate,* December 13, 1905. Neusner, "The Rise of the Jewish Community," p. 118. *Jewish Advocate,* December 1, 1909.

74. Marlene Rockmore, "The Kosher Meat Riots: A Study in the Process of Adaption Among Jewish Immigrant Housewives to Urban America, 1902–1917" (M.A. thesis, University of Massachusetts–Boston, 1980), pp. 35–57.

75. Boston Board of Election Commissioners, *Annual Reports for 1900–1910* (Boston, 1901–1911). *Jewish Advocate,* December 10, 1905.

76. Douglas L. Jones et al., *Discovering the Public Interest: A History of the Boston Bar Association* (Canoga Park, Calif.: CCA Press, 1993), p. 64.

77. Census data taken from Preston, "United States Census Data, 1910: Public Use Sample." See Statistical Appendix for data set construction.

78. Thomas O'Connor, *South Boston, My Hometown: The History of an Ethnic Neighborhood* (Boston: Quinlan Press, 1988), pp. 7–33, 87. Robert A. Woods and Albert J. Kennedy, eds., *The Zone of Emergence: Observations of Lower, Middle, and Upper Working Class Communities in Boston, 1905–1914* (Cambridge: M.I.T. Press, 1962), pp. 174–176. David Ward, "Nineteenth-Century Boston: A Study in the Role of Antecedent and Adjacent Conditions in the Spatial Aspects of Urban Growth" (Ph.D. diss., University of Wisconsin, 1963), pp. 223–228. Massachusetts Bureau of Statistics and Labor, *Census of Massachusetts: 1905,* pp. xcix, c, 638–639, and Preston, "United States Census Data, 1910: Public Use Sample." See Statistical Appendix for data set construction.

79. *South Boston Gazette,* October 6, 1906. O'Connor, *South Boston, My Hometown,* pp. 83–91.

80. John J. Toomey and Edward P. B. Rankin, *History of South Boston (Its Past and Present and Prospects for the Future with Sketches of Prominent Men)* (Boston: By the authors, 1901), p. 467. *South Boston Gazette,* October 13, 1916.

81. Toomey and Rankin, *History of South Boston,* p. 563. *South Boston Gazette,* September 4, 1909.

82. *Boston Post,* November 8, 1897. *Boston Herald,* November 25, 1941. Toomey and Rankin, *History of South Boston,* p. 558.

83. On Baldwin, see Toomey and Rankin, *History of South Boston,* p. 483; *Boston Post,* November 12, December 3, 6, 1902.

84. Boston Board of Election Commissioners, *Annual Report for 1902* (Boston, 1903), p. 71. Good Government Association Election Flyer, GGA, Files and History, file 2.

85. *South Boston Gazette,* October 13, 1906; August 31, 1907; November 16, 1907. See also September 14, 1907, for further proreform commentary. Toomey was not the only Irish editor in Boston who looked favorably on reform. John S. Flanagan, editor of the *Charlestown Enterprise,* encouraged many reforms and advocated nonpartisan political action in his Irish neighborhood. In his editorials he supported Democratic candidates but looked askance on the factional maneuverings of many neighborhood politicians, often attacking their self-serving political motivation and lack of public spirit. See for example *Charlestown Enterprise,* October 30, 1915.

86. *South Boston Gazette,* October 13, 1906; November 16, 1907; September 26, 1908.

87. *South Boston Gazette,* September 20, 1913; September 21, 1907; September 8, 1906; November 3, 1906.

88. *Charlestown Enterprise,* October 12, November 2, 1907; August 27, 1910.

89. *South Boston Gazette,* September 28, 1907; November 3, 1906. *Charlestown Enterprise,* November 10, 1906; November 9, 1907.

90. *South Boston Gazette,* September 21, 1909. *Charlestown Enterprise,* September 3, 1910. *South Boston Gazette,* September 19, 1908.

91. Polly Kaufman, "Boston Women and School Committee Politics: Women on the School Committee, 1872–1905," (Ed.D. diss., Boston University, 1978), pp. 341–378. Burns, "The Irony of Progressive Reform," pp. 140–141. *Charlestown Enterprise,* November 30, 1907; December 2, 1907; December 8, 1906; December 9, 1905. *South Boston Gazette,* December 1, 1906.

92. *Charlestown Enterprise,* December 2, 1905.

93. "Constitution and By-Laws of the League of Catholic Women," RG VI.4, box 1, folder 1, LCWP.

94. Paula M. Kane, *Separatism and Subculture: Boston Catholicism, 1900–1920* (Chapel Hill: University of North Carolina Press, 1994), p. 213.

95. Unidentified typescript, October 1920, Chancery Correspondence, Archives, Archdiocese of Boston, RG III.E.10, folder 14.

96. Elizabeth Dwight to Archbishop O'Connell, November 11, 1914, Chancery Correspondence, Archives, Archdiocese of Boston, RG III.E.10, box 1, folder 2. "Second Report of the League of Catholic Women, 1912–1913," Chancery Correspondence, Archives, Archdiocese of Boston, RG III.E.10, box 1, folder 2. Kane, *Separatism and Subculture,* p. 217.

97. Kane, *Separatism and Subculture,* p. 214. R. J. Haberlin to Msgr. Splaine, November 18, 1916, Chancery Correspondence, Archives, Archdiocese of Boston, RG III.E.10, box 1, folder 3.

98. Kane, *Separatism and Subculture,* p. 216.

3. The Politics of Municipal Reform

1. *South Boston Gazette,* September 8, 1906. *Boston Post,* September 1906 clipping (no specific date given), GGA, Scrapbook, vol. 14. See also *Boston*

Herald, September 13, 1905, GGA, Scrapbook, vol. 2, for descriptions of Linehan's attacks on the GGA.

2. Robert H. Wiebe, *The Search for Order, 1877–1920* (New York: Hill and Wang, 1967), pp. 111–132.

3. Ibid., pp. 164–195. Samuel Hays, "The Politics of Reform of Municipal Government in the Progressive Era," *Pacific Northwest Quarterly* 55 (1964): 157–169. Samuel Hays, "The Changing Political Structure of the City in Industrial America," *Journal of Urban History* 1 (1974): 1–32. Gabriel Kolko, *The Triumph of Conservatism: A Reinterpretation of American History, 1900–1916* (New York: Free Press of Glencoe, 1963). James Weinstein, *The Corporate Ideal in the Liberal State, 1900–1918* (Boston: Beacon Press, 1968). Richard L. McCormick, in *From Realignment to Reform: Political Change in New York State, 1893–1910* (Ithaca: Cornell University Press, 1981), pp. 271–272, argues that whatever the results of Progressive reform, most reformers believed their own democratizing rhetoric.

4. Terrence J. McDonald, *The Parameters of Urban Fiscal Policy: Socioeconomic Change and Political Culture in San Francisco, 1860–1906* (Berkeley: University of California Press, 1986), pp. 203–221. William Issell, "Class and Ethnic Conflict in San Francisco Political History: The Reform Charter of 1898," *Labor History* 18 (1977): 340–359. Philip J. Ethington, "Urban Constituencies, Regimes, and Policy Innovation in the Progressive Era: An Analysis of Boston, Chicago, New York City and San Francisco," *Studies in American Political Development* 7 (1993): 275–315. David Hammack, *Power and Society: Greater New York at the Turn of the Century* (New York: Sage Foundation, 1980), pp. 185–229. Kenneth Finegold, *Experts and Politicians: Reform Challenges to Machine Politics in New York, Cleveland, and Chicago* (Princeton: Princeton University Press, 1995). Maureen A. Flanagan, *Charter Reform in Chicago* (Carbondale: University of Southern Illinois Press, 1987).

5. Wiebe, *The Search for Order,* p. 181. Kenneth Fox, *Better City Government: Innovation in American Urban Politics, 1850–1937* (Philadelphia: Temple University Press, 1977), pp. 63–89. Jon C. Teaford, *The Unheralded Triumph: City Government in America: 1870–1900* (Baltimore: Johns Hopkins University Press, 1984). The more nuanced studies include Flanagan, *Charter Reform in Chicago;* Hammack, *Power and Society,* pp. 185–229; Issell, "Class and Ethnic Conflict in San Francisco."

6. Melvin Holli, *Biographical Dictionary of American Mayors, 1820–1980* (Westport, Conn.: Greenwood Press, 1981), p. 116. Doris Kearns Goodwin, *The Fitzgeralds and the Kennedys* (New York: Simon and Schuster, 1986), pp. 61–66, 68–69. John H. Cutler, *"Honey Fitz": Three Steps to the White House* (Indianapolis: Bobbs-Merrill, 1962), p. 52.

7. See Michael E. McGerr, *The Decline of Popular Politics: The American North, 1865–1928* (New York: Oxford University Press, 1986), pp. 138–183, for an analysis of these changes.

8. Richard M. Abrams, *Conservatism in a Progressive Era: Massachusetts Poli-*

tics, 1900–1912 (Cambridge: Harvard University Press, 1964), p. 146. *Boston Herald,* November 17, 1905. Thomas R. Mason, "Reform Politics in Boston" (Ph.D. diss., Harvard University Press, 1963), pp. 160–164.

9. Goodwin, *The Fitzgeralds and the Kennedys,* p. 106. *Boston Post,* December 13, 1905.

10. Fitzgerald quoted in Goodwin, *The Fitzgeralds and the Kennedys,* pp. 107–108; *Boston Herald,* November 7, 14, 9, 1905.

11. *Boston Post,* November 17, 1905. The count of ward organizations is from *The Mayors of Boston: An Illustrated Epitome of Who the Mayors Have Been and What They Have Done* (Boston: State Street Trust Co., 1914).

12. *Dorchester Beacon,* November 25, December 2, 1905. Abrams, *Conservatism in a Progressive Era,* p. 147.

13. *Boston Journal,* November 14, 1903, GGA, Scrapbook, vol. 3. Herbert M. Zolot, "The Issue of Good Government: James Michael Curley and the Boston Scene, 1897–1918" (Ph.D. diss., State University of New York at Stony Brook, 1975), p. 94. Abrams, *Conservatism in a Progressive Era,* p. 146.

14. McCormick, *From Realignment to Reform,* p. 206.

15. Boston Board of Election Commissioners, *Annual Report for 1905* (Boston, 1906), p. 171. Goodwin, *The Fitzgeralds and the Kennedys,* p. 109. Boston Board of Election Commissioners, *Annual Report for 1903* (Boston, 1904), p. 192. The strength of Fitzgerald's Irish support in 1905 is reported in Table 2.

16. "Inaugural Address of John F. Fitzgerald, Mayor of Boston," *Boston City Documents for 1906,* Document 1 (Boston: Municipal Printing Office, 1906), p. 4.

17. Thomas H. O'Connor, *The Boston Irish: A Political History* (Boston: Northeastern University Press, 1995), p. 168.

18. William Minot to George R. Nutter, April 7, 1936, GGA, Files and History, file 1.

19. Unidentified clipping, April 13, 1906, GGA, Scrapbook, vol. 14. *Boston Herald,* April 30, 1906, GGA, Scrapbook, vol. 14. See *Boston Advertiser,* April 30, 1906, GGA, Scrapbook, vol. 14, for an example of the press accusing Fitzgerald of seeking to divert attention from the sewer department investigation.

20. Martin J. Schiesl, *The Politics of Efficiency: Municipal Administration and Reform in America, 1800–1920* (Berkeley: University of California Press, 1977), pp. 99–132.

21. This account is pieced together from George Read Nutter Diaries, vol. 1, January 3, 16, 29, 30, 31, February 2, 6, 1907.

22. *Report of the Finance Commission of the City of Boston,* vol. 1 (Boston, 1908), pp. 5–12.

23. By late 1906 Fitzgerald was under steady attack from business-based reformers regarding the conduct of his administration. In November cries for an investigation grew louder. The *Boston Herald,* which maintained close ties to

the GGA, called on the state to commence an inquiry into the city's finances on November 6. Later in the month both the Republican state convention and the GGA had publicly endorsed the idea of a formal scrutiny of Boston's government. Sensing the inevitable, Fitzgerald beat his State House enemies to the punch. On December 13 he sent a message to the Board of Aldermen asking for the establishment of an investigative committee. Many saw through this transparent move; they echoed the views of a skeptical common councilman who asked "if there is anyone who believes that this order is not a humbug . . . a move to forestall a genuine investigation?" *Proceedings of the Common Council of Boston,* January 2, 1907. For details of the Commission's origins, see Zolot, "The Issues of Good Government," p. 104. Nutter Diaries, vol. 1, November 26, December 12, 15, 1906. See also Mason, "Reform Politics in Boston," pp. 170–172. Richard Abrams suggests that Fitzgerald hoped to gain wider support through his Finance Commission proposal because he had alienated Democratic leaders. Abrams, *Conservatism in a Progressive Era,* p. 147.

24. Nutter Diaries, vol. 2, July 15, 1907.

25. *The Republic,* August 31, 1907, GGA, Scrapbook, vol. 4. *Boston Transcript,* August 19, 1907, GGA, Scrapbook, vol. 4. Fitzgerald to finance commissioners, October 17, 1907, in *Report of the Finance Commission,* vol. 1, p. 47.

26. For a sample of the press coverage, see the *Boston Herald,* August 28, September 4, 6, 7, 8, 1907. For details of the Finance Commission hearings and reports, see *Final Report of the Boston Finance Commission,* vol. 4 (Boston: Municipal Printing Office, 1909). Mitchell eventually served a jail term for his connections to the illegal contracts. *Boston Herald,* November 9, 1909. On the limits of the Finance Commission's discoveries, see Constance K. Burns, "The Irony of Progressive Reform: Boston, 1898–1910," in Ronald Formisano and Constance K. Burns, *Boston: 1700–1980: The Evolution of Urban Politics* (Westwood, Conn.: Greenwood Press, 1984), pp. 133–164.

27. *Boston Herald,* September 6, 12, 1907.

28. *Report of the Finance Commission,* vol. 1, pp. 102–103. Mason, "Reform Politics in Boston," pp. 178–181. Goodwin, *The Fitzgeralds and the Kennedys,* pp. 148–149.

29. *Report of the Finance Commission,* vol. 2, pp. 211, 227.

30. *Gazzetta del Massachusetts,* September 21, November 11, 30, 1907. *South Boston Gazette,* September 14, 21, 1907.

31. *Report of the Finance Commission,* vol. 2, pp. 257–258. Frank M. Stewart, *A Half-Century of Municipal Reform: The History of the National Municipal League* (Berkeley: University of California Press, 1950), pp. 32–37.

32. *Report of the Finance Commission,* vol. 2, p. 195.

33. Ibid., pp. 198, 257, 252.

34. Ibid., pp. 194, 198.

35. Ibid., p. 196.

36. Nutter Diaries, vol. 2, January 5, February 13, March 24, 1909. Nutter cred-

ited former Boston Mayor Edwin U. Curtis with devising the compromise. See Nutter Diaries, vol. 2, April 23, 1909. The Republican leaders agreed to the deal because it gave their party a tighter grip on Boston's purse strings, allowing them to restrict the flow of patronage to Democratic city leaders while at the same time holding out the possibility of maintaining ward-based representation, a system that gave them at least a few seats in city hall.

37. Nutter Diaries, vol. 2, April 23, 1909. Mason, "Reform Politics in Boston," pp. 272–273.

38. Storrow quoted in Burns, "The Irony of Progressive Reform," p. 152. Nutter Diaries, vol. 2, March 27, February 13, 23, 1909.

39. *Boston Evening Transcript,* November 1, 1909.

40. *Boston Herald,* March 5, June 17, 1909.

41. *Boston Herald,* November 1, 1909.

42. *Charlestown Enterprise,* October 16, 1909. *Boston Herald,* October 5, 10, 12, 1909. *Gazzetta del Massachusetts,* October 30, 1909.

43. *Report of the Finance Commission,* vol. 2, p. 281.

44. For an example of suburban improvement association support for the charter, see *Dorchester Beacon,* March 20, 1909; *Jewish Advocate,* October 29, November 5, 1909; Allen F. Davis, *Spearheads for Reform: The Social Settlements and the Progressive Movement, 1890–1914* (New York: Oxford University Press, 1967), p. 178.

45. Flanagan, *Charter Reform in Chicago,* pp. 40–42, 143–144.

46. *South Boston Gazette,* October 16, September 18, 1909.

47. *South Boston Gazette,* October 2, 16, 1909. *Charlestown Enterprise,* October 16, 1909.

48. A separate model testing Irish and working-class support for Plan Two also showed no relationship, suggesting that Irish voters were also split on the issue. See Samuel H. Preston, "United States Census Data, 1910: Public Use Sample" (Ann Arbor: Inter-University Consortium for Political and Social Research, 1989), and Boston Board of Election Commissioners, *Annual Report for 1909–1910* (Boston, 1910), p. 142. Model: percent vote for Plan Two = intercept + percent Irish stock + percent working class. Model statistics: $N = 25$; $R^2 = .01$; adjusted $R^2 = -.08$; intercept = .51; percent Irish = .08 (p-value = .61); percent working class = $-.05$ (p-value = .86). See Statistical Appendix for construction of variables.

49. Burns, "The Irony of Progressive Reform," pp. 142–144.

50. Ibid., pp. 153–157. *Boston Transcript,* January 4, 1910. *Boston Herald,* December 29, 1909.

51. *Boston Transcript,* January 4, 5, 1910. On Storrow in the North End, see *Boston Post,* December 10, 1909, in Boston Election Department Scrapbook, Boston Public Library.

52. See Cutler, *"Honey Fitz,"* pp. 127–143, for an account of the campaign. *Charlestown Enterprise,* January 8, 1910. *Boston Transcript,* January 4, 1910.

53. Cutler, *"Honey Fitz,"* pp. 127–143.

54. Ibid., p. 92. According to Storrow's charge, Fitzgerald would submit an advance copy of a speech to newspaper reporters, who would print it verbatim, and then deliver a substantially different speech. *Boston Post,* December 5, 1909. On his purchase of *The Republic,* see Goodwin, *The Fitzgeralds and the Kennedys,* p. 106.

55. *The Republic,* December 4, 11, 18, 1909.

56. *The Republic,* December 25, 1909.

57. *The Republic,* January 8, 1910.

58. Ibid.

59. Burns, "The Irony of Progressive Reform," p. 151. Maurice Baskin, "Ward Boss Politics in Boston, 1896–1921" (senior honors thesis, Harvard University, 1975), p. 67. *The Republic,* December 11, 1909. Nutter Diaries, vol. 3, January 7, 1910.

4. The New Urban Political Terrain

1. The best description of these changes is Richard L. McCormick, *From Realignment to Reform: Political Change in New York State, 1893–1910* (Ithaca: Cornell University Press, 1981). See also Michael E. McGerr, *The Decline of Popular Politics: The American North, 1865–1928* (New York: Oxford University Press, 1986); Walter Dean Burnham, "The Changing Shape of the American Political Universe," *American Political Science Review* 54 (1965): 7–28; Paul Kleppner, *Continuity and Change in Electoral Politics, 1892–1928* (New York: Greenwood Press, 1987).

2. Samuel Hays, "The Changing Political Structure of the City in Industrial America," *Journal of American History* 1 (1974): 25.

3. Hays, "The Changing Political Structure of the City," pp. 1–32, is the principal statement of this thesis for urban politics. See also Robert H. Wiebe, *The Search for Order, 1877–1920* (New York: Oxford University Press, 1967); Louis Galambos, "The Emerging Organizational Synthesis in Modern American History," *Business History Review* 44 (1970): 279–290.

4. *Boston Herald,* November 10, 1909. *Boston Globe,* November 18, 1909, clipping, Boston Election Department Scrapbook, Boston Public Library.

5. Nutter Diaries, vol. 3, August 21, November 2, 1909. Unidentified clipping, n.d., MLS, vol. 17. *Boston Post,* November 9, 1909. *Boston Globe,* November 18, 1909, clipping, Boston Election Department Scrapbook. See Nutter Diaries, vol. 3, November 5, 1909, for a discussion of the long-planned Storrow candidacy and its appeal to Democrats.

6. See Boston Board of Election Commissioners, *Annual Reports for 1910–1914* (Boston, 1911–1915) for the results of City Council races.

7. Ibid.

8. Boston Board of Election Commissioners, *Annual Report for 1910–1911* (Boston, 1912), pp. 38–40. *Charlestown Enterprise,* September 9, 1911.

9. Boston Board of Election Commissioners, *Annual Report for 1908* (Boston, 1909), pp. 153–155. *South Boston Gazette,* September 26, 1908.

10. Paul Kleppner, *Who Voted? The Dynamics of Electoral Turnout, 1870–1980* (New York: Praeger, 1982), pp. 58–63. Burnham, "The Changing Shape of the American Political Universe," pp. 7–28. McGerr, *The Decline of Popular Politics,* pp. 12–68.

11. Unidentified typescript, box C36, folder 19, Allen-Lane Co. Collection, Baker Library, Harvard Business School, pp. 3–4. Benjamin Lane to H. Findlay French, April 5, 1915, box C36, folder 18, Allen-Lane Co. Collection.

12. *UIA Bulletin,* October 1910, p. 3.

13. Sam Bass Warner, *Streetcar Suburbs: The Process of Growth in Boston, 1870–1900* (New York: Athenaeum Press, 1962), pp. 41–42. Kenneth Jackson, *Crabgrass Frontier: The Suburbanization of the United States* (New York: Oxford University Press, 1985), pp. 138–148.

14. Massachusetts Bureau of Statistics and Labor, *Census of the Commonwealth of Massachusetts: 1905,* vol. 1, *Population and Social Statistics* (Boston: Wright and Potter Printing Company, 1909), p. xcii. William Marchione, *The Bull in the Garden: A History of Allston-Brighton* (Boston: Boston Public Library, 1986), p. 100.

15. Boston Board of Election Commissioners, *Annual Report for 1908,* pp. 84, 148. Idem, *Annual Report for 1904* (Boston, 1905), p. 80. *Brighton Item,* November 11, 1905.

16. *Brighton Item,* November 14, 21, 1908; December 29, 1906.

17. *Brighton Item,* November 21, 1908. See also *Brighton Item,* May 16, December 18, 1908.

18. *UIA Bulletin,* February 1911, p. 9. *Brighton Item,* January 8, 1910; February 25, 1911; February 26, 1910.

19. "List of Requests for Local Improvements," *Boston City Documents for 1910* (Boston, 1911), document 51, pp. 24–28. *Brighton Item,* February 19, 1910.

20. *Brighton Item,* May 14, 1910; April 1, 29, 1911; November 21, December 19, 1914. See also *UIA Bulletin,* January 1911, p. 11; *UIA Bulletin,* March–April 1911, p. 13.

21. "List of Requests for Local Improvements," p. 26. In the three nonmayoral city elections preceding charter reform, turnout averaged 66 percent, and an average of 67 percent of the district's adult males registered. In the first three elections under the new city charter, turnout dropped to an average of 42 percent and 62 percent of the district's adult males registered. See Boston Board of Election Commissioners, *Annual Reports for 1904, 1906, 1908, 1910–1911, 1911–1912, 1912–1913* (Boston, 1905, 1907, 1909, 1912, 1913, 1914). See also *Brighton Item,* January 14, 1911; January 18, 1912.

22. *Brighton Item,* October 16, 1909; February 21, 1914; February 5, 26, March 12, 1910. The registered voters total includes women who could vote at this time in School Committee elections but were not allowed to join the FIA.

23. Marchione, *The Bull in the Garden,* p. 101.

24. *Brighton Item,* October 26, December 21, 1912.

25. James R. Green and Hugh Carter Donahue, *Boston Workers: A Labor History* (Boston: Trustees of the Public Library of the City of Boston, 1979) p. 87. Allon Gal, *Brandeis of Boston* (Cambridge: Harvard University Press, 1980), pp. 58–59. See Allen F. Davis, *Spearheads for Reform: The Social Settlements and the Progressive Movement, 1890–1914* (New York: Oxford University Press, 1967), p. 107.

26. *Brighton Item,* February 21, 1914; January 13, 1917. Marchione, *The Bull in the Garden,* pp. 100–101. See *Brighton Item,* September 1, 1900, and January 22, 1910, for a sampling of the Associations activities on behalf of the neighborhood.

27. Marchione, *The Bull in the Garden,* pp. 100–101. "History" [typescript], p. 11, box 3, folder 4, LCWP.

28. *WMLB,* May 1913.

29. Sarah Deutsch, "Learning to Talk More Like a Man: Boston Women's Class-Bridging Organizations, 1870–1940," *American Historical Review* 97 (1992): 396, 399.

30. Robert Gillespie Blaine, "Birth of a Neighborhood: Nineteenth-Century Charlestown Massachusetts" (Ph.D. diss., University of Michigan, 1978), vol. 1, p. 307. Massachusetts Bureau of Statistics and Labor, *Census of Massachusetts: 1905,* vol. 1, *Population and Social Statistics,* pp. xcvi, xcvii, 638–639. The estimate of Irish population includes only first- and second-generation Irish immigrants. Since by the beginning of the twentieth century Boston was home to at least some third-generation Irish, this figure likely underestimates the size of the Irish presence in the district.

31. Blaine, "Birth of a Neighborhood," vol. 2, pp. 422–469; Maurice Baskin, "Ward Boss Politics in Boston, 1896–1921" (senior honors thesis, Harvard University, 1975), p. 25.

32. Boston Board of Election Commissioners, *Annual Report for 1908,* pp. 151, 153.

33. *Charlestown Enterprise,* November 23, 1912.

34. Blaine, "Birth of a Neighborhood," vol. 2, p. 490. Quote from "Constitution and By-Laws of the Charlestown Improvement Association, 1914," Boston Public Library. The Association's own assessment of itself was shared by the *Charlestown Enterprise,* whose editor, John S. Flanagan, was a prominent member: "every meeting of the past year of the Charlestown Improvement Association . . . is demonstrating its strength and influence in the interests of the district" (November 16, 1912).

35. *Charlestown Enterprise,* January 4, 1913; October 6, 1906; October 1, 1910; September 19, 1910.

36. "Constitution and By-Laws of the Charlestown Improvement Association, 1914."

37. Ibid. *Charlestown Enterprise,* October 2, 1909.
38. *Charlestown Enterprise,* September 16, 1911.
39. *Charlestown Enterprise,* January 3, 1914; September 13, 27, 1913.
40. The saga of the battle between Charlestown and the Elevated Company, and the Improvement Association's central role in it, can be gleaned from the pages of the *Charlestown Enterprise* between 1913 and 1917. For details on the events described in the text, see September 20, October 11, December 6, 13, 1913; September 19, November 21, 1914; December 25, 1915; June 2, 1917.
41. *Charlestown Enterprise,* November 5, 12, 1910.
42. Unidentified clipping, MLS, vol. 17.
43. For details of the 1909 campaign and Fales's role in it, see the *Charlestown Enterprise,* November 27, December 4, 1909. For future campaigns, see the *Charlestown Enterprise,* December 17, 1910; November 8, 1913. On Fales and McDonald, see the *Charlestown Enterprise,* December 16, 1916.
44. *Charlestown Enterprise,* December 31, 1910; December 7, 14, 1912.
45. Boston Board of Election Commissioners, *Annual Report for 1909–1910* (Boston, 1911), pp. 144–145. Idem, *Annual Report for 1910–1911,* pp. 145–146. South Bostonians had their representative selected for them in similar fashion. Under the old district system, reform candidate Thomas J. Kenny, a close ally of the South Boston Citizens Association, would have finished a lackluster fourth in the 1910 race for South Boston's Council seat. But bolstered by the Citizens' Municipal League endorsement, Kenny won enough votes to vault over the other three candidates from his district and take a seat on the new at-large City Council. Boston Board of Election Commissioners, *Annual Report for 1909–1910,* pp. 149–150.
46. On Lomasney, see Leslie Ainley, *Boston Mahatma* (Boston: Bruce Humphries, 1949). Lomasney's activities while serving in the State Senate are the source of his reputation as an urban liberal. See John D. Buenker, "The Mahatma and Progressive Reform: Martin Lomasney as Lawmaker," *New England Quarterly* 44 (1971): 371–419.
47. *Jewish Advocate,* December 30, 1910. GGA, Candidate Files, Ernest Smith file. Boston Board of Election Commissioners, *Annual Report for 1910–11* (Boston: 1911), p. 147.
48. "List of Requests for Local Improvements," pp. 16–17. *UIA Bulletin,* March–April 1911. "List of Requests for Local Improvements," p. 16. See *UIA Bulletin,* 1910–1912, for accounts of West End Improvement Society activities.
49. "List of Requests for Local Improvements," p. 16. *UIA Bulletin,* November 1910, p. 10. *UIA Bulletin,* March–April 1911, p. 9.
50. *Jewish Advocate,* November 26, 1909; July 15, November 11, 1910.
51. *Jewish Advocate,* November 26, December 24, 1909; January 7, 1910. Jacob Neusner, "The Rise of the Jewish Community in Boston, 1880–1914" (A.B.

thesis, Harvard University, 1953), p. 119. Boston Board of Election Commissioners, *Annual Report for 1909–1910*, pp. 145–146. Relations between the GGA and the CML had begun to sour by this time (see Chapter 5).

52. *Jewish Advocate*, March 17, 1911; January 12, 1912; July 29, 1910; January 26, 1912. Neusner, "The Rise of the Jewish Community," p. 63. Jacob Neusner, "The Impact of Immigration and Philanthropy upon the Boston Jewish Community (1880–1914)," *Publication of the American Jewish Historical Society* 146 (1956): 71–85.

53. On Lomasney's central place in the creation of the theory of latent functionalism, see Terrence J. McDonald, "The Problem of the Political in Recent American Urban History: Liberal Pluralism and the Rise of Functionalism," *Social History* 10 (1985): 335. See also Robert K. Merton, *Social Theory and Social Structure*, rev. enl. ed. (New York: The Free Press, 1968), p. 129. See "Introduction" for further discussion of this issue.

54. Boston Board of Election Commissioners, *Annual Reports for 1900–1908* (Boston, 1901–1909). Only the 1905 report provides the number of eligible voters. Still, it is important to examine the number of adult males who were actually mobilized, regardless of eligibility, because one purported "function" of the ward boss was the political acculturation of the immigrant.

55. Boston Board of Election Commissioners, *Annual Reports for 1905, 1907* (Boston, 1906, 1908). I focus on municipal candidates because city hall was the primary source of patronage for Boston Democrats. They had relatively little access to the Republican-controlled state government in this era.

56. Boston Board of Election Commissioners, *Annual Reports for 1900–1914*.

57. Nutter Diaries, vol. 6, October 2, 31, 1914. *UIA Bulletin*, February 1912, p. 1.

58. A. A. Fales to Daniel J. McDonald, October 17, 1914, GGA, Candidate Files, Daniel J. McDonald. *Charlestown Enterprise*, October 24, 31, September 26, 1914.

59. A separate regression testing the relationship of the native-stock and white-collar variables indicates a clear relationship between the two (the coefficient was .67, with a p-value of .004), suggesting that most of the Yankees voting against the Lomasney plan were also middle class. (The model is not powerful enough to indicate collinearity; its R^2 was .31.) The native-stock variable appears to have been so strong a predictor of opposition to Lomasney's plan that it obscures the effect of the white-collar variable on the equation. Indeed, a regression testing only the relationship between the size of a ward's middle-class population and the percentage of people in a district voting "no" on the 1914 referendum showed a significant correlation, albeit a smaller R^2 value. (Model: percentage "no" vote = percentage white-collar. Model statistics: R^2 =.25; adjusted R^2 =.22; percentage white-collar coefficient =.62; p-value =.01; standard deviation =.22; intercept =.39.) See Statistical Appendix for construction of variables. (Samuel H. Preston, "United States Census Data,

1910: Public Use Sample" (Ann Arbor: Inter-University Consortium for Political and Social Research, 1989; ICPSR, 9166), and Boston Board of Election Commissioners, *Annual Report for 1914*, p. 162.

5. James Michael Curley and the Politics of Ethnic Progressivism

1. See Nutter Diaries, vol. 2, June 8, July 8, 1908; E. Billings to E. Filene, July 1, 1908; H. W. Louis to Lincoln Steffens, October 6, 1909; H. W. Louis to E. Billings, August 11, 1909; Memorandum re: April 12, 1912, meeting between E. Billings and L. Steffens, GGA, Lincoln Steffens File, file 2. The GGA badly misread both Steffens's intentions and the character of *The Shame of the Cities* (New York: Hill and Wang, 1969). In his introduction to that essay collection, Steffens argued that the "big business man" was "the chief source of corruption," and his intention for Boston from the start was to write something more than a catalog of sensational corruption (p. 3). See Steffens to William C. Bobbs, May 13, 1908, in Ella Winter and Granville Hicks, eds., *The Letters of Lincoln Steffens*, vol. 1; *1889–1919* (New York: Harcourt, Brace and Company, 1938), p. 90.
2. This shift in political style is described in Michael E. McGerr, *The Decline of Popular Politics: The American North, 1865–1928* (New York: Oxford University Press, 1986), pp. 138–183. Quote from Nutter Diaries, vol. 3, February 27, 1911. Reaching voters in this new fashion was made possible by the explosion of the daily press in Boston and other big cities during this era.
3. Lincoln Steffens, "A Cure for Corruption," *Metropolitan Magazine* (March 1914), pp. 13, 68. The GGA, which owned the manuscript, authorized the publication of a three-part series in *Metropolitan Magazine* to help defray some of what it paid Steffens. The articles attracted little attention and apparently had no direct impact on Boston's public affairs, despite the parallels between its argument and the emerging themes of Boston's ethnic Progressivism. See Steffens to R. Bottomly, July 18, 1914, GGA, Lincoln Steffens File, file 4.
4. "James Michael Curley," in Melvin Holli and Peter d'A. Jones, eds., *Biographical Dictionary of American Mayors, 1820–1980* (Westport, Conn.: Greenwood Press, 1981), p. 83.
5. Jeffrey Tulis, *The Rhetorical Presidency* (Princeton: Princeton University Press, 1987), p. 4. Thomas R. Pegram, *Partisans and Progressives: Private Interest and Public Policy in Illinois, 1870–1922* (Chicago: University of Illinois Press, 1992), p. 220. George E. Mowry, *The California Progressives* (Chicago: Quadrangle Books, 1963), pp. 105–157. David Thelen, *Robert La-Follette and the Insurgent Spirit* (Boston: Little Brown, 1976). Melvin G. Holli, *Reform in Detroit: Hazen Pingree and Urban Politics* (New York: Oxford University Press, 1969), pp. 33–55. Hoyt Landon Warner, *Progressivism in Ohio, 1897–1917* (Columbus: Ohio State University Press, 1964),

pp. 22–41, 54–137. Edward Miller, *Mr. Crump of Memphis* (Baton Rouge: Louisiana State University Press, 1964). Holli and Jones, eds., *Biographical Dictionary of American Mayors* pp. 362, 176, 380.

6. James Michael Curley, *I'd Do It Again: A Record of All My Uproarious Years* (Englewood Cliffs, N.J.: Prentice Hall, 1957), pp. 30–43.

7. Jack Beatty, *The Rascal King: The Life and Times of James Michael Curley, 1874–1958* (Reading, Mass.: Addison-Wesley, 1992), pp. 56–63.

8. *Boston Evening Globe,* November 16, 1899. *Boston Post,* November 17, 1899. Herbert M. Zolot, "The Issue of Good Government: James Michael Curley and the Boston Scene, 1897–1918" (Ph.D. diss., State University of New York at Stony Brook, 1975), pp. 163, 193–195. *Boston Post,* December 6, 1903. Robert A. Woods and Albert J. Kennedy, eds., *The Zone of Emergence: Observations of Lower, Middle, and Upper Working-Class Communities in Boston, 1905–1914* (Cambridge: M.I.T. Press, 1962), pp. 135–137.

9. Beatty, *The Rascal King,* pp. 95–97.

10. Zolot, "The Issue of Good Government," pp. 193–195. Beatty, *The Rascal King,* pp. 68, 78. Woods and Kennedy, eds., *The Zone of Emergence,* pp. 135–137. *Boston Post,* December 6, 1903. "Report by Palfrey on Interview with Curley at the Tammany Club" [typescript], GGA, Candidate Files, James M. Curley File, box 9, file 5.

11. Terrence J. McDonald, "Introduction," in William Riordan, *Plunkitt of Tammany Hall: A Series of Very Plain Talks on Very Practical Politics,* edited with an Introduction by Terrence J. McDonald (Boston: Bedford Books of St. Martin's Press, 1994), pp. 20–25.

12. Zolot, "The Issue of Good Government," pp. 171–180. Charles H. Trout, "Curley of Boston: The Search for Irish Legitimacy," in Ronald Formisano and Constance K. Burns, eds., *Boston, 1700–1980: The Evolution of Urban Politics* (Westport, Conn.: Greenwood Press, 1984), pp. 175–178. Curley, *I'd Do It Again,* p. 115. *South Boston Gazette,* September 24, 1910.

13. *Roxbury Gazette and South End Advertiser,* December 27, 1913.

14. *South Boston Gazette,* September 24, 1910.

15. Thomas O'Connor, *South Boston, My Hometown: The History of an Ethnic Neighborhood* (Boston: Quinlan Press, 1988), pp. 97–100. *South Boston Gazette,* January 17, 1914. Boston Board of Election Commissioners, *Annual Report for 1913–1914* (Boston, 1914), pp. 153–156.

16. *Boston Daily Globe,* January 14, 1914. *Charlestown Enterprise,* January 17, 1914. Maurice Baskin, "Ward Boss Politics in Boston, 1896–1921" (senior honors thesis, Harvard University, 1975), pp. 80, 94; Zolot, "The Issue of Good Government," p. 566 (n. 36), 552.

17. Zolot, "The Issue of Good Government," pp. 327–328. Beatty, *The Rascal King,* p. 141.

18. Curley quoted in Beatty, *The Rascal King,* p. 141, and O'Connor, *South Boston,* p. 99.

19. Zolot, "The Issue of Good Government," pp. 339, 342. Beatty, *The Rascal King*, p. 123.
20. Curley, *I'd Do It Again*, pp. 102–104. *Congressional Record*, 62nd Congress, 2nd session, 1912, p. 10424. Trout, "Curley of Boston," pp. 180–181. Gustave Ralph Serino, "Italians and the Political Life of Boston: A Study of the Role of an Immigrant and Ethnic Group in the Political Life of an Urban Community" (Ph.D. diss., Harvard University, 1950), p. 70. *Jewish Advocate*, May 10, 24, December 20, 1912; December 19, 1913; January 9, 1914. *South Boston Gazette*, January 17, 1914.
21. A regression equation designed to measure the relationship between the size of an Irish population in a given ward and its vote for Curley (percent Curley vote = percent Irish stock) showed no such relationship (regression statistics: intercept = .48; coefficient = .28; standard error = .17; R^2 = .10; adjusted R^2 = .07; p-value = .11). For information on data set and statistical procedures, see Statistical Appendix.
22. Quoted in Beatty, *The Rascal King*, p. 159. See also Zolot, "The Issue of Good Government," p. 369.
23. Boston Board of Election Commissioners, *Annual Report for 1913–1914*, p. 159.
24. *Boston Journal*, January 15, 1915, clipping, JMCS, vol. A-10.
25. *Boston Advertiser*, February 3, 1914, JMCS, vol. A-1.
26. Zolot, "The Issue of Good Government" pp. 358–360. *Boston Journal*, February 3, 1914. *Boston Advertiser*, February 6, 1914. *Boston Herald*, February 6, 1914. Unlabeled clipping, March 1, 1914, JMCS, vol. A-1. Unlabeled clipping, March 3, 1914, JMCS, vol. A-2. Unlabeled clipping, April 14, 1914, JMCS, vol. A-3. Zolot, "The Issue of Good Government," pp. 370–371.
27. Beatty, *The Rascal King*, p. 157. Zolot, "The Issue of Good Government," pp. 378–388.
28. On charter campaign, see Nutter Diaries, vol. 5, October 21, 31, 1915; Zolot, "The Issue of Good Government," p. 267; *Boston Journal*, March 7, 1914, clipping, JMCS, vol. A-1.
29. Fliers in Nutter Diaries, vol. 5, October, 21, 31, 1915.
30. GGA comment in unlabeled clipping, March 2, 1914, JMCS, vol. A-1. *Boston Herald*, March 14, 1914, quoted in Zolot, "The Issue of Good Government," p. 378. *Boston Journal*, February 16, 1915, GGA, Scrapbook, vol. 14. *Boston Record*, December 4, 1914.
31. Zolot, "The Issue of Good Government," p. 484. *Boston American*, April 26, 1915, clipping, GGA, Candidate Files, James Michael Curley File, box C.2, file 3.
32. Jack Tager, "Reaction and Reform in Boston: The Gilded Age and the Progressive Era," in Jack Tager and John Ifkovic, eds. *Massachusetts in the Gilded Age: Selected Essays* (Amherst: University of Massachusetts Press, 1985), p. 241. Trout, "Curley of Boston," p. 178. *Boston Post*, March 12,

1917, GGA, Candidate Files, James Michael Curley File, box 10, file 5. *Boston American,* April 17, 1915, clipping, GGA, Candidate Files, James Michael Curley File, box C.2, file 1. Unlabeled clipping, March 29, 1914, JMCS, vol. A-3.

33. Zolot, "The Issue of Good Government," p. 596.

34. *Gazzetta del Massachusetts,* May 15, 22, 1915. *Boston Globe,* December 6, 1916, clipping, GGA, Candidate Files, James Michael Curley File, box 8, file 2.

35. Maguire's relationship with Curley later soured when Curley refused to back the East Boston publisher's congressional bid. See *East Boston Free Press,* August 13, November 19, 1921.

36. Unlabeled clipping, November 20, 1914, JMCS, vol. A-9. *Boston Record,* March 2, 1917, JMCS, vol. A-21. Unlabeled clipping, December 1, 1914, and *Boston Post,* January 1, 1917, JMCS, vol. A-20.

37. William Marchione, *The Bull in the Garden: A History of Allston-Brighton* (Boston: Boston Public Library, 1986), p. 105. *Brighton Item,* April 18, 1914. Lawrence Kennedy describes how Curley devoted increasing amounts of money to the city's ethnic neighborhoods while ignoring downtown business districts. See *Planning a City Upon a Hill: Boston Since 1630* (Amherst: University of Massachusetts Press, 1992), pp. 132–133.

38. Nutter Diaries, vol. 8, August 17, 1915. *Boston Post,* December 10, 1915, GGA, Candidate Files, James Michael Curley File, box 7, file 1. *Boston Labor World,* December 15, 1917, GGA, Candidate Files, James Michael Curley File, box 9, file 5. Real Estate Exchange statement from unlabeled clipping in Nutter Diaries, vol. 9, June 14, 1916. Records of the Boston Central Labor Union for 1916 (June 10), p. 82. *Boston Labor World,* December 15, 1917, GGA, Candidate Files, James Michael Curley, box 9, file 5.

39. J. Joseph Huthmacher, "Urban Liberalism and the Age of Reform," *Journal of American History* 49 (1962): 31–41. See also John D. Buenker, *Urban Liberalism and Progressive Reform* (New York: Charles Scribner and Sons, 1973).

40. Zolot, "The Issue of Good Government," pp. 315, 517–518. *Boston American,* March 31, 1915, clipping, GGA, Candidate Files, James Michael Curley File, box 7, file 3. Such claims could work both ways: one Boston minister responded to Curley by insisting that St. Patrick was Scottish. Beatty, *The Rascal King,* p. 168.

41. *Boston Post,* December 14, 1915, clipping, GGA, Candidate Files, James Michael Curley File, box C.2, file 2.

42. Kenneth Finegold, *Experts and Politicians: Reform Challenges to Machine Politics in New York, Cleveland, and Chicago* (Princeton: Princeton University Press, 1995), pp. 14–15, 52–133. Herbert F. Margulies, *The Decline of the Progressive Movement in Wisconsin, 1890–1920* (Madison: State Historical Society of Wisconsin, 1968), pp. 91–92, 283–285.

43. Zolot, "The Issue of Good Government," pp. 485–488, 490–491. *Proceed-*

ings of the City Council for 1915 (Boston, 1916), pp. 16, 50, 78–81. *Proceedings of the City Council for 1916* (Boston, 1917), pp. 61–105, 119–148. For evidence of the GGA's efforts to block Curley's loan and tax hike requests, see Nutter Diaries, vol. 8, April 5, 18, 1916.

44. Nutter Diaries, vol. 8, April 17, 1916. *Boston Journal,* (n.d.), JMCS, vol. A-11. *Boston Herald,* May 17, 1915, GGA, Scrapbook, vol. 14. Curley quoted in unidentified clipping, Nutter Diaries, vol. 8, April 19, 1916. *Boston Journal,* June 30, 1916, clipping, GGA, Candidate Files, James Michael Curley File, box 8, file 1. See also Nutter Diaries, vol. 8, April 18, 1916; Zolot, "The Issue of Good Government," pp. 508–510; *Proceedings of the City Council for 1916,* p. 67.

45. Zolot, "The Issue of Good Government," pp. 476–479.

46. Unlabeled clipping, Nutter Diaries, vol. 7, December 1, 1915.

47. Richard L. McCormick, *From Realignment to Reform: Political Change in New York State, 1893–1910* (Ithaca: Cornell University Press, 1981), pp. 251–272. Thomas R. Pegram, *Partisans and Progressives: Private Interest and Public Policy in Illinois, 1877–1922* (Chicago: University of Illinois Press, 1992), pp. 213–223.

48. See unlabeled clippings in Nutter Diaries, vol. 6, May 19, 1915, and vol. 7, November 26, 30, December 12, 1915; *Boston Advertiser,* May 18, 1915, GGA, Scrapbook, vol. 14.

49. *Charlestown Enterprise,* December 11, 1915.

50. *East Boston Free Press,* December 2, 1915.

51. *South Boston Gazette,* November 27, 13, 1915. See also *Boston Globe,* December 6, 1916, GGA, Candidate Files, James Michael Curley File, box 8, file 2, for Curley's cooperation with the South Boston Trade Association and its support of him.

52. *East Boston Free Press,* October 30, December 4, 1915.

53. Unlabeled clipping, Nutter Diaries, vol. 6, May 30, 1915.

54. On the GGA's attitude, see Nutter Diaries, vol. 6, November 4, 1914, and vol. 9, January 16, 1917.

55. *South Boston Gazette,* December 16, 1916. *Boston Daily Globe,* December 18, 1916. Nutter Diaries, vol. 8, April 10, 18, 1916. Zolot, "The Issue of Good Government," pp. 506, 511. It is important to remember that the split between the GGA and Irish politicians occurred *inside* the terms of Progressivism. Both Curley and the GGA claimed to be reformers. The timing and character of this split parallel similar divisions within other Progressive coalitions, including those in New York City, Cleveland, Chicago, and Wisconsin. See Finegold, *Experts and Politicians,* and Margulies, *The Decline of the Progressive Movement in Wisconsin.* See also J. Joseph Huthmacher, *Massachusetts People and Its Politics* (New York: Athenaeum, 1969), pp. 64–65.

56. Beatty, *The Rascal King,* p. 169.

57. Ibid., pp. 169–170. *Boston Journal* clipping (n.d.), JMCS, vol. A-1. See also Zolot, "The Issue of Good Government," p. 531.

58. On O'Connell, see James M. O'Toole, *Militant and Triumphant: William Henry O'Connell and the Catholic Church in Boston, 1859–1944* (Notre Dame: University of Notre Dame Press, 1992). (Quotation from p. 121.) See also Paula M. Kane, *Separatism and Subculture: Boston Catholicism, 1900–1920* (Chapel Hill: University of North Carolina Press, 1994), pp. 13–21.

59. Beatty, *The Rascal King,* p. 170. The reference to "dog-raising matrons" was a common (and traditional) critique of women reformers that implicitly questioned their maternal character. They had dogs instead of children.

60. *Boston Herald* (n.d.), JMCS, vol. A-22.

61. After the January 1914 election in which Curley was elected, the date of municipal election was moved from January to December, so the 1917 election occurred nearly four years after the 1914 vote.

62. Unlabeled clipping in Nutter Diaries, vol. 10, December 10, 1917. See also *Boston Globe,* December 11, 16, 1917, GGA, Candidate Files, James Michael Curley File, box 3, file 4, and Curley campaign circular, GGA, Candidate Files, James Michael Curley File, box 9, file 5, for further details of the 1917 campaign.

63. Unlabeled clippings, Nutter Diaries, vol. 10, December 10, October 17, 1917.

64. *The Hibernian,* December 13, 1917, clipping, MLS, vol. 26.

65. John J. Toomey and Edward P. B. Rankin, *History of South Boston (Its Past and Present) and Prospects for the Future with Sketches of Prominent Men* (Boston: by the authors, 1901), p. 508. *Boston Post,* December 17, 1917. *Jewish Advocate,* April 2, 1915. Boston Board of Election Commissioners, *Annual Report for 1917* (Boston, 1918), pp. 143–151.

6. Ethnic Progressivism Triumphant: Boston Public Life in the 1920s

1. *Boston Telegram,* October 19, 1921. Jack Beatty, *The Rascal King: The Life and Times of James Michael Curley, 1874–1958* (Reading, Mass.: Addison-Wesley, 1992), pp. 226–228.

2. Lynn Dumenil, *The Modern Temper: American Culture and Society in the 1920s* (New York: Hill and Wang, 1995), pp. 22–26. William E. Leuchtenberg, *The Perils of Prosperity, 1914–1932* (Chicago: University of Chicago Press, 1958), pp. 84–103, 120–139, 204–224. James T. Kloppenberg, *Uncertain Victory: Social Democracy and Progressivism in European and American Thought, 1870–1920* (New York: Oxford University Press, 1986), pp. 391–392.

3. Richard Hofstadter, *Age of Reform: From Bryan to F.D.R.* (New York: Alfred A. Knopf, 1985), p. 280. Among those pointing to the persistence of parts of Progressive reform are Arthur S. Link, "What Happened to the Progressive Movement in the 1920s?," *American Historical Review* 64 (1959): 833–851; Robyn Muncy, *Creating a Female Dominion in American Reform, 1890–1935* (New York: Oxford University Press, 1991); J. Joseph Huthmacher,

Massachusetts People and Politics, 1919–1933 (New York: Atheneum, 1969); Ellis Hawley, *The Great War and the Search for a Modern Order: A History of the American People and Their Institutions, 1917–1933* (New York: St. Martin's Press, 1979); Joan Hoff Wilson, *Herbert Hoover: Forgotten Progressive* (Boston: Little, Brown, 1975). For another approach that emphasizes the continuities between the Progressive Era and the 1920s, see Morton Keller, *Regulating a New Economy: Public Policy and Economic Change in America, 1900–1933* (Cambridge: Harvard University Press, 1990), and idem, *Regulating a New Society: Public Policy and Social Change in America, 1900–1933* (Cambridge: Harvard University Press, 1994).

4. Curley campaign letter, GGA, Candidate Files, James Michael Curley File, box 10, file 6. *Boston Telegram,* November 10, 1921, clipping, GGA, Candidate Files, James Michael Curley File, box 10, file 2. *South Boston Gazette,* December 10, 1921.

5. *Boston Globe,* October 27, 1921, clipping, GGA, Candidate Files, James Michael Curley File, box 10, file 2. Curley circular, GGA, Candidate Files, James Michael Curley File, small box (no number), file 1.

6. On Murphy, see the *Charlestown Enterprise,* January 18, 1919; campaign letter, GGA, Candidate Files, James Michael Curley File, box 10, file 6; *Boston Telegram,* October 27, 1921, clipping, GGA, Subject Files, Loyal Coalition File.

7. Studies that trace machine politics through the 1920s and 1930s include Steven Erie, *Rainbow's End: Irish-Americans and the Dilemmas of Urban Machine Politics, 1840–1985* (Berkeley: University of California Press, 1988); M. Craig Brown and Charles Halaby, "Bosses, Reform, and the Socioeconomic Bases of Urban Expenditure, 1890–1940," in Terrence J. McDonald and Sally K. Ward, eds., *The Politics of Urban Fiscal Policy* (Beverly Hills: Sage, 1984), pp. 69–100; Bruce M. Stave, *The New Deal and the Last Hurrah: Pittsburgh and Machine Politics* (Pittsburgh: University of Pittsburgh Press, 1970); Alan DiGaetano, "The Rise and Development of Urban Political Machines: An Alternative to Merton's Functional Analysis," *Urban Affairs Quarterly* 24 (December 1988): 242–267.

8. *South Boston Gazette,* February 26, November 26, December 17, 1921. The *Gazette*'s celebration of Curley's victory is even more remarkable because one of Curley's opponents, Charles S. O'Connor, was from South Boston. Further evidence of Curley's Irish base is evident in Table 8. Curley carried the city's working- and lower-middle-class ethnic districts, including Murphy's home district of Charlestown and O'Connor's South Boston. Murphy carried the Back Bay and the suburban sections. Even the presence of three Irish candidates did not break the Progressive pattern in Boston, a testimony to the power of Curley's rhetoric. See Boston Board of Election Commissioners, *Annual Report for 1921* (Boston, 1921), pp. 22–30.

9. Beatty, *The Rascal King,* pp. 230–231.

10. *South Boston Gazette,* January 7, 1922. See *East Boston Argus-Advocate,* December 31, 1921; *Italian News,* April 14, June 2, 1923, for examples of Curley's cooperation with local civic leaders.

11. Frederick A. Bushee, *Ethnic Factors in the Population of Boston* (Boston: South End House, 1903), p. 132. Gustave Ralph Serino, "Italians in the Political Life of Boston: A Study of the Role of an Immigrant and Ethnic Group in the Political Life of an Urban Community" (Ph.D. diss., Harvard University, 1950), p. 34. Robert A. Woods, *Americans in Process: A Settlement Study by Residents and Associates of South End House* (New York: Garrett Press, 1898), pp. 64–65. Gerald Gamm, *The Making of New Deal Democrats: Voting Behavior and Realignment in Boston, 1920–1940* (Chicago: University of Chicago Press, 1989), p. 185.

12. *Boston Globe,* August 2, 1922, clipping, JMCS, vol. B-2. *Italian News,* May 27, August 19, July 29, 1922; April 14, June 2, 16, September 8, 1923. For the donation to the Home for Italian Children, see *Italian News,* November 12, 1922.

13. *Italian News,* April 7, March 31, March 4, 1923.

14. *South Boston Gazette,* March 4, May 20, 1922; August 4, 1923. On the size of the Evacuation Day allotment, see *South Boston Gazette,* February 18, 1922.

15. See *South Boston Gazette,* July 22, 1922; March 23, 1924, for Bigney's public correspondence with city hall. See *Gazette,* June 3, 1922, for Daly's letter and July 28, 1923; May 3, 1924, for other examples.

16. On fiscal debates, see *Proceedings of the Boston City Council for 1922* (Boston, 1923), p. 88; *Proceedings of the Boston City Council for 1923–1924* (Boston, 1924), p. 20; *Proceedings of the Boston City Council for 1924–1925* (Boston, 1925), p. 37; *Proceedings of the Boston City Council for 1925–1926* (Boston, 1926), pp. 71–72. See also *City Affairs,* vol. 11, no. 1 (July 1923); Beatty, *The Rascal King,* p. 231.

17. Unidentified clipping, Nutter Diaries, vol. 16, June 14, 1923. Unidentified clipping, Nutter Diaries, vol. 18, September 11, 1925.

18. Kenneth Jackson, *Crabgrass Frontiers: The Suburbanization of the United States* (New York: Oxford University Press, 1985), pp. 174–177. Stephan Thernstrom, *The Other Bostonians: Poverty and Progress in an American Metropolis, 1880–1970* (Cambridge: Harvard University Press, 1973), pp. 9–28. One political history that does take into account demographic change is Kenneth J. Winkle, *The Politics of Community: Migration and Politics in Antebellum Ohio* (New York: Cambridge University Press, 1988).

19. Henry C. Binford, *The First Suburbs: Residential Communities on the Boston Periphery, 1815–1860* (Chicago: University of Chicago Press, 1984). Sam Bass Warner, *Streetcar Suburbs: The Process of Growth in Boston, 1870–1900,* 2nd ed. (Cambridge: Harvard University Press, 1978), pp. 21–29.

20. Thernstrom, *The Other Bostonians,* pp. 9–11; see Table 2.1 (p. 11) on population stagnation after 1920. Population figures derived from U.S. Bureau of

the Census, *Twelfth Annual Census of the United States: Population Schedule, Massachusetts* (Washington, D.C., 1901), p. 11; idem, *Thirteenth Annual Census of the United States: Population Schedule, Massachusetts* (Washington, D.C., 1911), p. 890; idem, *Fourteenth Annual Census of the United States: Population Schedule, Massachusetts* (Washington, D.C., 1921), p. 457. The twelve adjacent cities and towns were Brookline, Cambridge, Chelsea, Dedham, Everett, Milton, Newton, Quincy, Revere, Somerville, Watertown, and Winthrop. Boston's annexation of Hyde Park in 1912—the city's only territorial expansion during the period of this study—accounts for a large piece of its 33 percent population growth from 1900 to 1930. On the issue of continued population migration and turnover within Boston after 1920, something on which Thernstrom is noncommittal, see Ronald Tobey, Charles Wetherell, and Jay Brigham, "Moving Out and Settling In: Residential Mobility, Homeowning, and the Public Enframing of Citizenship, 1921–1950," *American Historical Review* 95 (1990): 1395–1422.

21. Boston Council of Social Agencies, Bureau of Research and Studies, *Social Statistics by Census Tract in Boston: A Method of Neighborhood Study* (Boston: Boston Council of Social Agencies, 1933), p. 5.

22. Statistics derived from U.S. Bureau of the Census, *Twelfth Annual Census of the United States: Population Schedule, Massachusetts*, p. 11; idem, *Thirteenth Annual Census of the United States: Population Schedule, Massachusetts*, p. 890; idem, *Fourteenth Annual Census of the United States: Population Schedule, Massachusetts*, p. 457. Figures for churches taken from *The Boston Catholic Directory for 1992* and Parish Census Files, Archives of the Archdiocese of Boston, Brighton, Mass.

23. George Read Nutter, "Political Boston" [typescript], pp. 34–35, GGA, Candidate Files, George Read Nutter File.

24. See *Constitution and By-Laws of the Charlestown Improvement Association, 1914,* Boston Public Library, for a list of members in 1914 and *Boston City Directory for 1928.* Quotation from *Charlestown News,* May 25, 1929.

25. *UIA Bulletin,* May 1911. *Boston City Directory for 1928.*

26. John Higham, *Strangers in the Land: Patterns of American Nativism, 1860–1925* (New York: Atheneum, 1973), pp. 264–299. Leuchtenberg, *The Perils of Prosperity.* J. Joseph Huthmacher, *Massachusetts People and Politics, 1919–1933.* Allan J. Lichtman, *Prejudice and the Old Politics: The Presidential Election of 1928* (Chapel Hill: University of North Carolina Press, 1979).

27. On the origins and impact of mass culture in this era, see Lizabeth Cohen, *Making a New Deal: Industrial Workers in Chicago, 1919–1939* (New York: Cambridge University Press, 1990), pp. 99–101; Stuart Ewen, *Captains of Consciousness: Advertising and the Social Roots of Consumer Culture* (New York: McGraw Hill, 1976); Ronald Edsforth, *Class Conflict and Cultural Consensus: The Making of a Mass Consumer Society in Flint, Michigan* (New Brunswick: Rutgers University Press, 1987).

28. Barbara Miller Solomon, *Ancestors and Immigrants: A Changing New England Tradition* (Cambridge: Harvard University Press, 1956), pp. 99–102, 136. *Boston Transcript,* March 20, 1920, GGA, Loyal Coalition File. For a full account of the police strike, see Francis Russell, *City in Terror: The 1919 Boston Police Strike* (New York: Penguin Books, 1977).

29. *Charlestown News,* December 20, 1924. *Jewish Advocate,* September 11, 1924. *Italian News,* February 19, 1921.

30. *Charlestown News,* July 16, 1927. *Italian News,* April 15, 1922. On links between Progressivism and moral reformism of the 1920s, see Hofstadter, *Age of Reform,* pp. 287–295; Leuchtenberg, *The Perils of Prosperity,* pp. 203–224. On Prohibition, the Anti-Saloon League, and reform, see K. Austin Kerr, *Organized for Prohibition: A New History of the Anti-Saloon League* (New Haven: Yale University Press, 1985), pp. 7–9.

31. Curley quoted in *Boston Herald,* January 20, 1923, clipping, GGA, Candidate Files, James Michael Curley File, box 11. See the *Boston Globe,* January 9, 1923, on rumors of a kidnapping plot. On the cross-burning incident, see the *Boston Globe,* May 17, 1924, and Beatty, *The Rascal King,* p. 244. On the Loyal Coalition, see *Boston Daily Advertiser,* January 18, 1923, clipping, GGA, Ku Klux Klan File. On immigration restriction, see *Italian News,* February 17, March 24, July 14, 1924, and *Gazzetta del Massachusetts,* February 2, 9, 16, 24, 1924.

32. Unidentified clipping, Nutter Diaries, vol. 16, June 14, 1923. Unidentified clipping in Nutter Diaries, vol. 18, September 11, 1925.

33. Huthmacher, *Massachusetts People and Politics, 1919–1933,* p. 55. Arthur Warner, "Blackmail a la Boston," *Nation* 63 (November 2, 1921), p. 499–500.

34. Unidentified clippings in Nutter Diaries, vol. 14, November 2, 17, October 12, 28, 1921.

35. Huthmacher, *Massachusetts People and Politics, 1919–1933,* p. 55. Nutter Diaries, vol. 16, December 22, 1922.

36. "Report of the Executive Secretary, Annual Meeting, March 23, 1922," Wenona Osborne Pinkham Papers, WRC, folder 1028.

37. Louise M. Young, *In the Public Interest: The League of Women Voters, 1920–1970* (Westport, Conn.: Greenwood Press, 1989), pp. 34–35. Anna L. Harvey, "The Political Consequences of Suffrage Exclusion," *Social Science History* 20 (1996): 116.

38. "Report of the Executive Secretary, March 21, 1921," Wenona Osborne Pinkham Papers, WRC, folder 1028. *Boston American,* October 5, 1921, clipping and *Boston Traveler,* October 13, 1921, clipping, GGA, League of Women Voters File.

39. "Report of the Executive Secretary, March 21, 1921," Wenona Osborne Pinkham Papers, WRC, folder 1028. "Report of the Executive Secretary, March 23, 1922," WRC, folder 1028. *Boston Advertiser,* June 5, 1921, clip-

ping, Elizabeth Lowell Putnam Papers, Schlesinger Library, Radcliffe College, Cambridge, Mass.

40. League of Women Voters flier, enclosed in Virginia Moore to Elizabeth Lowell Putnam, November 10, 1921, Elizabeth Lowell Putnam Papers, box 31, folder 527.

41. *Boston Traveler,* October 12, 1921, clipping and *Boston Post,* December 10, 1921, clipping, GGA, League of Women Voters File. The approach taken by the Boston branch of the League differed from the neutral approach recommended by Carrie Chapman Catt and the League's national leadership, although Boston's women claimed to be acting in a nonpartisan manner. Young, *In the Public Interest,* pp. 57–58.

42. *WMLB,* February 1917, pp. 12–13. *Boston Post,* March 12, 1913, clipping, GGA, Candidate Files, James Michael Curley File, box 10, file 5. *Boston American,* April 17, 1915, clipping, GGA, Candidate Files, James Michael Curley File, box C.2, file 1.

43. *Boston Telegram,* December 7, 1921, clipping, GGA, League of Women Voters File. Sheehan received an appointment as assistant election commissioner from Curley during his second term. See *Boston Globe,* May 17, 1922, clipping, JMCS, vol. B-1.

44. *Boston Traveler,* September 12, 1921, clipping, GGA, League of Women Voters File.

45. Unidentified clipping in Nutter Diaries, vol. 14, November 15, 1921. "Letter to the Women of Boston from Mary E. Curley," GGA, Candidate Files, James Michael Curley File, small box (no number), file 1. *Boston Telegram,* October 14, 1921, clipping, GGA, Candidate Files, James Michael Curley File, box 10, file 2.

46. Regression equations designed to measure the relationship between the rate of female turnout in a ward and support for either Curley or Murphy found no significant relationship in either case. While far from conclusive, these results suggest that neither man ran more strongly in districts where larger proportions of eligible women voted. The regression coefficient for Curley's vote was .32, the p-value was .36, and the R^2 equaled .03. The regression coefficient for Murphy's vote was −.38, with a p-value of .35 and an R^2 of .04. See the Statistical Appendix for details on the construction of the female turnout variable. Boston Board of Election Commissioners, *Annual Report for 1921* (Boston, 1922).

47. The problems encountered by the Boston LWV in its efforts to speak for the women of the city in municipal politics clearly parallel the difficulties faced by the national LWV and other women's groups seeking to mobilize women as women on a national scale after the passage of the Nineteenth Amendment. The ethnic conflict that undermined these efforts in Boston represents but one of the many divisions, including race, class, party, and ideology, that presented obstacles to a united politics among women during the 1920s. For a

discussion of this issue, see Nancy Cott, *The Grounding of Modern Feminism* (New Haven: Yale University Press, 1987), pp. 85–114; idem, "Across the Great Divide: Women in Politics Before and After 1920," in Louise A. Tilly and Patricia Gurin, eds., *Women, Politics, and Change* (New York: Russell Sage), 1990, pp. 153–176; Harvey, "The Political Consequences of Suffrage Exclusion," pp. 105–128; Sara Alpern and Dale Baum, "Female Ballots: The Impact of the Nineteenth Amendment," *Journal of Interdisciplinary History* 16 (1985): 43–67.

48. *WML,* December 1917, February 1918, December 1919, April 1922, October 1922, April 1922, May 1922.

49. *Gazzetta del Massachusetts,* February 2, 1924. *Jewish Advocate,* April 11, 1918; November 24, 1921.

50. "List of Chairwomen and Standing Committees, 1920," RG VI.4, box 3, folder 16, LCWP. Paula M. Kane, *Separatism and Subculture: Boston Catholicism, 1900–1920* (Chapel Hill: University of North Carolina Press, 1994), p. 217. On the child labor issue and O'Connell, see also James M. O'Toole, *Militant and Triumphant: William Henry O'Connell and the Catholic Church in Boston, 1859–1944* (South Bend: University of Notre Dame, 1992), pp. 132–135.

51. Unidentified typescript, October 1920, RG VI.4, box 3, folder 14, LCWP.

52. Kane, *Separatism and Subculture,* pp. 213, 218.

53. "History of the League of Catholic Women" [typescript], n.d., RG IV.4, box 2, folder 9, LCWP.

54. *Boston Transcript,* November 15, 1920, clipping, Nutter Diaries, vol. 13, November 15, 1920.

55. *South Boston Gazette,* December 11, 1920. *New York Times,* December 18, 1921, clipping, Nutter Diaries, vol. 15, December 19, 1921.

56. *South Boston Gazette,* December 16, 1922; December 8, 1923.

57. Unidentified clipping in Nutter Diaries, vol. 16, December 10, 1923.

58. *City Affairs,* vol. 10, no. 1 (July 1922).

59. Nutter Diaries, vol. 15, December 15, 1921; vol. 16, December 20, 1922.

60. Nutter Diaries, vol. 13, November 11, 1920.

61. Nutter Diaries, vol. 16, April 9, 27, 1923. *Boston Transcript,* December 10, 1923. Nutter quoted in Nutter Diaries, vol. 16, April 9, 1923. For a full roster of the executive committee, see GGA letterhead in Nutter Diaries, vol. 18, September 1, 1925.

62. Nutter Diaries, vol. 18, October 23, 1925.

63. William Marchione, "The 1949 Boston Charter Reform," *New England Quarterly* 49 (1976): 374.

64. "Statement of Dr. Morton Prince," March 11, 1920, GGA, Subject Files, Charter Association File (Prince was chairman of the Charter Association). Marchione, "The 1949 Boston Charter Reform," p. 375. Boston Board of Election Commissioners, *Annual Report for 1924* (Boston, 1925), p. 238.

Idem, *Annual Report for 1909–1910* (Boston, 1910), p. 129. Idem, *Annual Report for 1914* (Boston, 1915), p. 162.

65. Douglas L. Jones et al., *Discovering the Public Interest: A History of the Boston Bar Association* (Canoga Park, Calif.: CCA Press, 1993), pp. 77–91.

Epilogue

1. *Charlestown News,* September 11, 1926.
2. *Charlestown News,* August 6, 1927. *South Boston Gazette,* August 23, 1924.
3. *South Boston Gazette,* November 24, 1923. Boston Board of Election Commissioners, *Annual Report for 1928* (Boston, 1929), pp. 97–103. Ward committees remained insignificant in Boston politics in ensuing decades. See Murray B. Levin, *The Compleat Politician: Political Strategy in Massachusetts* (Indianapolis: Bobbs-Merrill, 1962), p. 244.
4. Jack Beatty, *The Rascal King: The Life and Times of James Michael Curley, 1874–1958* (Reading, Mass.: Addison-Wesley, 1992), p. 258.
5. J. Joseph Huthmacher, *Massachusetts People and Politics, 1919–1933* (New York: Atheneum, 1969) p. 177. *Boston Herald,* October 1, 1928. Curley and Glynn both planned to run for mayor in 1929 and undoubtedly formed separate Smith organizations to promote their own fortunes.
6. Huthmacher, *Massachusetts People and Politics, 1919–1933,* pp. 177–178. *Charlestown Enterprise,* May 12, 1928. *Boston Herald,* October 2, 1928.
7. Boston Board of Election Commissioners, *Annual Report for 1924* (Boston, 1925), p. 238. William Marchione, "The 1949 Charter Reform," *New England Quarterly* 49 (1976), pp. 390, 396.
8. Charles H. Trout, *Boston, the Great Depression, and the New Deal* (New York: Oxford University Press, 1977). Beatty, *The Rascal King,* pp. 249–398.
9. John F. Stack Jr., *International Conflict in an American City: Boston's Irish, Italians, and Jews, 1935–1944* (Westport, Conn.: Greenwood Press, 1979), pp. 50–57, 63–72.
10. Ibid., p. 140.
11. James Michael Curley, *I'd Do It Again: A Record of All My Uproarious Years* (Englewood Cliffs, N.J.: Prentice Hall, 1957), pp. 1–2.
12. Arthur M. Schlesinger, *The Politics of Upheaval* (Boston: Houghton Mifflin, 1960), pp. 441–443. Nancy J. Weiss, *Charles Francis Murphy, 1858–1924: Respectability and Responsibility in Tammany Politics* (Northampton, Mass.: Smith College Press, 1968), p. 94. Edward C. Banfield, ed., *Urban Government: A Reader in Administration and Politics,* rev. ed. (New York: Free Press, 1969), pp. 165–166. For those contesting this view, see Bruce M. Stave, *The New Deal and the Last Hurrah: Pittsburgh and Machine Politics* (Pittsburgh: University of Pittsburgh Press, 1970); Lyle Dorsett, *Franklin Delano Roosevelt and the City Bosses* (Port Washington, N.Y.: Kennikat Press, 1977); Alan DiGaetano, "The Rise and Development of Urban Political Ma-

chines: An Alternative to Merton's Functional Analysis," *Urban Affairs Quarterly* 24 (1988): 242–267; M. Craig Brown and Charles Halaby, "Bosses, Reform, and the Socioeconomic Bases of Urban Expenditure, 1890–1940," in Terrence J. McDonald and Sally K. Ward, eds., *The Politics of Urban Fiscal Policy* (Beverly Hills: Sage, 1984), pp. 69–99.

13. Terrence McDonald, "The Problem of the Political in Recent American Urban History: Liberalism and the Rise of Urban Functionalism," *Social History* 10 (1985): 331–332. See also Michael Rogin, *McCarthy and Intellectuals: The Radical Specter* (Cambridge: M.I.T Press, 1967), pp. 9–31.

14. Richard Hofstadter, *The Age of Reform: From Bryan to F.D.R.* (New York: Alfred A. Knopf, 1985), pp. 12–22.

15. Ibid., pp. 176, 177–180.

16. Ibid., pp. 180–181.

17. Even now, when research has established the "Progressive" credentials of a myriad of social groups, the emphasis on the native-born, middle-class nature of Progressivism persists. See for example Richard McCormick, "Public Life in Industrial America, 1877–1917," in Eric Foner, ed., *The New American History* (Philadelphia: Temple University Press, 1990), p. 107. See also John D. Buenker, *Urban Liberalism and Progressive Reform* (New York: W. W. Norton, 1973), and Kenneth Finegold, *Experts and Politicians: Reform Challenges to Machine Politics in New York, Cleveland, and Chicago* (Princeton: Princeton University Press, 1995), pp. 18–22.

18. Hofstadter, *The Age of Reform*, p. 181, n. 1. Terrence McDonald, "The Problem of the Political," p. 332, notes Hofstadter's reliance on Handlin's interpretation of the political boss and his supporters. Oscar Handlin, *The Uprooted: The Epic Story of the Great Migrations that Made the American People,* 2nd ed., enl. (Boston: Little, Brown, 1973), pp. 190–194. Idem, *Boston's Immigrants: A Study in Acculturation,* rev. and enl. ed. (Cambridge: Harvard University Press, 1979), pp. 228–229. See Robert Sean Wilentz, "Industrializing America and the Irish: Toward the New Departure," *Labor History* 20 (1979), pp. 580–586, for a critical discussion of *Boston's Immigrants.*

19. Maureen Flanagan, *Charter Reform in Chicago* (Carbondale, Ill.: Southern University Press, 1987), pp. 110–135. Thomas R. Pegram, *Partisans and Progressives: Private Interest and Public Policy, 1870–1922* (Urbana: University of Illinois Press), pp. 87–119.

20. Paul Kleppner, *Chicago Divided: The Making of a Black Mayor* (DeKalb: Northern Illinois University Press, 1985), pp. 71–72. See also John M. Allswang, *A House for All Peoples: Ethnic Politics in Chicago, 1890–1936* (Lexington: University Press of Kentucky, 1971). I am not arguing that this political system always benefited black Chicagoans. The Democratic machine was often an impediment to civil rights progress, and discrimination against African Americans in the city was rampant and often violent. See Arnold R. Hirsch, "Massive Resistance in the Urban North: Trumbull Park, Chicago, 1953–1966," *Journal of American History* 82 (1995): 522–550.

21. Kleppner, *Chicago Divided,* pp. 73–74.
22. Jim Sleeper, *Closest of Strangers: Liberalism and the Politics of Race in New York* (New York: W. W. Norton, 1990), pp. 53–67.

Statistical Appendix

1. See Steven Ruggles and Matthew Sobek, *Integrated Public Use Microdata Series, IPUMS-95, Version 1.0,* vol. 1, *User's Guide* (Minneapolis: Social History Research Laboratory, Department of History, University of Minnesota, 1995).
2. Samuel H. Preston, "United States Census Data, 1910: Public Use Sample" (Ann Arbor: Inter-University Consortium for Political and Social Research, 1989; ICPSR 9166). For an additional discussion of the 1910 dataset, see Philip J. Ethington, "Recasting Urban Political History: The Public Household and Political Participation in Boston and San Francisco during the Progressive Era," *Social Science History* 16 (1992): 312–313. Professor Ethington and I collaborated on the preparation of the dataset for Boston.
3. Linear regression was performed using the PROC REG procedure described in Sandra D. Schlotzer and Raymond C. Littell, *SAS System for Elementary Statistical Analysis* (Cary, N.C.: S.A.S. Institute, 1987), pp. 266–285.
4. Konrad H. Jarausch and Kenneth A. Hardy, *Quantitative Methods for Historians: A Guide to Research, Data, and Statistics* (Chapel Hill: University of North Carolina Press, 1991), pp. 67, 151.
5. See Jarausch and Hardy, *Quantitative Methods for Historians,* p. 78, on degrees of freedom. The number of wards in Boston increased to twenty-six in 1912, with the annexation of Hyde Park. This change does not significantly affect the degrees of freedom.
6. Alba M. Edwards, "A Social Economic Grouping of the Gainful Workers of the United States," *Journal of the American Statistical Association* 27 (1933): 377–387. Stephan Thernstrom, *The Other Bostonians: Poverty and Progress in the American Metropolis, 1880–1970* (Cambridge: Harvard University Press, 1973), pp. 289–302.
7. Robert A. Woods and Albert J. Kennedy, *The Zone of Emergence: Observations of Lower, Middle, and Upper Working Class Communities in Boston, 1905–1914* (Cambridge: M.I.T. Press, 1962). Zane Miller, *Boss Cox's Cincinnati: Urban Politics in the Progressive Era* (New York: Oxford University Press, 1968), pp. 3–56. Richard Wade, "Urbanization," in C. Vann Woodward, *The Comparative Approach to American History* (New York: Basic Books, 1968), p. 196. For a dissenting view, see David Ward, "Nineteenth-Century Boston: A Study in the Role of Antecedent and Adjacent Conditions in the Spatial Aspects of Urban Growth" (Ph.D. diss., University of Wisconsin, 1963).
8. M. S. Lewis-Beck, *Applied Regression: An Introduction* (Beverly Hills: Sage, 1980), pp. 58–63.

Index

Curley, James Michael *(continued)*
1914 mayoral election, 139, 140–142;
imprisoned, 140; and immigration
restriction, 141; policies as mayor,
143–145, 167–168; and ethnic
neighborhoods, 146–147, 155–156; and
neighborhood improvement
associations, 146–147; and North End,
146–147, 166–167; and fiscal issues,
147, 151, 155; and labor unions,
147–148; and 1921 election, 147–148,
161, 162; and Boston history, 148–150;
and Brahmin Boston, 148–150,
154–158; compared to John F.
Fitzgerald, 150, 158; and South Boston,
155–156, 167–169; and 1917 election,
159–160; and Irish independence, 163;
and Loyal Coalition, 163, 173, 175; and
woman suffrage, 179–181
Curley, Thomas, 137

D'Alessandro, Dominic, 57, 59
Daley, Richard, 198
Dean, Josiah, 68–69
De Haas, Jacob, 63, 64, 127, 128
Democratic Citizens Association, 33
Democratic city committee, 28
Democratic Party: links Irish and Yankees,
2–3, 16; power of, 27–28, 32;
factionalism in, 32–36; revived, 152–153
Denison House, 47
Dewey, Henry, 83
Dolan, Arthur, 71, 82
Donnaruma, James, 57–58, 60, 89, 147
Donovan, Edward, 82
Donovan, Jim, 45, 46, 98
Donovan, William J., 34
Dorchester, 127, 147
Duff, Julia, 72

East Boston Free Press, 147, 155
East Boston riot, 23–24
Efficiency rhetoric, 70. *See also*
Progressivism
Eliot, Charles, 20
Ellis, David, 63
Ethnic conflict, 22–24; party politics and,
28–36; sources of, 169, 170–171,
172–178; Progressivism and, 188–189
Ethnic identity, 55–56. *See also* Narratives

Ethnic nationalism, 13–14
Ethnic Progressivism: John F. Fitzgerald
and, 3, 83–85, 100–101, 102; defined,
3–4; James Michael Curley and, 3–9,
132, 134–135, 146–147, 158–159,
162–164, 177–178; impact of, 14,
190–200
Ethnic Progressivism, 56; Italians and,
56–61; Jews and, 61–66; Irish and,
66–75. *See also* Progressivism
Evacuation Day, 165

Fales, Augustus A., 121, 123–124, 130,
171
Faneuil Improvement Association (FIA),
113–117, 147
Fenway scandal, 45–46
Filene, Edward A., 39
Finegold, Kenneth, 78–79
Fiscal policy, 151
Fitzgerald, John F.: use of Progressivism, 3,
83–85, 100–101, 102; background of,
58, 80–81; and Finance Commission,
58–59, 80, 85–90, 102–103; Italian
opposition to, 58–60; political style of,
81–83, 100–102; electoral support for,
89–90, 98–99, 132; as Mayor, 123;
compared to James Michael Curley, 150,
158
Fitzgerald, William T. A., 82
Fitzgerald Club, 115
Flanagan, John, 121, 122
Flanagan, Maureen, 79
Frances E. Willard settlement, 127
Frothingham, Louis A., 46, 82–84
Fulton, Justin, 19

Gallivan, James A., 160
Galvin, Owen, 19
Gazzetta del Massachusetts, 57–58, 59–60,
89, 95, 141
Gender: and Progressivism, 10, 158; and
politics, 100–101; as basis for political
action, 164, 178–184. *See also* Women,
activism of; Women's Municipal League
General Federation of Women's Clubs, 182
Good Government Association (GGA):
origins of, 37, 41–47; membership in,
42–43; power of, 43–47; investigations
by, 45–46, 59